Three Years of Hate: The Very Best of In Mala Fide

by In Mala Fide

Copyright © 2013-2014 Matt Forney. All rights reserved.

ISBN-13: 978-1481881876

Short quotes from this book can be used so long as I am credited. To use longer quotes, email me at the address below using subject line "Attention: Permissions Coordinator."

For further information, email me at admin@mattforney.com.

To Annie,

but I know you're never going to read this.

TABLE OF CONTENTS

Preface	1
I: Sexuality	9
II: What's Wrong with the World	172
III: The Tao of Ferd	336
IV: Humor and Satire	438
Endnotes	463

PREFACE

A few months ago, I was on a pub crawl with my friend Mark Zolo in Manhattan. We were relaxing at a hole-in-the-wall bar in Greenwich Village, chatting with the bartender and another patron, when the subject turned to our jobs.

"We're authors," Mark exclaimed. I nodded along, half-gone.

"Really?" That always gets people attention. "What have you written?"

"Well, his book is more interesting. It's a memoir of his experiences traveling the world." Which is the truth: Mark's book is titled the same as his blog, *Naughty Nomad*.

"And can you get these on Amazon and wherever?"

"Yeah."

"What have you written?" the guy asked me.

"Oh, Matt's written a whole bunch of stuff," Mark interjected, "but his best book is *Three Years of Hate*. You should check it out."

"Yeah," I grinned and took another swig of Blue Moon. I didn't have the heart to mention that I'd pulled the book off the

PREFACE

market.

Anthony Burgess' most famous novel was *A Clockwork Orange*, which he knocked off in three weeks because he needed the cash. I slapped *Three Years of Hate* together in half that time for the same reason. I had just completed a six month hitchhiking tour, landing in Portland, Oregon, and cranked the book out over the Christmas season to pay the bills. Were it not for my desperate financial situation, I would have been happy to leave the legacy of "Ferdinand Bardamu" dead and buried.

Unfortunately, while I may not have been interested in *In Mala Fide*, *In Mala Fide* was interested in me.

You don't get to walk away from a site that had been a mainstay of the alternative media—at one point drawing 50,000 unique visitors a month—without it catching up to you. I transitioned to writing under my real name and killed the site in 2012 because I wanted to make a clean break from the *In Mala Fide* legacy of vituperation and anger. My big secret lasted about two months after the site's close, when everyone of importance in the manosphere came together on the sly and started comparing notes. *"How likely is it that there are TWO guitar-playing writers from the same small city who have similar writing styles?"* By the time I'd arrived on the West Coast, I'd embraced my former alter ego and the perks it brought me, which included meeting three of my favorite writers and long-time influences (Jack Donovan, Trevor Blake of *OVO*, and W.F. Price of *The*

PREFACE

Spearhead) and a week-long stay at a groupie's house, among other things. Though not everyone took the news the same way: Davis Aurini, who contributed to *In Mala Fide* in its last days, half-jokingly called me a "cocksucker" over Skype before calming down. (Strangely enough, we're closer friends now then when he was actually writing for me.)

In Mala Fide was birthed by alcoholism, amphetamine abuse, and bitterness. I began writing in 2009 shortly after my 21st birthday, a period in my life where everything was coming apart at the seams. At the same time I was transitioning to the comfy but soul-deadening life of a government bureaucrat, I had seen both my social life dwindle and the most meaningful relationship I'd ever had collapse, the latter due almost entirely to my own stupidity. Back home, a death in the family had thrown everything into chaos. I was progressively unhappy with the direction my life was going in, and nothing I did to change it seemed to take.

So the logical conclusion was to sublimate my rage in a way that was productive yet wouldn't affect my real life in any significant fashion. From that foundation, the rest of the pieces fell into place. "Ferdinand Bardamu" was the ideal pen name for a depressive, egotistical nobody on the edge of nowhere; I had spent the previous year plowing through Céline's bibliography and identifying with his self-abasing cynicism. While I later tried to attach a philosophical meaning to the name "In Mala Fide," it mainly came about because I felt that titling the blog *Journey to the End of the Night* would have been laying it on too thick.

The way my blog suddenly became popular was a shock, but makes sense in retrospect. In 2009, there was no "manosphere," "alternative right," "Dark Enlightenment" or any sort of cohesive online culture, just a bunch of disparate blogs discussing interrelated ideas. The "game" segment was confined to *Roissy in DC*, *Roosh V* and a handful of other sites; neoreaction had not yet caught on, with Mencius Moldbug spinning book-length articles to an attentive but unmotivated audience; obsessing over "HBD" (human biodiversity) was still a thing; the men's rights' "movement" was a collective of scattered sites that didn't engage in anything that could remotely be called "activism"; and the Men Going Their Own Way were, well, Going Their Own Way. The closest thing to a "connecting" blog was *2Blowhards*, which shuttered its doors months after I began writing at *In Mala Fide*.

That was part of my success: I came into the blogosphere at precisely the right time. I had stumbled across all of these online communities at some point during my college tenure, and I drew at least *some* inspiration from all of them. Additionally, a few months in, I started collecting links to my favorite articles and blog posts out of boredom, posting them every Sunday in a series I called "Linkage is Good for You" (which, like *In Mala Fide* itself, had no grand intellectual pedigree; I just picked it because it was catchy). The combo of articulate-yet-vengeful articles and constant backscratching was a hit, the first hit I'd ever managed in

PREFACE

years of trying–and failing–to get people to read the blogs I started up. In *In Mala Fide's* first month, July 2009, the blog got around 3,000 hits total; that number rose to *30,000* in August. No other project I've launched has seen that degree of initial success before or since. By the following year, I had a dedicated audience of 30,000 visitors per month, and I had attracted the attention and praise of many of the writers I respected. Later on, the site played a role in some pivotal events, including helping to popularize the names of Julian Assange's and Dominique Strauss-Kahn's false rape accusers in the English-language media.

So why quit?

I'll freely admit that my experiment in turning *In Mala Fide* into a magazine-style blog with multiple contributors was a failure. While I did help promote some good writers (such as Maximus, Bronan the Barbarian, and Frost), I had no experience running a project like that and it showed; my inability to institute quality control drove away many longtime readers. Additionally, rather than try and adhere to some set of ideological principles or goals, I just opened the doors to everyone with an anti-establishment bent, letting the conversation become dominated by the craziest nuts in the asylum. And as crass as it sounds, money played a part in my decision as well; editing other peoples' work and moderating comments was *far* more time-intensive than I thought it would be, detracting from ventures that actually helped me make a living.

PREFACE

But the main reason I no longer wanted to write as "Ferdinand Bardamu" was because I no longer *felt* it. *In Mala Fide* was the product of a particular period of my life, and by the time 2012 rolled around, I had changed so much that I couldn't maintain the facade. Writing as "Ferdinand," I felt constrained by a voice I'd cultivated years ago but no longer represented me or my beliefs. Additionally, I realized that if the "movement," "culture" or whatever the manosphere happens to be was ever going to get anywhere, pseudonymity would not be enough. Eventually, we would have to emerge, show our faces and be *leaders*.

As I mentioned already, the reason why I refused to divulge my authorship of *In Mala Fide*, at least initially, was to free myself from three years of baggage and start anew. Cowardice played a role as well; just prior to the site's closure, *In Mala Fide* had been targeted by the Southern Poverty Law Center as a "hate group," though they were forced to backpedal after being mocked by the mainstream media. The issues that would result from making my identity as "Ferdinand" known were not something I had wanted to deal with.

What I slowly realized, as I made my way across America, was that even as I had grown dissatisfied with *In Mala Fide's* legacy, countless men and women had been partially or wholly inspired by my writings to change their lives. Not only that, as the truth about my alter ego started to circulate in the manosphere's back rooms, people actually respected me *more* for what I was

PREFACE

doing, not less. Even still, I would have preferred not to revisit my old articles... until now.

I've come to accept that my writing career will always in part be defined by what I did as "Ferdinand Bardamu." Even as I disagree with a lot of what I wrote back then (if not in content, then in style), these writings are valuable enough to preserve for future generations of men to learn and study. If nothing else, they show how I've evolved and changed in the past few years.

As a result, here is *Three Years of Hate*. Originally hastily assembled in a few days for quick dough, I've re-edited (and in the case of the paperback edition, re-typeset) the book to be more professional-looking. The sixty plus essays in this book are those that I believe are the finest I wrote during that era; there are a couple of others I had to exclude for copyright reasons.

Flipping through the essays, first when I was putting the book together a year ago and again now, is like stepping into a time warp. The blogosphere that I stepped into on July 15, 2009 has metamorphosed into a completely different animal five years later. The emergence of the manosphere as a unique entity, disparate from both the men's rights' activists and the seduction community. The renaming of *Roissy in DC* to *Chateau Heartiste*. Roosh becoming the most widely read anti-feminist author today, both as a result of his own blog and books and his site *Return of Kings*. The coalescence of neoreaction as a worldview. The organization of the men's rights' movement into

PREFACE

something resembling a *movement* (not withstanding the idiocy of their goals). The death of Lawrence Auster and the spiraling of his cultish fan base into intellectual onanism. The co-opting of MGTOW by Forever Aloners who haven't even *heard* of zed, Rob Fedders or the men who laid down its core tenets.

The creation of a culture that counters the lies of mainstream society and exists outside of it: *that* is In Mala Fide's legacy. And for all the mistakes I've made, I can say that I'm glad to have been a part of it.

Illegitimi non carborundum, indeed.

Matt Forney

January 2014

I

SEXUALITY

The Eternal Solipsism of the Female Mind

If I had to pick a random word to describe women, one of the ones I could choose is "solipsistic." Solipsism is defined according to the *Merriam-Webster Online Dictionary* as "a theory holding that the self can know nothing but its own modifications and that the self is the only existent thing" or "extreme egocentrism." The female of the species is a master at absorbing herself in her own thoughts and neuroses and projecting them onto men.

Granted, not all women are equally solipsistic. It's like breasts. Some women have dainty, delicate A-cups; some very fortunate girls have heaving, delicious double-Ds; still more unlucky gals have barely noticeable bee stings. So it is with self-absorption: some women are more self-centered and clueless than others. A woman's inherent solipsism is also affected by her surrounding environment. On a scale of 1 to 10, where 1 represents almost no solipsistic tendencies and 10 represents near-fatal levels of solipsism, American women would clock in at 9. For comparison's sake, Canadian women would be 8, Brits would be 10, Chinese women would be 5, and Russians would be 3. These are completely unscientific estimates based on a combination of personal experience and crude stereotypes, but I stick by them.

It's no accident that American women and other women from Western, feminist countries are utterly self-absorbed and ignorant. Much like how the FDA's policies encourage Americans to wolf down junk food until they're fat enough to crush asteroids in their Roche limits, Western pop culture in general and American culture in particular impute all sorts of idiotic and self-defeating ideas in the minds of women. American female solipsism is so pervasive and commonplace that no one notices it anymore; it's like air.

The raging solipsism of the American female mind is most obvious when it comes to the realm of sexual attraction. Virtually all women in the U.S. suffer from the delusion that men find the same qualities attractive in them that they find in men. From career women who lament that their accomplishments don't give men erections to living lardballs claiming that men aren't lining up to date them because of peer pressure against "plus-sized" gals, women are unparalleled when it comes to assigning their prejudices and desires to the male. Even on issues on which men and women are visibly different, such as the effect of aging on sexual attractiveness, women can't stop digging in their hole of projection, as evidenced by the myth of "andropause" (male menopause) and the ludicrous new claim that men have a biological clock. The popularity of *Eat, Pray, Love*, a memoir (and movie) about a woman who divorces her husband to travel the world sucking and fucking exotic cock and shoveling down pallets of fattening Italian food is just one example of how modern society encourages women to be selfish and solipsistic.

All this is not to imply that men are incapable of solipsism and projection. To paraphrase Mark Twain, all I care to know that a man is a human being: that is enough for me; he can't possibly be any worse. Men are certainly capable of projecting their desires onto women, but the crucial difference is that male solipsism isn't encouraged by society and pop culture, and men who are solipsistic are mocked by everyone and sometimes prosecuted. See the case of New York congressman Anthony Weiner, who became a national laughingstock in 2011 when he was caught sending pictures of his dick to women he was chatting up over the Internet. Men, being visual creatures first and foremost, can and will get turned on by the wiggly bits of any attractive girl they lay eyes on; women typically don't get horny looking at the private parts of strange men. When a girl a man doesn't know flashes her tits at him, he thinks *"Awesome!"*; when a man a girl doesn't know flashes his penis at her, she thinks *"Eww, gross!"*

Female sexual solipsism and projection are the primary

reasons why women's dating advice is useless. Let's look at the Bible of modern dating advice for women, *The Rules: Time-Tested Secrets for Capturing the Heart of Mr. Right*. What *The Mystery Method* is to men, *The Rules* is to women; it's sold millions of copies since it was published in 1995, it's been featured on Oprah, its authors Ellen Fein and Sherrie Schneider have written numerous sequels, and the two even run a dating advice firm to help women unlucky in love. What kind of attitudes does *The Rules* try to inculcate in women? Not good ones:

"Rule 1: Be a "Creature Unlike Any Other"

"Rule 2: Don't Talk to a Man First (and Don't Ask Him to Dance)

"Rule 3: Don't Stare at Men or Talk Too Much

"Rule 4: Don't Meet Him Halfway or Go Dutch on a Date

"Rule 5: Don't Call Him & Rarely Return His Calls

"Rule 6: Always End Phone Calls First

"Rule 7: Don't Accept a Saturday Night Date after Wednesday

"Rule 8: Fill Up Your Time before the Date

"Rule 11: Always End the Date First

"Rule 12: Stop Dating Him if He Doesn't Buy You a Romantic Gift for Your Birthday or Valentine's Day

"Rule 13: Don't See Him More than Once or Twice a Week

"Rule 14: No More than Casual Kissing on the First Date

"Rule 15: Don't Rush into Sex and Other *Rules* for Intimacy"

Sexual politics, like all politics, is about gaining the upper hand. These rules are intended to help women extract as much out of men as possible with minimal effort, which is fair enough, but they don't work because they don't take into account the different criteria by which men and women evaluate prospective mates.

Women ascertain a man's sexual desirability primarily through his social dominance. This is a multifaceted criterium, incorporating not only looks, but physical fitness, the power he wields in society (e.g. how much money he has), his personal confidence and other factors. Because of this quirk of the female psyche, a man who isn't naturally attractive can make himself more desirable by becoming successful in his career, working out at the gym, and/or altering his behavior (typically referred to as "game").

Men ascertain a woman's sexual desirability through her looks, and all other metrics are tertiary at best. If she makes his penis hard, she's a worthy conquest. This ensures that women who aren't wildebeests will have an endless stream of dudes looking to bring their battering rams crashing through her iron gates of life, but it has a downside; a woman's options for improving her sexual market value are limited. The reason a 20-year old co-ed can play the coy coquette and a 35-year old cougar has to force herself onto guys is because the former has qualities men desire (youth and beauty) that the latter doesn't and can never get back. Exceptionally attractive girls have a good deal of leeway in regards to their behavior, but an unattractive woman who prances about like she's a perfect 10, like *The Rules* says she should do, isn't going to suddenly make men think that she's a 10. They'll just avoid her in favor of girls who are still on the same plane of reality. Men instinctively know the difference between fool's gold and the real deal, and no games played by girls can convince them otherwise.

This is why *The Rules* doesn't work; because the authors are projecting their sexual desires onto men. Many of the Rules themselves exist in the literature of game; writers like Roosh,

Heartiste and Mystery encourage men to be aloof, to avoid paying for dates/buying women drinks, and to carefully ration the amount of time they spend on the phone with their girl, among other things. In his pick-up manual *Bang*, Roosh even goes into detail as to how many days a guy should wait before he calls back a girl he met at the bar. In their solipsism, having imbibed decades worth of feminist propaganda claiming that men and women are the same, women assume that men want the same things that they want, only to end up getting burned again and again when reality doesn't conform to their fantasies.

Another example of female solipsism can be found in this post from the blog *Gucci Little Piggy*, "From the Mouths of Babes":

> "Watching a girl teach another girl how to go about picking up a guy is like watching two retarded kids teach each other Advanced Thermodynamics. Last week, I witnessed a female friend trying to give a mutual female friend of ours pointers on picking up our mutual male friend. The female friend's advice was similar to the stuff that works for guys when picking up girls. She advocated playing hard-to-get, not standing too close to him, and walking away whenever he came near. My advice was this: 'Rub your tits on his nose.' Plain. And. Simple."[1]

Even when we leave the realm of sex, women are still deeply solipsistic. Feminism, the Western ideology that purports to empower women, is in fact a massive projection of female attitudes and beliefs onto men. Take the oft-repeated feminist claim that there is a patriarchy, an "old boys' club" that exists to give men special treatment and keep women down. As the anti-feminist writer Rob Fedders points out in his essay "When Shit Gets Sold as Soap...," not only is the "old boys' club" a myth, there in fact exists an "old girls' club" in female-dominated workplaces that promotes women at the expense of men:

> "I have never worked at a place where the men secretly conspired to give each other advantages over female co-workers... *but I have experienced working at places where myself and my male co-workers have caught several women conspiring in secrecy to make sure that women outperformed their male co-workers.* It happened when I was working in a high-pressure commission sales environment. It was a fair sized staff, 12 in sales (11 men, 1 woman), 3 in management (2 men, 1 woman), and 3 receptionists (all women). Now, don't go thinking it was discriminatory that there were 11 men and only 1 woman on the sales staff. The General Manager tried and tried to increase the

ratio of women on his staff, and hired several women while I was there, but the women he hired just kept quitting, some in tears, because they couldn't cope with the high pressure of commission sales.

"What was discovered by myself and my male co-workers, however, was that the three receptionists were sending double the amount of first-time customers & phone calls to the lone saleswoman, and the female manager was turning over double the amount of clients to the saleswoman as she was to the men.

"When it was brought to the attention of the General Manager, by 11 pissed off employees, he called *the only 5 females* that worked at the place into a meeting and after some intense grilling, the women finally admitted that they were purposefully sending more business to the woman than the men, because they wanted to make sure that a woman was the top salesperson. And not only that, *but they had discussed, in secret, how they were going to go about doing it!* And let's make this clear, every single woman that worked at that outfit was in on this secret conspiracy. Gee... sounds an awful lot like that far-fetched notion of patriarchy that women keep accusing men of... except the patriarchy-boy's club is the wrong gender, because what was really going on there was a matriarchal girl's club, which designed itself to discriminate based on gender.

"So, I maintain that women believe in so many of these far flung notions about men because women know that *women* themselves do these things and therefore they rationalize that if they were men, they would discriminate against women in the same way.

"There is no secret patriarchy – but there is a secret matriarchy."[2]

Fedders goes on to name other examples of feminist projection, such as how women view men as chattel "to provide...food, clothing, shelter and luxuries for herself and her children" while simultaneously accusing men of viewing women as "objects" and chattel.

Where does the extreme, unprecedented sexual solipsism of modern females come from? While I'd argue that women are naturally more inclined to solipsism than men, the human personality is very malleable, with culture and the surrounding environment being the sculptors. The deep, abiding cluelessness of Homo americanus womanus is a product of nurture, not nature.

I personally blame the average woman's complete disconnect from reality, owing in part to two realities of sex and biology. Women are the gatekeepers of sex; exempting rape, sex never happens unless the woman *wants* it to happen. Western dating and marriage culture is organized around this reality; in most cases, men are the ones who ask women out on dates and propose marriage. Additionally, female sexual power peaks long before mens' does. Because men find youth and beauty attractive, starting in her teen years, a reasonably attractive and sociable young woman can just sit back and watch the gentleman callers line up to kiss her feet. Not until her late twenties (give or take a few years depending on race and/or nationality) does her sexual power begin to wane. In contrast, no one but female pedophiles like Debra Lafave consider teenage boys to be desirable over all other age groups. Most men don't begin to hit the peak of their sexual power until their mid- to late twenties, when they've established themselves in their careers and matured a little. This is why, despite feminist propaganda, most intergenerational relationships and marriages consist of an older man and a younger woman, not the other way around. Because of these factors, Western women can spend a good portion of their lives sailing on a cloud of fantasy.

Not only that, what Heartiste terms the "Four Sirens of the Sexual Apocalypse," the four great social and technological changes that have enabled unrestrained female hypergamy (the desire for men at the top of the socioeconomic food chain to the exclusion of everyone else), also enable female solipsism.[3] These Sirens are:

1. Effective, cheap, legal and widely available contraception (condoms, birth control pills, abortion).
2. No-fault divorce.
3. Economic emancipation for women (letting them go to college and join the workforce).
4. Feminist-created laws like the Violence Against Women Act and child support laws that encourage women to divorce their husbands.

The Sirens enable female solipsism by shielding women from the consequences of their bad behavior. Cheap and freely available contraception, for example, removes most of the ill effects of being a slut. In the not-too-distant past, sexual promiscuity was a recipe for social censure and life-threatening diseases. No-fault divorce makes getting out of a marriage as easy as getting in for wives, with alimony and child support sweetening the deal. In the past, women were cautioned against these actions by their mothers and grandmothers; this knowledge was junked in the sexual revolution in favor of the "if it feels good, do it" mantra of liberalism. Think of a spoiled brat who has everything he wants handed to him without complaint (lest he throw a tantrum) and who is rescued by daddy whenever he gets himself into trouble. In our modern world, women are basically spoiled children, constantly running to Daddy Government in tears whenever their stupid choices blow up in their faces.

As I stated earlier, men aren't immune to being solipsistic, but on average they are less self-absorbed then women for the aforementioned reasons. We men are forced to confront reality from the outset because we are the dominant sex, expected to approach girls and direct our relationships with them. The overwhelming majority of guys have been slapped with rejections from girls from the day they first worked up the nerve to ask one out to the prom, forcing them to analyze their behaviors in order to either adapt to the sexual marketplace or drop out entirely in a world of video games and porn. The only men who can afford to engage in woman-esque solipsism without becoming late-night show punchlines are famous, wealthy or otherwise natural ladykillers; the rest of us grinders have to stay on our toes at all times.

Another factor in female sexual solipsism is how sexual promiscuity affects the minds of women. A comment from a now-defunct blog states this:

"That may or may not be true: most slutty women I

SEXUALITY

know could take on entire football teams without noticing the nature of male sexuality. They're that self absorbed in their emotional turmoil, they don't notice men look at them like a hungry man looks at a piece of meat. Prudes notice more, probably because they had fathers who were decent men."

The sexual double standard arises from the reality that getting sex is easy for women but hard for men. Women being the gatekeepers of sex, the reason studs are respected and sluts are derided is because being a stud requires skill, while being a slut merely requires a pulse and a lack of impulse control. As the folk saying goes, a key that can open many locks is a master key; a lock that can be opened by many keys is a faulty lock.

The unsung flip side of the double standard, however, is that female virgins are cherished whereas male virgins are ridiculed. A man who can't get laid signals to the world that he is a loser who repels girls, while a woman who resists spreading her legs for every scumbag who winks at her signals that she is a sober, selective person. Because women can get laid easily but have a much harder time wrangling commitment out of a man in the form of marriage or a long-term relationship, women who cannot or will not stay in a relationship are poor sources of information on men. The male virgin and the female slut are mirror images of each other in terms of attractiveness to and knowledge of the opposite sex.

The solipsism of the fairer sex will ultimately be their undoing. The social conditions that have empowered women are on the verge of collapse. The article "The Misandry Bubble" from *The Futurist* names the "Four Horsemen of Male Emancipation," four factors that will ensure the destruction of feminism by the end of this decade:

1. Game, the art of seduction, teaching men how to manipulate female psychology to their advantage in the mating dance.

2. Adult entertainment technological such as virtual reality sex simulators, allowing men to have sex without the hassle of having to seduce an actual woman.

3. Globalization, which encompasses the expatriation of Western men to non-feminist countries outside the West as well as immigration from those same countries to Western countries, weakening popular support for feminism.

4. Male economic disengagement due to the poor economy and progressive taxation that benefits women at the expense of men. Even with our current "mancession," men still dominate job fields that are necessary to keep the economy going, such as construction, manufacturing, mining, law enforcement and the military; women dominate ancillary fields such as education, healthcare,

and the civil service. The latter needs the former to function, but the former doesn't need the latter.[4]

Coupled with how women typically desire marriage more than men and women's hypergamous mating preferences, this is going to lead to a massive shift of power in the mating market from women to men. *The Futurist* terms the moment when a woman realizes her sexual power has fallen off a cliff the "Wile E. Coyote Moment":

> "...In the past, the steady hand of a young woman's mother and grandmother knew that her beauty was temporary, and that the most seductive man was not the best husband, and they made sure that the girl was married off to a boy with long-term durability. Now that this guidance has been removed from the lives of young women, thanks to 'feminism', these women are proving to be poor pilots of their mating lives who pursue alpha males until the age of 34-36 when her desirability drops precipitously and not even beta males she used to reject are interested in her. This stunning plunge in her prospects with men is known as the *Wile E. Coyote* moment, and women of yesteryear had many safety nets that protected them from this fate. The 'feminist' media's attempt to normalize

'cougarhood' is evidence of gasping desperation to package failure as a desirable outcome, which will never become mainstream due to sheer biological realities...

"The big irony is that 'feminism', rather than improving the lives of women, has stripped away the safety nets of mother/grandmother guidance that would have shielded her from ever having to face her Wile E. Coyote moment. 'Feminism' has thus put the average woman at risk in yet another area."

With the coming economic meltdown and the end of the "sheconomy," a great many Strong, Independent Women™ are going to find themselves up Shit Creek without a paddle. While marriage served the function of keeping good women out of total poverty in the past, the current generation of men will be too burned out by feminism to play Captain Save-a-Ho this time around. In the war between the sexes, the ultimate losers will be *women*, not men.

October 6, 2009, revised and expanded November 2011

The Emptiness of Modern Manhood

If I had a loonie for every cubicle jockey I've known

who's huffed and puffed about quitting their office slave job and going on an trip abroad, I'd have enough money to do it myself. Roosh is one of the few men who had the brains and balls to follow through. After ditching his career as an industrial microbiologist and finishing his first book, Bang, Roosh took a trip through South America that lasted six months and took him to eight countries. Now, he has transcribed the events of his trip into a travel memoir. Don't be dissuaded by his cliché-laden description of *A Dead Bat in Paraguay* as being about "suffering and pain and hardship and darkness": Roosh's book is a glorious triumph of low comedy and high adventure, a breezy and worthwhile read.

      Unfortunately, as this is Roosh's first foray into literary writing, his inexperience shines through at regular intervals. While he narrates his misadventures with a wry tone that readers of his blog ought to be familiar with, every so often he breaks voice to go on a sentimental missive. Take for instance, this snippet in which Roosh tries really, really hard to convince us that he gives a shit about poor miners in Bolivia:

> "Until the output of the Potosí mines cease to be profitable—and it is a matter of when, not if—these men and future generations who follow will die miners, much younger than is fair… I felt small for complaining about my relatively easy job at home that paid me a salary the miners could only dream

of. How did I come to the conclusion that a professional job with fair pay in a modern building was actually torture?"

My God, someone has it worse off than you! What an original observation! Please, shut the fuck up and spare me the bathos.

But aside from these trite diversions, *A Dead Bat in Paraguay* maintains a breakneck pace from beginning to end. The story begins in Washington, DC, where Roosh relates the story of his life and the factors that led to him giving the bird to the 9-to-5 life and heading to South America. The sequence of events will be familiar to longtime Roosh readers, both of his current blog and his previous incarnation as DC Bachelor, but Roosh fills in details about his career and family life that are new and interesting. In particular, his description of his close relationship with his sister is moving, showing a side of Roosh that we don't see in his other writings.

An important part of any book is its diction, and on this front, *A Dead Bat in Paraguay* is as smooth and pleasing to read as a good wine is to drink. An acolyte of the Hemingway school of literary writing, Roosh shies away from flowery descriptions and overblown metaphors, relaying his story with an understatement that conveys imagery and emotion in its own way. His bone-dry sense of humor pervades his prose at almost all times, with lines like "I made love with the toilet." Roosh is awfully fond of toilet humor in the literal sense: a lot of the laughs come from his loving descriptions of the painful, explosive bowel movements he had while on the road. No mere clown, though, he also retells the struggles of his journey with a bluntness that gets the reader invested emotionally. A large part of the narrative is Roosh's attempts to hook up with the local women in the various places he visits, only to be met with repeated failure. His constant battle to adapt his game to the cultural idiosyncrasies of the women who he tries to bed is so compelling that when he finally meets success, you'll want to cheer.

The frankness and honesty of *A Dead Bat in Paraguay* is a refreshing change from the fake, phony, and fraudulent memoirs that have flooded the book world in recent years, but it also hurts the book in some ways. Any good storyteller has the ability to bullshit with aplomb, and Roosh isn't quite there yet. His emphasis on relaying the details of his trip has too much of a "just the facts, ma'am" feel to it, as if he was writing a college paper and not a commercial book. The weakness of this approach culminates in the book's ending, which just sucks. In fact, it isn't really an ending: the book just sort of stops.

In pointing out these issues, I don't want come off as being too critical. In a literary world full of flotsam, jetsam, and other varieties of garbage, Roosh has produced something remarkable and memorable. Beyond its other qualities, *A Dead Bat in Paraguay* speaks to something deeper: the dissatisfaction so many men these days have with their lives. Writers sublimating their existential angst into grand adventures which they later published is nothing new, as we can see from this stanza from Lord Byron's *Childe Harold's Pilgrimage*:

> "Childe Harold bask'd him in the noontide sun,
> Disporting there like any other fly;
> Nor deem'd before his little day was done
> One blast might chill him into misery.
> But long ere scarce a third of his pass'd by,
> Worse than adversity the Childe befell;
> He felt the fulness of satiety:
> Then loathed he in his native land to dwell,
> Which seem'd to him more lone than Eremite's sad cell."

What *is* different is that ennui with one's existence is no longer confined to misfits like Byron. Last year, former *Lonely Planet* guidebook writer Thomas Kohnstamm published his own travel memoir, *Do Travel Writers Go to Hell?*, in which he stated similar reasons as Roosh for abandoning his high-paying corporate job in Manhattan to roam northeastern Brazil. In fact, Kohnstamm is mentioned in passing in Roosh's book, though not by name (Kohnstamm achieved some notoriety when he revealed that he had fabricated parts of his guidebooks, even claiming he wrote the *Lonely Planet* guidebook to Colombia without having visited there). This concept of men being unsatisfied with their lives has become clichéd to the point where we now have "mid-life crises" and "quarter-life crises." What is it about the modern West that sucks the joy out of being a man? To quote John Derbyshire:

> "The modern workplace has also been de-masculinized. I have spent many years working in the offices of big corporations, among the vast clerical middle class of the Information Age. It has often struck me how much more suitable this work is for women than for men—how, in fact, men seem rather out of place among the "tubes and cubes" of the modern office. No masculine values are visible here. The mildness of manners, the endless tiny courtesies, the yielding and compromising, the cheery assertions of labor-room stoicism ("Hangin' in there!") that are necessary to get this kind of work done, leave little outlet for masculine forcefulness. Such outlets as did once exist have been systematically sealed off by the feminists and "sexual harassment" warriors. Was it really only twelve years ago that my mixed-sex office in a big Wall Street trading house celebrated the boss's birthday by bringing in a full-monty stripper to

entertain us? Yes, it was. If we did that today, we should be the subject of a *60 Minutes* segment.

"The more boisterous manifestations of masculinity—physical courage, danger-seeking, the honor principle, belligerence, chivalry, endurance, small-group loyalty—which were once accessible to all men, in episodes of war or exploration if not in everyday life, have now been leached out to the extremes of our society—to small minorities of, at one extreme, super-rich sports and entertainment stars, and at the other, underclass desperadoes. There is no place now for a brilliant misfit like the Victorian explorer Sir Richard Burton, whose love of danger and of alien cultures led him to be the first, and quite probably the only, non-Moslem ever to penetrate the holiest sanctuary of Islam, the Ka'aba in Mecca—he even had the audacity to make a surreptitious sketch of the place while he was supposed to be praying. (Burton, by the way, was a holy terror as a boy—would be a sure candidate for heavy Ritalin treatment nowadays.)"[5]

With the government and society out to crush any

expression of manliness beyond servile boot-licking, we are forced into feminized roles in order to survive. Any expression of true masculinity is suppressed. As men, we have allowed ourselves to be mentally and emotionally gelded by a culture that seeks to abuse us for its own immoral ends. But you don't have to be a slave. Rebellion doesn't necessarily entail ripping up stakes to settle in an alien nation on another continent. It begins when you become cognizant of the system and how to avoid being enmeshed in its grinder. The revolution begins with you.

In the meantime, feel free to give Roosh your greenbacks. He's earned them.

The Spearhead, September 25, 2009

Sluttiness Implies Consent

Some time ago, I came across a manifesto entitled "Sluts Against Rape" posted at a blog entitled *Bitch Brat*.[6] Opposing rape is such a brave and daring position to take—right up there with supporting world peace and opposing punting puppies into lakes—especially coming from a class of women whose weekends usually involve taking multiple foreign objects in multiple orifices. I'm in a *really* good mood, so I'm going to rip this essay apart and impart a valuable lesson in the process.

The post is prefaced with this note:

"This piece from the Women's Direct Action

> Collective reflects my belief that a woman should be able to dress, act and live her life exactly as she wants and not be persecuted or prosecuted for it..."

What utter narcissism. No one on earth, man or woman, can "live [their] life exactly as [they] want": if everyone did that, organized society would crumble as the force of six billion atomized entities following their whims collided like particles in a nuclear reactor. Civilization is a compromise between individuals, and its a compromise I've been all too happy to make.

Also note: why is it that feminists demand total autonomy for women, something men have *never* had throughout the history of the civilized world?

> "...Of course that would be the ideal world, but then no one ever listens to me cos I'm apparently a whore. Ha ha..."

I remember listening to the Tom Leykis show years ago when a female caller came on the air accusing him of saying something that he hadn't. To his credit, he refrained from insulting her off the bat, simply telling her that she was wrong. She then declared that he was "picking a fight with [her] because [she was] a woman," to which Leykis replied, "No, I'm picking a fight with you 'cause you're *stupid!*" Anonymous whore blogger, nobody listens to you for the same reason.

SEXUALITY

The manifesto begins proper:

"We are feminists. We call ourselves 'Sluts Against Rape' because we believe that a woman should have the right to be sexual in any way she chooses and that she is never at fault for rape."

Yes, a woman is "never at fault for rape," like how a white supremacist who walks into a black neighborhood wearing white sheets and throwing burning crosses onto front lawns isn't at fault if he gets the shit beaten out of him and possibly arrested. It's not like he put himself in a bad situation or did something incredibly stupid!

Fact of the matter, sexual arousal in men is an involuntary reaction. Unless a man is gay, a eunuch, or medically impotent, his dick will get hard if he sees an attractive woman. There's also a small segment of men who are deranged enough to act on their erections in a violent and unacceptable way, a segment of men who cannot be eliminated from the population. Ladies (and I use that term with the utmost sarcasm), if you put yourself in dangerous situations, such as walking alone in a crummy neighborhood in the middle of the night or getting in a car with a bunch of strangers, you are partially culpable if something bad happens to you. Ignorance of reality is not an excuse.

"...We choose to focus on sexual promiscuity–
straight or queer–as a positive assertion of sexual

SEXUALITY

> identity and to focus on women as sexual agents as opposed to sexual victims. We remember that this embrace of sexuality in the public sphere has been particularly difficult for people of color, women–especially sex workers–and queer women..."

"Queer women?" Yes, that epidemic of straight men raping lesbians has been all over the news lately.

> "...Each of these group's "supposed" inability to sexually control themselves has been used as justification for violence..."

Funny, going by what the media says, it's sheltered, middle-class, straight white chicks who are the most clueless on this issue.

> "...At the same time, each of these groups have continued to explore and refine the place of sexuality in their lives and insist that public spaces remain open to them."

I tried feeding that line into my Bullshit-to-English translator, and now it's throwing out sparks and smoke. Anyone care to decipher this nonsense?

> "Promiscuity is often used as a justification for rape

> and violence—it is used as a justification for rape by rapists, by the legal system, and even at times by other women who attempt to impose their own rigid morality upon others..."

"Justification" does not mean "factor that increased the chances of the crime happening." If you stop smoking, you reduce your risk of dying from lung cancer. If you stop being a slut—including stopping engaging in the activities that are usually associated with sluttiness, such as barhopping at 3am, binge drinking, and taking random cocks in the keister—you'll reduce the chances of running into a psycho who'll rape you. Try taking some personal fucking responsibility for your actions. And while you complain of "women who attempt to impose their own rigid morality upon others," you chicks don't have a problem with imposing your *own* morality on the rest of us: namely, your insane contention that the members of the less-fair sex should be allowed to do whatever they want without facing the consequences.

> "...Discourse on male violence tends to centralize male sexuality and demand women's safety in relationship to it. In this context, our own sexualities become peripheral, almost non-existent..."

Uh yeah, because men are both physically stronger then

women and a greater percentage of them are inclined to use that strength to sick ends. Christ, it's like I said: sluts are as clueless about men as guy virgins are clueless about women. It's like there's a chemical in semen that kills girls' brain cells if they imbibe too many different varieties. Too much dick makes Jane a dumb girl, too much dick makes Jane a dumb girl...

> "...When female sexuality does become visible—when we put on a sexy dress and say naughty things—we are seen as colluding in our own oppression (read: we invite rape)..."

"When alcoholism does become visible—when we uncork a bottle of vodka and start doing shots—we are seen as colluding in our own oppression (read: we invite cirrhosis)."

> "...When women's innocence is invoked as a reason to curb male sexual violence, the usual assumption is that this innocence is only something white, middle class, heterosexual women can have, all women of color are presumed to be already sexually available. Thus, we argue, innocence has never protected any of us and we need to recognize the racist and classist assumptions behind any embrace of innocence."

This is a typical leftist debate tactic in regards to race:

throwing out naked assertions with no proof. Press them for facts and they fold like a two-dollar bill. What evidence is there that only "white, middle class, heterosexual women" can have "innocence?"

> "We participate in this year's 'Take Back the Night March' to protest rape and to protest the lack of safety in public spheres shared by all women, all people of color and all sexual minorities. But we will not erase our own sexual adventures, our own sexual displays to occupy this public space."

A TBTN rally is one of the most unintentionally funny events you can witness. There's just something hilarious about watching "liberated," "empowered," "independent" women who think that hammy speeches and candlelight vigils will stop a deranged madman from forcing his crotch rocket into their baby pockets. The ones that allow men are the funniest of all, because you get to see the sorts of empty-sacked, limp-wristed, easily-cuckolded eunuchs who consider themselves feminists. Seriously, drop in to one if you can.

> "We support the rights of prostitutes to be prostitutes, the rights of strippers to be strippers..."

Hooking and stripping aren't "rights," they're choices... and choices have consequences.

> "...We support the rights of porn stars,
> transgendered people, transsexuals, lesbians,
> bisexuals, gay men, all self-defined sluts (and there
> is no hegemony of style here), and all sexual
> minorities made invisible by the institution of
> compulsory heterosexuality..."

"Compulsory heterosexuality?" The really sad part is that these jokers believe their own bullshit. Hint: minorities are minorities because they constitute a small fraction of a given population. And none of these so-called minorities are "invisible": in fact, at no point in history have homosexuals and bisexuals had as much freedom to live their lives as they wish as they do now.

> "...Though we are often victimized, we will not be
> passive victims. We are active sexual agents
> strutting our stuff in the face of rape."

All the "strutting" won't save you when a sicko overpowers you in a dark alley.

This sort of thing is a prime example of how feminists encourage women to do stupid things that get them hurt or killed. They kvetch on about how women should be able to do what they like and not get raped or murdered, *but it is precisely the mentality that women should be able to do what they like, including doing monumentally moronic things, that leads to them getting raped or murdered.* That's right, you go girl! Go ahead, pound Jagerbombs until four in the morning, then walk home alone! Anything the boys can do, you can do better! And when the girls who do those things end up violated or on a mortuary slab, the very same people who encouraged them to engage in the behavior that lead to them being raped and/or killed turn around and tell the rest of us that we're not allowed to criticize them for engaging in that behavior by bleating, *"Don't blame the victim!"* Can anyone else see just how fucked up this is?

Well, I've had enough. Every time a woman does something dumb that leads to them getting hurt, we shouldn't be afraid to call her out on it. Roosh wrote recently on the case of a dumb bitch who poured her drink on Joe Francis' shoulder and got her ass kicked as a result. He concludes:

> "Do think Jayde would have attacked a man like that in a Middle Eastern country? Hell no because she knows she'd be **murdered.** I'm definitely not saying that's what we need, but our culture has taught women that they can disrespect men without repercussion, and has taught men to accept that disrespect like little punks. Well there are men who haven't bought that view and are making the world a better place by teaching women like Jayde that

you can't go around attacking men. I guarantee you she will never pour a shot on a man again in her life."[7]

Am I saying we should go around excusing rape or violence against women? No. I oppose those things, as does anybody else with a semi-functioning moral compass, and anyone who commits those crimes should be punished. But allowing the feminists to browbeat society with their "don't blame the victim" chanting has done nothing but harm the lives of women. The next time something bad happens to a girl who helped bring it upon herself, we should scream this fact from the rooftops. And it may be time to bring back that dreaded four-word sentence, that phrase that instills fear in the hearts of knowing fools. That most hated line is:

"I told you so."

October 29, 2009

Women Don't Get to Define Female Beauty

I've got lots of ideas knocking around my skull, but it sometimes takes external stimuli in order to get them out of my head and in comprehensible form, like this catty blog post by real-life libertarian girl Ilana Mercer concerning Christian martyr-cum-amateur porn star Carrie Prejean:

"**Blond Squad'** is a synonym here for the

conservatives' chick of choice. She can be brunette, although that is not preferable. She *has to be* dumb. [...]

[...] "Prejean's looks comport with what I've termed the **porn aesthetic**. She is most certainly not beautiful.

"Those who've been conditioned to consider beautiful women who look well-used, cheap, unrefined, and whorish even in their youth will object. But you only have to think of **Audry Hepburn** [sic], or the bare-faced **Julie-Christie** to remember what natural, striking beauty is."[8]

Following Mercer's link leads us to a post where she defines the "porn aesthetic":

"...they represent what I call the **porn aesthetic**, the essence of which is not true sensuality or real physical beauty, but something that corresponds to the lowest form of sex. They are pornographic phenoms theirs are faces that men want to see on hookers; on women they have plain crude sex with. They look well-used, cheap, unrefined, and whorish even in their youth."[9]

That post serves as a teaser for this column she wrote for *WorldNetDaily*, "Sluts Galore: Scenes from 2006":

"Ideas about feminine beauty are bust. The sublime 1350 B.C. bust of Queen Nefertiti showcases her fine cheekbones and graceful neck. Her Western contemporary look-a-like, down to the perfectly shaped dainty face, was Audrey Hepburn. Catherine Deneuve embodied the French ideal of female beauty, immortalized in the bust of Marianne.

"But forget these regal beauties; they, apparently, have nothing on the double-chinned, large, flat expanses that make up Britney Spears' crude mug. Nefertiti, Hepburn, Deneuve—your patrician pulchritude no longer excites the "porn generation"; the sly, weasel-like looks of a Paris Hilton do.

"The culture's aesthetic preferences are now shaped by the basest of instincts. I call it the porn aesthetic, another example of which is Hugh Hefner's harem of hos. The three kept creatures are currently starring in a reality show called 'The Girls Next Door.'

"According to Wikipedia, "The prototype of the girl next door is often invoked in American contexts to indicate wholesome, unassuming, or 'average' femininity." Like Ali MacGraw in "Love Story," perhaps? Hef's hos have bleached, cotton-candy hair, augmented by extensions, silicone breasts, and demented, syphilitic grins. But according to an entirely new sensibility, they are the girls next door."[10]

So, according to Miss Mercer, Carrie Prejean isn't beautiful because she looks like a woman that men instinctively want to bang, and Audrey Hepburn *is* beautiful because she looked like a woman that men instinctively *didn't* want to bang. That's a statement so retarded only a libertarian woman could argue it in earnest.

Manosphere writers have argued in the past that women, not men, determine which males are alphas in the context of mating and sex. The flip side of this is that *men, not women, determine which females are beautiful.* The primary purpose of female beauty is to help us men determine who is most worthy of receiving our sperm-missiles, and the yardstick we use to measure it is the penis. The harder the dick, the hotter the girl; it is that simple.

Now, I'm sure some of you are thinking, *"Ferdinand, you reductionist, cock-centered, evo-psych-loving pig-dog, you're wrong! In past epochs, women's beauty was determined by higher concepts then what men got off to!"* Take your romanticist golden age crap and stick it where the wind breaks. The female beauty ideal has *always* been determined by what men wanted to nail, as Lynne Lawner wrote in *Lives of the Courtesans:*

> "Falling in love with statues and paintings, even making love to them is an ancient fantasy, one of which the Renaissance was keenly aware. Giorgio Vasari, writing in the introductory section of the Lives about art in antiquity, tells how men violated the laws, going into the temples at night and making love with the statues of Venus. In the morning, priests would enter the sanctuaries to find stains on the marble figures."

Yes, that's right. Those beautiful Greek marble statues that are supposedly symbolic of a higher ideal of beauty? Guys were so turned on by them that they dry-humped them and shot their sticky loads in their crevices. I hope that visual is permanently burned into your brain. And all of those paintings of beautiful women from the Renaissance? They were the jerk-off fantasies of the men who created them. Yes, we of the male species really do think with our little heads that much.

Now, if Miss Mercer wanted to argue that women are becoming less feminine, I'd agree. If she wanted to argue that women are becoming more crass and vulgar, I'd wholeheartedly agree. But the cock doesn't care about a woman's class or behavior; it just wants a nice, warm, attractive place to snuggle for the night. Mercer's notion of "true" female beauty springing from something other then what men want to fuck is pure bullshit. Her vision blinded by female solipsism and her mind dulled by historical ignorance, she can't help but get it wrong.

And, ladies, if you think it's unfair that we get to determine what we find attractive in you, keep in mind that it's also unfair that you get to determine what you find attractive in us. We can't help our dicks any more then you can help your pussies. This is the Age of Flesh, where the desires of the loins rule all. I don't make the rules, I just point them out.

November 17, 2009

Marriage is Dying: How Will Women Respond?

Yesterday, I read a story from *The Frisky* on older American women seeking European men for long-term relationships and marriage. The primary complaints of both writer Amelia McDonell-Parry and Irina Aleksander (who wrote the

New York Observer article that McDonell-Parry based her post on) is that American men are "commitment-phobic" and "emotionally unavailable": the usual whiny, self-centered crap. A couple of telling quotes:

> "The collective sigh that evening was in reference to the stubborn, New York man-child with his perpetual fear of marriage and confused ("I love you, now go away") approach to relationships. It is now an entrenched cultural truth: A desirable woman in her 30s could meet someone, date for a while, enter a relationship, spend Thanksgiving at her boyfriend's parents' house, rent an apartment together, adopt a pet, wash his skivvies for years and still: Long-term commitment is not guaranteed. [...]
>
> [...] "After all, there's no way I'm the only 30-year-old who met a man, dated him for 4.5 years, spent countless holidays with his family, lived with him, adopted a dog with him, and did his laundry before being unceremoniously dumped (for someone younger and probably more willing to have anal sex)."[11]

SEXUALITY

A long long time ago, I recall reading a feminist somewhere on the Web write that going on a date with a girl (and paying) didn't entitle a man to sex, or even to a kiss goodnight. Well ladies, the flip side of that truth is that getting banged stupid by a guy doesn't entitle you to marriage (or any kind of relationship). It doesn't even entitle you to a phone call back the next day. Gender parity is a bitch, bitches.

More to the point, these posts got me thinking. Everyone is familiar with the pattern that women in our hypergamous culture follow: they spend their prime, fertile years getting fucked left, right, up and down by alphas, and when they hit the big 3-0 and find themselves stretched out, aging, and alone, they settle for a near-virginal nice guy beta. But if girls of a certain age are now finding it difficult to get hitched, to the point where they now consider expatriating to find foreign men who *don't* know that they spent the better part of their lives as the town doorknob, this may signal that a change is in the air.

Extrapolating this from a couple of articles may seem far-fetched, but there's sufficient empirical evidence to show that we're witnessing a slow, steady shift in the sexual marketplace. Alphas are more often then not averse to marriage because they have so many options in women and subsequently zero incentive to exclusively commit to any one. But if betas, the safety school of the urban slut machine, are wising up to the fact that marrying one of their same-aged chick compadres is the sexual equivalent of paying full price for a busted Yugo, along with the mancession and the already-existing disincentives for men to marry, this spells doom for the marriage industry.

If marriage is indeed dying due to women's collective abuse of the institution, how will they react? Despite feminist fish and bicycle chanting, accepted wisdom shows that women are far more interested in marriage then men. If in fact more and more men are refusing to commit, how will women cope? Let's take a look:

1. Shaming tactics.

We already see the attempts by our cultural overlords to slander single men as "manboys" who are "afraid to grow up," trying to guilt us guys into binding ourselves in chains. Unfortunately, women have overplayed this card to the point where its effectiveness is rapidly approaching zero. I remember once reading on an MGTOW site that shaming language is like a scalpel, in that it is intended to be used in a surgical, precise manner, aiming right for vital spots. Modern women wield shaming language like a mallet, trying to beat down men with a tiny little knife. They've so abused shaming tactics that the blade has broken off, leaving them with nothing but a handle stained with their sweat.

2. Expatriating, like the articles recommend.

Some individuals will do this, but it will never catch on for two primary reasons. One, women are the more parochial sex, less willing to date outside the tribe.[12] Two, foreign men already think of American women as fucked-in-the-head harpies only good for pumping and dumping.[13]

3. Legal coercion.

This has historical precedent; during the waning years of the Roman Empire, taxes were levied on unmarried men in an attempt to get them to settle down.[14] Bachelor taxes have been proposed and passed at various times in America's history.[15-16] I've predicted in the past that feminists and conservatives in Congress would join forces to try to pass a bachelor tax into law in the coming years. I don't think such proposals will go through, but given that the two groups have pushed through anti-male legislation before, its not impossible. Unmarried men will likely react to a bachelor tax by leaving the country, renouncing their American citizenship, or by simply utilizing less-than-legal methods to hide their income from the IRS.

4. Girl game.

Women will start learning tactics to rope their men into commitment. Unfortunately, on this topic, most female writers have their heads rammed so far up their asses they can see daylight out the other end. And the problem with girl game is that its utility is much more limited than guy game. No amount of game can turn a wrinkled 36-year old into a tight-bodied teenager, a clap-infected slut into a virgin, or a monster from the black lagoon into a hottie. The sad reality of female sexual market value is that most of it is determined by factors that are either outside the woman's control or the result of choices that can't be reversed.

5. Wisdom.

Younger women will witness the sorry state of their thirty-something spinster sisters and begin pursuing commitment and marriage when they're still at the peak of their value, averting a potential crisis and saving Western civilization in the process. They'll also begin agitating for social reform that will make marriage a more viable option for men. Yeah right, and I'm a Canadian Mountie.

Not too long ago, the woman MRA blogger Hestia asked what Marriage 3.0 would look like. (Pre-Sexual Revolution marriage was Marriage 1.0, while modern marriage is Marriage 2.0.) Frankly, the idea of a Marriage 3.0 is ludicrous, like the concept of trans-transhumanism. There will be no Marriage 3.0 because marriage as an institution is on its deathbed. Single ladies interested in settling down should be very, very concerned. Men can live without marriage; in fact, we'd be better off without it in many ways. As has been said before, the biggest losers in the coming hell will be women, not men.

January 20, 2010

Pornonomics

Living in our modern world with its various creature comforts, it's easy to forget the struggles that our forbears had to go through in order to enjoy the things we take for granted. Take porn as an example. You kids don't realize how easy you've got it! When I was your age, trying to find decent porn on the internet was nearly impossible. Half of the porn sites out there were nothing but teaser pages with nothing good on them that did nothing but redirect you to other worthless teaser pages. And on the off chance you *did* find something to fill the spank bank with, good luck downloading it over a 56k modem. We had to resort to swiping dirty mags from the convenience store, stealing our parents' hidden VHS tapes, or **gasp** using our imaginations! Nowadays, you whippersnappers have got broadband internet and your own private laptops to access a universe of smut in all sizes and flavors floating around on torrent networks and video upload sites like *YouPorn* and *RedTube*. Sons of guns.

    If you're curious as to what inspired the above bit of curmudgeonry, for the past few weeks, I've been getting emails from a porn site I briefly subscribed to years ago begging me to re-join by lowering their prices. This was during the uncomfortable period when internet smut emerged from the anarchic Scam Era of the late 90's, but before it blossomed into the anarchic File Sharing Era that we live in today. Aside from the usual deluge of virus-laden spam mails with near-incomprehensible subject lines (*"H0t brun3tte lo\/35 \/\/3ll-hung 5t/_/d!"*) that my filters catch most of the time, I haven't heard from the site since I canceled my subscription. And now, years after I forgot about them, they want me back? Not only that, they've also been offering me a reduced subscription fee to one of their competitors if I sign back up with them. That's kind of like Apple offering discounts on Motorola Droids if you buy an iPad.

If this piece from *Freakonomics* is any indication, the porn industry is among the many whom the Internet has eagerly turkey slapped:

> "The biggest of the sites, Pornhub, is currently the 53rd most heavily trafficked site on the Internet. By contrast, CNN.com is No. 59, the website of the *New York Times* is No. 96, and vivid.com (the site of the best-known high-end porn producer in the U.S.) is No. 19,543. (YouTube is no. 3.) Sales of porn DVDs are collapsing, and the revenues of subscription-based porn sites are drying up. Vivid did sue one of the porn-tube sites for copyright infringement, but that suit was dropped in 2008 and the targeted site continues to operate. There is some talk within the porn industry of a coordinated litigation strategy a la the recording industry's campaign against Internet file-sharers. But there are other insiders who note that copyright suits have done little to stop the implosion of the major record companies, and who despair of any

litigation-based solution. And, unlike the record industry, pornography producers have shown no interest thus far in suing their customers for illegally downloading porn."[17]

From the looks of things, the porn industry will be joining the newspaper industry in the Graveyard of Technological Anachronisms. But who can feel sorry for them when they put out pathetic PSAs like this?[18]

God, that video was hilarious. When the movie got to the black chick talking about "creative artists," I started laughing my ass off. What creativity? *You fuck on camera for money, honey.* The most "creative" you can get is deciding whether to use mayonnaise or egg yolk for the money shot.

That's one of the industry's biggest problems: the nature of porn precludes creativity. Individual fetishes aside, the only point of smut is to help the viewer get off. The artistic evolution of pornography in the past forty years has moved towards making arousing the viewer quickly enough to get him to come as efficient as possible. From classic-style movies with plots, storylines, and Hollywood knockoff titles, we've descended to "gonzo" porn, which dispenses with the formalities and just gets straight to the fucking. It's a formula so simple that anyone can pull it off, and lots of people in our debased world do. And who cares about the "actors?" Can any of you normal people name any of the folks who have sex on film for your masturbatory pleasure? When every Dick and Jane with a digital camcorder can film themselves getting it on doggystyle on the dining room floor, the value of the average porn star falls through the floor.

Porn's other problem is that it's *porn*. It's a vice, sinful, pure evil in fleshy, carnal motion. Because of its inherently shameful nature, people are probably more likely to illegally download porn then any other form of media, and they can rationalize their actions more easily. Nobody will defend porn in court, on TV or in the hallways of respectable opinion if they want to keep their reputations intact. There will be no bailout for *Hustler* and *Vivid*. Hell, if I was a moralizing, short-sighted, uptight conservative, I'd clandestinely encourage file sharing porno movies to hasten the collapse of the industry. Pirates for Jesus!

The democratization of information access that has forced a reconfiguration of journalism is also forcing a change in mainstream pornography. Gone are the days of big-budget productions and highly-paid, household name stars and directors. The smut of tomorrow will be simpler and more cheaply produced, made by and starring people who either get paid shit or do it as a hobby. The *Freakonomics* piece lays out a probable future for porno:

> "In short, the porn-tube sites probably won't kill the porn industry. But they will change it. Production is

likely to shift even more from 'features' to short porn-tube-friendly clips. At the moment, the commercial porn industry, concentrated in L.A.'s San Fernando Valley, turns out more than 1,000 new feature films every month. This model probably cannot be sustained in a porn-tube world. Pornography is, in large part, a utilitarian product, and for most consumers, the purpose for which it is employed is served just as well by a five-minute porn-tube clip."

Of course, this will all become moot when the sexbots and VR sex simulators hit the stores.

This post has been rated D for Degenerate and has been approved by the *In Mala Fide* Rule 5 Committee. Heil Satan!

May 18, 2010

In(t)activism

One of the various hobbyhorses of the manosphere is "intactivism," opposition to circumcising boys when they're too young to decide for themselves. I've read the facts. I've heard the horror stories of guys with mutilated dicks and that poor kid in Canada who had his gender re-assigned because a surgeon screwed up a routine operation. I know that cut guys have less pleasurable orgasms because of decreased sensitivity and all the other problems. Blah blah blah.

Maybe I'm just a bad men's rights supporter, but I simply can't get worked up over circumcision. I don't disagree with the intactivists' arguments, but I can't pretend to care even one iota about the issue.

I'm among the many men in America who were cut at a young age. Specifically, according to my mom, I was circumcised the day after I was born. From what I recall her telling me (this was a long time ago), it was apparently against her will: the surgeons snuck in to do the dirty deed while she was in the bathroom or something and no one else was around to stop them. I've never cared to press her for details, largely because I don't consider my dick to be an appropriate topic of conversation when my mom is around. Really, that's it. I would have prefer to have not been snipped, but I don't claim to be traumatized for having a non-essential part of my anatomy removed when I was too young to tell the difference.

But there are people who are really, seriously into fighting this thing. The number one search for "intactivism" (sans quotes) on Google turns up *The Intactivism Pages*, a site about "the struggle for genital integrity and against the involuntary genital modification of children of any sex."[19] These people are nothing if not serious. They've got reams of documents debunking every justification for male circumcision that exists. They've got photo galleries comparing cut vs. uncut schlongs. They've even got a poem attacking willy-whacking, "The Rape of the Cock," which ends like this:

> "To cut a cock's a load of crock, no matter how they cut it.
> These words beware: "Just sign down there."
> They'll try to scare you but it
> Would do your son a wondrous boon to treat them with derision:
> 'You'd dock his dick? My God, that's sick!' To hell with circumcision!"[20]

Alexander Pope truly is rolling in his grave.

Honestly people, is defending the physical integrity of the penis the best you can come up with? Is it an issue of importance for MRAs on the level of no-fault divorce, alimony/child support, false rape accusations, and the myriad other problems that face men today? Hardly. Circumcision may suck, but it's not the end of the world. Even without a foreskin, you can still pee like a man and fuck like a champ. Having a bit of skin amputated from your peter is far from the worst thing that could happen to you.

But what really gets on my nerves about intactivism are the idiots who claim circumcision is as bad as female genital mutilation. No, it's not, and here's a reminder why it isn't:

"Female genital mutilation is classified into four major types.

- Clitoridectomy: partial or total removal of the clitoris (a small, sensitive and erectile part of the female genitals) and, in very rare cases, only the prepuce (the fold of skin surrounding the clitoris).

- Excision: partial or total removal of the clitoris and the labia minora, with or without excision of the labia majora (the labia are "the lips" that surround the vagina).

- Infibulation: narrowing of the vaginal opening through the creation of a covering seal. The seal is formed by cutting and repositioning the inner, or outer, labia, with or without removal of the clitoris.

- Other: all other harmful procedures to the female genitalia for non-medical purposes, e.g. pricking, piercing, incising, scraping and cauterizing the genital area."[21]

There's no male circumcision procedure that comes anywhere close to what victims of female genital mutilation have gone through. Sorry guys, but having your foreskin removed in a sterile, first-world hospital when you were a newborn is not the same as a ten-year old girl in some African village having her vaginal lips and clitoris ripped off by a bunch of primitives with blunt scalpels. Equating the two only serves to dilute the true horror of the latter.

I will say one thing for the intactivists, though: this claim that reducing your chances of contracting HIV is a good reason to get snipped is beyond stupid. Unprotected anal sex is the only form of intercourse from which you stand a chance of getting HIV. Ergo, the only people who have to worry about it are homosexuals and losers who rawdog IV drug using skanks in the ass. Oh wait, we're not allowed to mention that the spread of AIDS is related to the activities of certain protected groups! My bad.

While I essentially agree that forced circumcision is bad, I remain unconvinced that intactivism should occupy any more real estate in my cerebrum then any of the other things I don't give a shit about. Anyone care to persuade me otherwise?

June 8, 2010

Male Promiscuity and the Lover/Provider Complex

In the manosphere's haste to tear down the oh-so-pretty lies of the feminist-industrial complex, many of its inhabitants have a tendency to go too far in the opposite direction, inventing their own myths that are just as absurd. Like chilblains on the naked foot of a skier in the winter, these half-truths fester, propagate across the 'sphere, and itch like a real motherfucker. Because I specialize in pissing on peoples' myths, no matter who they are, I'm going to dissect and take down a particularly popular and persistent one: the myth of female attraction to male promiscuity.

The conventional wisdom of game is that women, being hypergamous, are attracted to men whom other women find attractive; they love men who are loved by other women. This truth has been proven and demonstrated over and over again in so many different places that I don't need to re-state it again. The lesser mind looks at the above reality and thinks, *"Well, if women want men who are wanted by other women, that means having sex with lots of women will make them want me more!"* BZZZT! Wrong answer!

This is where the Lover/Provider complex comes in. The Lover/Provider complex is basically the female equivalent of the Madonna/Whore complex. Much in the same way men desire a woman who both utterly chaste and is totally sexually debauched, women desire a man who both excites them down under and will stick around to provide for them. In other words, women ultimately want a man who embodies alpha and beta traits: the "gamma male," as Athol Kay has termed it.[22]

Since there are few if any gammas in the wild, women

will prioritize one side of the coin over the other. At the peak of their sexual power (late teens/early 20's), hormone-flushed, emotional girls will favor the Lover; older women will gravitate to the Provider as the estrogen drains from their veins and the biological clock tick-tocks away. Hence the phenomena of girls hopping aboard the alpha cock carousel when young and settling for a beta when they age out of peak attractiveness.

So what does this have to do with promiscuity? In a clamshell, the female fantasy of an attractive man is one who is wanted by many women but resists the temptation to shag them all rotten by committing to her and only her. As an example, take a look at romance novels, which usually all have the same plot: girl meets a dashing hunk who ravishes her like the sexy rapist that she is, and she subsequently tames him into a monogamous marriage, ending with the emasculating clang of wedding bells. Acting like a blow addict in a crackhouse is not a turn on.

Note that I did *not* say that manwhoredom is necessarily a turn *off*. The double standard is still in play. Because male promiscuity doesn't cause as much damage to women as female promiscuity does to men, women don't value chastity in men as highly as men do in women. However, all else being equal, give a woman a choice between two men and she will likely pick the one with the lower notch count. Since sexy, abstinent men are nearly nonexistent (outside of strict religious communities) in the Bacchanalia that is the modern sexual marketplace, this is one of the first requirements women will sacrifice when seeking out a mate.

Additionally, women's reactions to caddishness run along a continuum. I would argue that women who react more positively to male promiscuity are attracted *not* to the promiscuity itself, but to the danger it represents and its taboo nature.

I would attribute females' lack of attraction to male promiscuity to three reasons, since the biggest reason why men are wary of sluts—paternity certainty—doesn't apply:

1. Resources.

A polygamous man is likely to be dividing his assets up between his paramours, leaving less for each individual one. Plus, each woman risks impoverishment if the man abandons them.

2. Social standing and pussy price control.

Women who can ensnare men into long-term relationships gain prestige among other women, like how men who bang a lot of women are admired by other men. A girl who gets played by a known stud both signifies that she is low-value and lowers the price that other women can demand from men in exchange for sex, opening her up to attack from her peers. (As an aside, the latter reason is why it is women, and not men, who are the primary proponents of slut-shaming. Men don't hate sluts; we wouldn't marry 'em, but we love having 'em around for easy sex.)

3. The threat of STDs.

Men who stick their dicks in anything will inevitably pick

up all sorts of gross, exotic diseases, and women are at a greater risk for disease transmission during sex because vaginal tissue tears and breaks more easily than penile tissue, allowing said diseases to enter the bloodstream. Condoms protect you from many STDs, but not all, and the Law of Large Numbers means that the more you engage in a certain activity, the more likely something will go wrong. This is probably less of a concern to most women (despite their protestations to the contrary) due to the fact that it isn't part of their unconscious, hindbrain thinking. If women truly prioritized avoiding contracting VD, extramarital sex would vanish overnight.

I originally started drafting this article way back in February, when a now-vanished rookie blogger wrote a post in which he claimed that feminists are now trying to slut-shame studly men:

> "Recently, however, I have been attacked for my traditional 'stud-ness' by men as well as women. I am no longer a 'stud.' I am now a 'man-whore.' This shift in attitudes is important for two reasons. First, it categories those that are labelled with it in the same class as female whores. It is another arrow in the quiver for feminists to have their cake and eat it too. More importantly, by making the term acceptable for men to call other men 'man-whores'

means that 'stud-ness' is no longer something to be aspire to. Instead, studs are being attacked by beta men, who are only doing what they think women want."[23]

I don't think feminists will be leading a charge to shame caddish men into monogamy, largely because it was they who opened the floodgates of promiscuity to begin with. If there is a stud backlash, it will come from non-feminist women. Back in April when I took a break from blogging, Susan Walsh posted on a study that confirms the above observations:

"...A study at the University of Illinois by Allison and Risman surveyed 20,000 undergraduates at 20 colleges and universities. Their conclusion:

"COLLEGE STUDENTS LESS LIKELY HOLD TO A SEXUAL DOUBLE STANDARD. AND SOMETIMES THE DOUBLE STANDARD GOES AGAINST MEN. [...]

[...] "They found that 63% of men lose respect for women who hook up frequently, hardly surprising. What's more surprising is that 41% of men lose respect for other men who hook up frequently. This may reflect the resentment of men who feel like "have nots." Or it may be that men who are more relationship-oriented disrespect the "pump and dump" mentality.

"When it came to women, Allison and Risman found that 60% of women lose respect for other women who hook up frequently. Again, this is not surprising, and speaks to female intrasexual competition. Women who prefer to abstain from casual sex are well aware that promiscuous women are depressing the number of men willing to commit. What is very surprising is that **70% of women lose respect for men who hook up frequently.**"[24]

Susan also cites a study which shows that women who are more chaste are less likely to support the double standard:

"In a direct test of the double standard, the students were asked whether or not they would discourage either a female or a male friend from dating someone who had had intercourse with more than 10 partners. Contrary to our hypothesis, the women did not personally endorse the double standard. In fact, they were more likely to discourage a female friend from dating a highly experienced male than to discourage a male friend from dating a highly experienced female. These findings again suggest that women today may be judging highly experienced men more negatively than experienced women (a reverse double standard). This might be explained by the traditional script: Men are seen as strong and capable of self-preservation, whereas women are seen as potential victims who need to be defended. O'Sullivan (1995) noted that a highly experienced male might be seen as someone who is more likely to ignore signs of resistance during a sexual encounter."

I should state that women losing respect for promiscuous men will not necessarily translate into said men being shunned in the dating dance. Like I said above, women as a rule value chastity less than men, and are more willing to overlook a high notch count if the guy is attractive. This is college after all, where most men worth a damn in the girls' eyes are playing the field *and* the cards are stacked against women. There's also no evidence that these changed attitudes are leading to changed behavior. It's not like women's mouths are known for writing checks that their vaginas can cash.

However, if college girls are indeed starting to disapprove

of caddishness, this means that outwardly chaste alphas will be favored over outwardly promiscuous ones. The big losers will be the loudmouth dudebro douchebags who run around high-fiving their frat buddies after they score. *"OMIGOD DUDE I HOOKED UP WITH KATRINA LAST NIGHT!!!" "SHE'S SO HOT!!! AWESOME, BRO!!!"* More quiet types will reap the pussy bounty. If you're a guy worried that your predilection for bed-hopping could hurt your sex life, I've got some tips.

For starters, be discrete. Mystery mentioned this in *The Mystery Method*, but it bears repeating: no girl worth having wants the whole world to know that you banged her silly in the bar men's toilet. Keep a lid on your conquests: if you're in the game to impress people with your notch count, you're playing for the wrong reason. The exception is if the girl is on vacation; she'll be more likely to let her hair down since her friends won't be around to hear about it. Remember, "don't talk about the secret society."

If confronted by a girl about your number, you need a way to defuse her curiosity. This is a common shit test during the pick-up phase, and Roissy wrote on ways to pass it here.[25] All of his suggestions work – I personally prefer the cocky-type answers because they're short and snappy. My method is to give a deliberately outlandish number with deadpan seriousness. *"Millions."* Smirk while you're delivering, so she gets the joke. If you're in an LTR and she asks, tell her the truth straight up: no lies, no games, and no apologies. If she's really into you, she

SEXUALITY

won't care.

    When girls meet you, one of the first things they do when you're not around is Google your name to suss out more info about you. Therefore, you need to limit the amount of information about yourself that you put on the Internet. Facebook is the biggest problem. Keep your profile spartan and don't use it too frequently. Depending on the niche of girls that you exploit, you may be able to dump Facebook altogether, which you should if you can. Frankly, I hate Facebook and wish it had never been invented–I'm tired of people using it as a substitute for real-world interaction–but for me it's become a necessary evil.

    Travel frequently or live in cities with transient populations. This will decrease the likelihood that you'll develop a negative reputation in a particular area and allow you to shed it when you leave. And for God's sake, don't try to live the player lifestyle in small cities and towns, unless you want to screw yourself.

    Good luck my brothers, and may the poon be with you!

June 30, 2010

The Sheep in Wolf's Clothing

    When I was in college, the spot where all the students went to party was a dumpy house not far from the campus called 35 Main for its street address. It was targeted specifically at

SEXUALITY

underage college students looking to get drunk and mingle. The place was run quite professionally; a bouncer charged you five dollars to enter, and the kegmaster charged another five if you wanted to drink, all-you-could-chug so long as you held on to your plastic cup. To dissuade cops looking to bust young drunkards, the bouncer actively discouraged loitering outside, telling offenders to "keep moving." The inside of 35 Main wasn't too impressive, consisting of just a tiny foyer, a little living room, a kitchen (complete with beer pong table), and a side room used mostly by potheads and partygoers looking for peace and quiet. Still, the promise of alcohol for minors ensured that the place was packed every weekend. And it was there that I met one of the stranger girls I've ever known, not so much because she herself was strange, but because of the circumstances surrounding what she was.

It was a Saturday night and I had managed to swipe a seat on one of the couches in the living room, having been separated from my friends by the tight-as-sardines crowd. Next to me was an bored-looking girl dressed in jeans and a tank top. Fueled by liquid courage, I opened my mouth.

"Gee, you look excited to be here."

She turned her eyes towards me. "Heh. You'd be mad too if your friends had up and vanished."

"My friends *have* vanished," I parried. "Looks like we've got something in common."

SEXUALITY

We hit it off from there. Her name was Stacy and she was from Ohio (or "Ah-hi-ah," as she pronounced it in her cutesy hick accent), from a small town along the Ohio River across the border from West Virginia. A freshman majoring in Communications, she was on the plain side of average: cute if oddly flat face, a distracting gap between her two front teeth, short brown hair, B-cups and a bit of a tummy, and a flat ass like most non-obese white girls. Thirty minutes later, after our friends had run into us, I convinced her to move to the side room for some privacy.

It was about a little less than an hour in, when she was drinking beer from my cup (she had lost hers) and laughing at my bad jokes, when things started to get weird.

"So, what's the wildest thing to happen to you sexually?" she blurted out.

"Um," Caught off-guard, I started bullshitting. "I don't really do that sort of thing anymore. What kind of guy do you think I am?"

"Oh, I slept with lots of guys back home in Ohio," she explained. "I've got some great stories, like the guy I had sex with in my parents' backyard."

"...What?"

"Oh yeah, I love having sex. I've got a vibrator I use all the time, but it just isn't the same."

That should have been red flag number one. Talkers aren't doers. My gut feelings of unease with a girl I barely knew openly talking about sex were overpowered by my ignorant, foolish thoughts of *"Oh yeah, this chick is a real freak! I'm gonna get laid tonight!"* I was smart enough to not get all puppy-dog excited, but I ignored the flashing lights in front of me.

Somehow, I managed to not fuck up with Stacy long enough to start kissing her. An hour-and-a-half in, I persuaded her to come to my dorm to show her the nice view of the lake I had from my bedroom window. Fifteen minutes later, we were back at my eighth-floor room, where one thing lead to another and we started making out. We fell atop my bed, and Stacy paused to ask, "Could you get the light?"

That should have been red flag number two. In my experience, high-mileage women don't care whether the lights are on or not, but I didn't know that then. I just reached behind me to switch off the lamp.

We kept at it, Stacy pressing my head back into my filthy pillows as she pulled her top off and I slipped out of my shirt. I got lucky by unhooking her bra from behind on the first try and she started fumbling with my belt buckle. This was it. I unclasped my belt and started wriggling out of my pants. She grabbed my trouser snake, which was poised and ready to strike. Omigod omigod omigod I'm gonna fuck her oh hell yeah omigod…

…And then she started yanking on my dick. Not sliding

her hand up and down in the gentle-but-firm motion that every man makes when masturbating and expects girls to do the same, but tugging at it like she was a gardener trying to pull a flower out of the ground. And my eyes, slowly adjusting to the darkness, could see a twinge of disgust in her face. Something was wrong.

After about a minute of her trying to tear my cock off, I pushed her hand away saying, "I-I think I'll just finish it myself." My erection was deflating like a balloon being stomped on by a fat kid. "I think we should just... let me see yours."

"Okay." Stacy undid her belt and slid her pants off. As she pulled down her panties, I stifled a gag. This girl had the thickest, gnarliest bush I'd ever seen in my life. Even with the tiny amount of light streaming in under the door, I could tell she had a regular forest growing down there. Ungroomed, unshaved, untouched. I have an allergic reaction to that much bush and what was left of my boner was sounding the retreat. Suddenly, I put two and two together.

"You lied to me."

"What?" she retorted, offended.

"You've never had sex before." I sat up. "You've probably never even touched a cock before."

"No! I've fucked dozen of guys..."

I cut her off. "You don't know how to give a handjob. You don't shave. Admit it: you're a virgin."

"I don't know *what* your problem is…"

Angered by her snottiness, I lept up and grabbed her by the shoulder. "Are you a virgin?"

Cowed by my rage, her attitude gave way to sheepishness. "A guy went down on me last month…"

I wasn't satisfied. "Answer the question!" I yelled, staring her in the eye. "Has a guy put his penis in your vagina or not?"

After an awkward pause, she replied. "No…"

With her confession, my mind was officially blown. I leaned back against the wall, befuddled.

"So all that stuff you talked about back at the party; is any of it true?"

She shook her head in shame.

"But why? If you're a virgin, why lie about being a slut?"

"I… I don't know." She stared at the floor, avoiding my gaze. "None of the guys I meet here want to see me after I tell them I'm a virgin. I wanted you to like me…"

"Have you gone out with *any* guys?"

"I had a boyfriend in high school. We went out for two years and kissed a lot, but we never had sex."

If it wasn't for my inexperience with girls and repulsion at her tangled undergrowth, I might have tried to salvage this into a bang. But I was a total jackass in college and I felt cheated. Instead of getting the wild slut who would do all sorts of crazy shit that I expected, I had a girl who couldn't even jerk me off right. And my erection had completely vacated the battlefield at this point.

"I-I think you should leave," I exhaled.

"Could you at least walk me..."

"No." I stopped her in mid-sentence. "Just get the hell out."

She dressed herself in silence and left. I never saw her again.

***

I was inspired to share this story after having a phone conversation with my mom. My youngest sister, Claire, was going off to college next month and had just come home from her orientation. My mom was worried that some douchebag would take advantage of her last baby bird now that she would be leaving the nest.

"You think she's going to be fine at college?" my mom worried.

"Mom, Claire is a geek," I fired back. "She's into anime and video games, she doesn't dress like a girl, she doesn't like going to parties, and her idea of a fun Saturday night is playing *BioShock* alone on her laptop. She's a Computer Science major for God's sake! She'll be fine."

"Guys aren't going to try to, you know…"

"College guys typically try to get with girls who are hot and look like they'll put out. A shy, glasses-wearing tomboy doesn't exactly scream 'hot and easy.'"

"What about her male friends? Won't they try to sleep with her?"

"Those nerds she hangs out with?" I was incredulous. "They won't even have the nerve to ask her out! You didn't worry like this when Cécile went to college!"

"I don't know, Ferd." my mom sighed, in that tone of perpetual worry all mothers speak in. "Guys were always trying to take advantage of girls when I was Claire's age [my mom was in college in the early 70's, the height of the Sexual Revolution], but if you say so…"

"Mom, listen to me," I stated. "The girls who 'get taken advantage of' put themselves in that position. Claire isn't going to do that and you know it."

Only a fool thinks the girls he picks up for one-night stands are innocent, chaste things being defiled by his rakish dong. If she's willing to go home with you after only a couple hours and a few drinks, chances are she's had her own share of bedroom adventures. It's not like it matters; you're looking for a night of carnal ecstasy, not the One. In fact, a slutty chick is preferable to a virgin if quick sex is what you want, since she'll be more likely to both give it up and do fun stuff in bed. But occasionally you end up as that one in a million, the guy who takes home a angel who dances with the devil.

I never did find out what happened to Stacy. Maybe another guy who didn't mind excessive pubic hair took her virginity in the same way I almost did. Maybe she straightened herself out and found herself a meek nice guy with slack wrists. Maybe my freakout screwed her up for good. A small part of me hopes she had a happy ending, but I'm not that naive. There is no god or karma to punish the wicked and reward the just: there is only the universe, which is amoral and turns a deaf ear to the suffering of the good and the triumphs of the evil.

All I know is that sheep shouldn't pretend to be wolves.

July 20, 2010

Sweet Statutory, Batman!

Statutory rape and age of consent laws are something of a touchy issue among anti-feminists. Anyone who argues against sodomizing every adult who fucks a sixteen year-old girl with the police state jackboot is tarred as a "pedophile." Pedophiles, of course, are America's Dalit class, despised and spit on by everyone regardless of age, class, race or ideology. You can destroy the life savings of millions of people in a Ponzi scheme and get a slap on the wrist, like Bernie Madoff; you can murder policemen in cold blood and get millions of limp-wristed liberals to march in support of you, like Mumia Abu-Jamal and the dozens of black cop-killers imprisoned or executed over the past few decades; but if you get caught leering at a minor the wrong way, God help you. Even in prison, pedophiles get no respite; it's a well-known fact that "sex offenders" are at the bottom of the American prison food chain, below mass murderers and thugs who rob little old ladies.

This isn't a NAMBLA recruiting push: people who molest children deserve to be jailed. The problem is that feminists, working in concert with religious conservatives, have been continuously defining childhood upward, laughably trying to argue that fully pubescent teenagers, who would have been married with children in previous eras, are the same as pre-pubescent elementary schoolers. The gerontocratic trajectory of American society, prolonging adolescence by making it impossible for young people to join the middle class without taking on crippling amounts of college loan debt, is also part of this trend.

The issue with statutory rape becomes obvious when you read about some of the absurd examples of men getting nailed under these laws. Take Italian prime minister and noted ladies' man Silvio Berlusconi getting busted for paying for sex from a Moroccan stripper earlier this year:

"ROME—Premier Silvio Berlusconi has sat down

with the enemy, telling an opposition newspaper that he is too old to have had all the sexual encounters he is accused of by Italian prosecutors.

"The 74-year-old faces trial in Milan next month over charges he paid for sex with a Moroccan minor and used his influence to try cover it up. In court documents, prosecutors have identified 33 women, including the Moroccan teenager, who allegedly prostituted themselves during parties at Berlusconi's villa near Milan. [...]

[...] "Paying for sex is not a crime in Italy, but it is if the prostitute is under the age of 18.

"The Moroccan teen, Karima el-Mahroug, known by her nickname Ruby, turned 18 in November, but was a minor at the time of the alleged encounters."[26]

Note the illogic here. It's legal to have sex with 17-year olds in Italy, and they can be employed as exotic dancers, but you can't pay them for sex. It calls to mind George Carlin's routine about prostitution: "Selling is legal, fucking is legal. So why is it illegal to sell fucking? Why is it illegal to sell what is perfectly legal to give away?" Plus, what separates a 17-year old from an 18-year old? Does turning 18 magically endow someone with maturity and wisdom that they didn't have before? I don't recall becoming privy to any secrets of the universe on my 18th birthday: I was the same man I was the day before, only I could now vote, smoke and watch porn.

This is where the feminists interject with their sob stories of prostitutes being trafficked in from third-world countries to suck strange men off all day, get paid close to nothing, live in squalor and be flogged by their pimps when they don't perform. Ruby Rubacuori is being exploited! This poor young thing was forced against her will to have sex with this creepy old lecher!

The problem is that sex slavery and sex trafficking are myths. Complete and total lies. The men's rights blogger Schopenbecq has compiled a long list of links and news items showing how feminists and anti-sex trafficking organizations regularly fabricate statistics and outright lie in order to mislead the public, as well as proof that sex trafficking occurs in negligible numbers across the globe.[27] The blog *Gucci Little Piggy* also has a series of articles debunking the claims of massive sex slavery at the Super Bowl.[28] The reality is that women who prostitute themselves do so because they *want* to: but I digress.

Or consider another story from 2010 on a man who was jailed because he had a porno flick starring a 23-year old actress whose claim to fame is looking underage:

"Before returning home to New York from Venezuela, Carlos Alfredo Simon-Timmerman stopped in Puerto Rico. He was arrested for possession of child pornography – and he almost went to prison for it – even though a reasonable person could have discovered that the pornography was not illegal.

"The man had in his possession: "Little Lupe the Innocent; Don't Be Fooled By Her Baby Face." The movie stared noted film actress Lupe Fuentes – who is also know as Wikipedia. [sic] Since 2007, Lupe Fuentes has had a Wikipedia entry. It's right here for anyone to see. Anyone could have Googled the name of the alleged child pornography; found Little Lupe; and verified Fuentes' age."[29]

The prosecutor in the case, Jenifer Yois Hernandez-Vega, couldn't be bothered to perform a simple Google search, and Simon-Timmerman was only freed after Fuentes herself intervened:

"Thus, Simon-Timmerman's hope lay in one long-shot gamble: Little Lupe herself would have to fly to Puerto Rico, show her passport to the prosecutor, and testify under oath that she was really, really not 13 years old.

"'My fans mean everything to me,' Fuentes told Asylum via her publicist. 'It was important to me to make the trip to Puerto Rico to show support to someone who did no wrong.'"[30]

It's like something out of a Douglas Adams novel, if Adams wasn't a grotesque nerd.

These two stories show how the age of consent issue is used to pathologize and criminalize normal, healthy male sexuality. Virtually all the arguments in favor of our present regime, whether feminist or conservative, are wrongheaded and moronic.

1. "Raising the age of consent was a response to the Sexual Revolution to protect teenage girls from being taken advantage of."

Wrong. Abnormally high ages of consent are largely unique to America and the Anglosphere in general; in most continental European countries, the age of consent is lower.

- In the U.S., age of consent laws are largely left to the states.[31] The lowest age of consent is 16 in 31 states, including Pennsylvania, New Jersey and Massachusetts. Nine states, including New York, Texas and Illinois, have ages of consent of 17; the remaining eleven states, which include California and Florida, have an age of consent of 18.

- In Canada, the age of consent is 16; it was raised from 14 in 2008 as a result of the Tackling Violent Crime Act.[32] The United Kingdom and New Zealand also have an age of consent of 16, as does Australia with the exception of the states of South Australia and Tasmania, where it is 17.

- In contrast, the age of consent is 15 in France and Sweden, 14 in Germany and Italy, and 13 in Spain.

The genesis of statutory rape laws in the U.S. has little to do with the Sexual Revolution and everything to do with America's Puritan roots, beginning in the late 19th century with women-led "social purity" movements like the temperance movement and Prohibition:

> "In the late nineteenth century, 'Age of consent' referred to the legal age at which a girl could consent to sexual relations. Men who engaged in sexual relations with girls who had not reached the age of consent could be criminally prosecuted. American reformers were shocked to discover that the laws of most states set the age of consent at the age of ten or twelve, and in one state, Delaware, the age of consent was only seven.

Women reformers and advocates of social purity initiated a campaign in 1885 to petition legislators to raise the legal age of consent to at least sixteen, although their ultimate goal was to raise the age to eighteen. The campaign was eventually quite successful; by 1920, almost all states had raised the age of consent to sixteen or eighteen."[33]

2. "Statutory rape laws keep girls from getting pregnant at an age when they are unable to care for a child properly."

Also bunk. The same European countries that have low ages of consent also have lower rates of teen pregnancy than those prim and proper Anglosphere countries. According to *Advocates for Youth*, the pregnancy rate per thousand women aged 15-19 is 79.6 in the U.S., compared to 20.2 for France, 16.1 for Germany and 8.7 for the Netherlands.[34] The United Kingdom, which has a higher age of consent than most European countries, also has one of Europe's highest teen pregnancy rates.[35] Plus, with the advent of effective contraception, sex no longer has the consequences it used to, and even a girl gets knocked up, we have safe and legal abortion to get rid of any unwanted rugrats.

3. "Statutory rape laws keep teenage girls from being sexually exploited at a naive age."

This rests on the assumption that all teen girls are asexual angels who are being taken advantage by those dastardly lecherous men. Only someone who has never spent any time around teenagers (or who can't remember their high school years) could seriously argue this. Most teenagers are very aware of their sexual power and frequently use it to get what they want. Blogger Agnostic writes about an experience he had at a teen dance club:

> "But what has irrevocably adulterated my being happened at the end of the night tonight. I've been keeping to myself at the club mostly because I'm paranoid that if I am too pro-active, I will come off as the creepy old guy (relatively speaking). Maybe it was too cautious, but now I have all the evidence I need that these girls want to press their bodies against mine, and I will be back for more. [...]
>
> [...] "I can't help making eye contact, though, and this time one of the girls made a final move as the club was about to close, abandoning all pretense of subtlety in her signals. She marched straight up to me, violating my space, turned around, bent over, and began working her ass around in my lap like an eyeball during deep sleep wiggling wildly around in its socket. Unlike almost every girl below the age of 22, she was well endowed back there, and she had a delightful hourglass figure. Tawny flesh covered

her pelvis as melted caramel over an apple, and like a kid at a carnival I let my hands stick right to it, not caring about how I would wash off the residue later."[36]

I can back this up with my own observations. I went to a private Catholic high school, and my lady peers were always flirting with the male teachers. While not overt, their mannerisms and attitude became more seductive whenever they spoke to a teacher they either thought was cute or wanted to get something out of. I recall one incident that sticks out in my mind. I was a freshman trudging to a classroom for… something (this was a lifetime ago, I don't recall the details) when I saw three of my classmates catcalling our biology teacher in unison with a cutesy pun on his name in the "Oh my God, he's so dreamy" tone that teen girls specialize in. I can't reveal the pun, as it would reveal the teacher's identity (I think he still works there), but I do remember that he ate the attention up. These were 14-year olds, for crying out loud. And if you own a used book that once belonged to a teenage girl, you will probably be able to find paeans to the dreaminess of whatever teacher she crushed on at the time scribbled in the margins.

The fact is if you're a teacher who is in good physical shape, dresses well and has a bit of savvy, there's no way to *not* get hit on by your female students. At one point in my life, I was striving to become a high school teacher; if I had followed through on my plans to get my master's degree and certification, I could easily clean up with the junior and senior girls of any school I taught at (and subsequently get fired for sleeping with students). The point is is that the average teen girl is anything but naive when it comes to sex.

4. "Statutory rape laws prevent teenage girls from making stupid decisions."

If that's the case, why is it that the girls in statutory rape cases are never punished? Or, more appropriately, why aren't their *parents*, who are the ones responsible for making sure their babies don't grow up to be sluts, never punished? If the goal is to prevent people from doing stupid things, the best way to do that is to make stupidity painful and costly, yet in this case the stupid people always get off scot free. It's like Scandinavian feminist prostitution laws that allow whores to sell themselves freely but prosecute the men who take advantage of their services.

5. "Statutory rape laws protect female sexuality."

Then why do we have Romeo and Juliet laws? Why is it traumatizing for a sixteen-year old girl to have sex with a twenty-four year old guy but not with a sixteen-year old? Most teenage boys in America are unholy terrors because they mature slower than girls. When I was in high school, I was an immature, mouth-breathing hormonal asstard who couldn't think beyond his inappropriately erect cock. Girls avoided me because I was a repellent, braying jackass, and it's a wonder how I even managed

SEXUALITY

to not only get a girlfriend, but cash in my V-card. Most teen boys are like that: antisocial horrors with no class or culture. A sixteen-year old penis robs a teenage womb of its value as much as a twenty-four year old one, so why is the former let off the hook?

6. "Wanting to do a teenager under 18 is something only an emotionally stunted pervert who can't get a date with a woman his own age would do."

Feminist drivel. Teenage girls are acutely aware of human status hierarchies; men who have trouble with women their own age will never have a chance with the PYTs. If the older men they do lust after are "losers," they're losers with fame and money: think rock stars, celebrities or drug dealers. As for the feminists' attempts to demonize men for being attracted to teenage girls, this is laughable. Most girls are fully developed by the time they hit their late teens, possessing most if not all of the physical aspects that they'll carry into their legal years. They don't call 'em "jailbait" for nothing.

7. "There's no historical precedent for an adult-on-teen sex free-for-all."

There's no historical precedent for many of the other factors that make our current general sexual free-for-all possible either. There's no historical precedent for a lot of what's going on today. Relying on the past as a roadmap for the future is only useful up to a certain point.

The fact is that there's no justification whatsoever for leaving statutory rape law the way it is. It's a clusterfuck of religious moralizing, feminist pussy price control, and lazy parents expecting everyone else to raise their kids but them. It's not unlike the bogus War on Drugs, which has done nothing to stop drug trafficking and usage but has succeeded in getting a lot of nonviolent drug users having their rectums split open by HIV-positive convicts in penitentiaries across America. There is no reason to ruin the lives of men who have consensual sex with teenage girls and don't cause any real harm.

At the same time, while the card-carrying members of the He-Man Woman Haters Club will get mad at me for saying this, there are some legitimate reasons to protect minor teens from the potential predations of older men. Therefore, my proposal to remedy the situation is to drop the age of consent to 15 or 14 for females, raise it to around 17 or 18 for males (since boys mature more slowly than girls), and add an age of consent to be impregnated.

Under my system, any man who impregnates a girl at or above the age of consent but legally a minor gets his ass sent to prison. We could also force him to pay for an abortion (if the girl or her parents decide to get one) or child support bills (if she doesn't). Although I'm in favor of reforming the anti-male child support laws that oppress divorced men in America, I'd support them in this instance because unlike adult women with full legal rights and earning potential, teenagers are vulnerable and

SEXUALITY

inexperienced with the realities of living independently. I'd also add prohibitions for relationships in which the senior partner has power over the junior one (the above mentioned example of high school teachers, for instance) that carry a light sentence. Any man who has sex with a girl below the age of consent gets tried as a pedophile and molester. Rapists get tried as normal.

Alternately, we can get serious about defending the virtue of women by making having sex with any girl under 18 illegal for any man of any age, save for husbands. No more Romeo and Juliet laws: same-aged teen guys and adult men *both* get sent to Prison Block D where they can be the passaround bitch for the local Aryan Brotherhood cell. It's only fair, after all.

Under my preferred arrangement, the onus for making sure teenage girls don't get sexually exploited falls on the parents to safeguard her and teach her how to weed out dirtbags and scumfucks: which is where it should be. If you've raised your daughter right, she should be fine. And if that fails, daddy can always smash the sleazy bastard's skull in with a rock. There are a lot of problems in this world that could be solved with the frequent and strategic application of shotgun shells.

I don't think the statutory rape issue should be a big concern for anti-feminists. There are bigger—and less controversial—fish to fry. Still, it's something worth thinking about.

July 29, 2010, revised and expanded November 2011

Women Get the Men They Deserve

A couple of weeks ago, there was a bit of a brouhaha over at Dalrock's blog. The man himself had penned a post back in July in which he half-jokingly outlined a plan that beta men in their thirties could use to exact revenge on their same-aged lady peers who rode the alpha cock carousel when they were young and hot and are now looking for a provider to slap a ring on their clap-addled rear-ends.[37] A commenter, name of Marcos, left a reply saying that he did just that:

> "Actually, I've done this for the last six years or so. Dalrock is correct, there really isn't any challenge to it at all. I've shagged quite a few over-30 year olds in that time. To be honest, I'm a pretty good-looking guy (7 to 8 range, I'm told I'm cute a lot) and minimally tall (5'11" barefoot – taller with shoes). So maybe I'm not a fair test case.
>
> "In any case, it's really a matter of positioning yourself into a social group where a lot of those women socialize. Usually the uber-professional crowd. The average looks are women who were in the 6 to 8 range but over-played their hands expecting Mr. Perfect to marry them. Most of the women were what I would call "A la carte" feminists,

too. About 40% of my marks were the bitter type. You know, angry that life didn't turn out like that little fairytale in her head. Others were not so bitter but more focused on just finding a decent guy. These girls were the ones who just plum forgot about marriage or kept pushing it to the back burner because they focused on career or didn't want to deal with the tough world of the marriage market thinking it would "happen to them when they least expect it." Yep, that old canard. The Dane Cook of all dating advice.

"If you're not into social groups per se, then you could go the mass marketing route: Online Dating. Trust me, it's just as effective. No matter what lake you find them in, the bait is the same. When they ask you (Trust me – they will! Several times) why you're 34, 35 whatever years old and never married you just take a moment and say, "Candidly? I haven't found the right girl. I'm a traditional man and was raised to believe the man takes care of all the bills and financial responsibility. You know, where the woman doesn't mind taking care of the home. I don't mind that a woman has a job/career or whatever...In fact that's great! But I don't want her to feel that she has to work. That's my job. Also, I've been working all these years to get to a position financially to where I can afford the lifestyle my kids deserve and now I'm ready to focus on the right girl and settle down. You'd be surprised how hard it is to find a woman who wants to have kids and settle down these days." Say this very relaxed, matter-of-factly tone and it will work. Especially if she's over 32. Result: deer in headlights. And they buy it..."

A few of Dalrock's schoolmarm commenters started clucking in disapproval, enough so that he wrote his own post addressing Marcos' comment:

"However, if they are trying to trade sex for financial security, how innocent can they be? I think this is the fundamental question. **Marcos' con won't work on any woman not looking to trade sex (outside of marriage) for financial security.** The old saw *you can't con an honest man* comes to mind. If the nuns in question are chaste, Marcos isn't going to waste any time on them. He didn't say he is marrying them or even getting engaged. He's dating them and sending signals that he would be a great man to try to get into a binding agreement to support her and any future children. If the woman isn't looking to have him support her, she won't be attracted by his 'bait.' **Moreover, if she isn't willing to provide plenty of easy sex to lure him into a trap of her own, he isn't going to waste his time with her."**[38]

From my look at Dalrock's posts, most of Marcos' detractors seem to be women, while most of his defenders (or at least, the people trying to explain the context behind his behavior) seem to be men. One goes so far as to call him a hero. Wanna know what I think?

I don't consider Marcos to be a hero, but I won't shed a single tear for his "victims."

Long-time readers will know that I am a fanatical proponent of Spengler's Universal Law of Gender Parity. Unfortunately, I haven't had the opportunity to rub your faces in it recently, so sit down and quiet down, because class is in session:

> "In every corner of the world and in every epoch of history, the men and women of every culture deserve each other. Permit me to call this conjecture 'Spengler's Universal Law of Gender

Parity.' Of all the silly plans advanced by Americans to remake the world in their own image, raising the banner of women's rights has the smallest chance of success. Where men subjugate women physically, women ravage them psychologically. That may explain why violence toward women and secret homosexuality so often are endemic in the same cultures."[39]

The existence of this Law is not because of some sort of supernatural entity meting out salvation or damnation from on high. There is no god and no karma, just a vast, amoral universe that is blind to your pleas and deaf to your cries. Every day, saints and sinners suffer in silence while villains and rogues live in the lap of luxury. The Law doesn't necessarily guarantee that one or two skanks-turned-monogamists won't find that beta schlub who is happy to be dick number 121.

What the Law *does* guarantee is that on the macro level, every injury inflicted on one sex by the other will eventually, in some form, be repaid in full. When men become simpering, cowardly weaklings, women become ball-busting sluts. When women become ball-busting sluts, men become exploitative cads. When men become exploitative cads, women become tyrannical shamers. It goes on and on, transcending individuals and generations in a neverending feedback loop until equilibrium is reached.

A system in which women to shun men who don't meet their exacting standards to get banged by alpha stud after alpha stud only to reverse course when her youth and beauty are gone and her ovaries are shriveling up is one in which a predator like Marcos can arise to screw them over. Used-up old skanks deserve amoral predators. Marcos and his ilk are bringing balance to our sexual ecology, no matter how loudly his enemies whine in protest.

To those who condemn him on the basis of morality, why should he care what you think? You're not in a position to punish him or otherwise enforce your beliefs. To the women who claim they Aren't Like That and don't deserve to be played, I'm pretty sure not everyone in Dresden was a goose-stepping Nazi. That didn't stop the Allies from bombing it into oblivion anyway. To those who will attack me for pointing any of this out, all the highfalutin insults you can pull out of your quiver won't change the facts on the ground. Ignore reality at your own peril.

As I am fond of repeating, women are free to make any choices they please. But they must also know that *choices have consequences*. Marcos is just the latest progeny of a feedback loop engendered in part by the behavior of American women. Bastard he may be, he is still your son, ladies. Karma isn't a bitch: bad faith is.

October 27, 2010

SEXUALITY

Ehe Macht Frei

Laura Wood, of *the (Un)Thinking Housewife*, was a blogger who I used to read up until she revealed herself to be as loopy and mentally ill as her intellectual mentor (whose name is not to be spoken on this blog ever again). She has been lambasted in the past as a proponent of "conservative female supremacism," toting around a coterie of sycophantic "traditionalist" male commenters who furiously suck up to her. But Laura has managed to outdo herself on this front. In a post entitled "Does Society Need Men's Rights?", she and her compadres have revealed, once and for all, why they simply don't get it.[40]

Before I leap into the fray, I should mention that while I have described myself and been described by others as an "MRA," I've decided to eschew the label for two reasons:

1. It doesn't describe me. MRA is taken to be shorthand for "men's rights activist," and blogging is not activism. Angry Harry is an activist. Paul Elam is an activist. A pseudonymous blogger living on the far side of civilization is not an activist.

2. I'm tired of the alphabet soup of acronyms that are frequently slung around this part of the blogosphere. PUA, MRA, HBD, MGTOW: they all sound stupid. No more acronyms for me.

I have my own criticisms of the men's rights movement (namely the concept of rights, which is bogus, and the idea that they can achieve true gender equality where the feminists have failed) but I consider them fellow travelers because I believe they are a force for good in the world. It would be more accurate to describe me as a *men's rights supporter*.

All that aside, let's get back to the topic at hand. In the past I have criticized conservatives and traditionalists for "not getting it" in regards to sexuality and the feminist dystopia, without fully articulating what the "it" is. Gay marriage? Abortion? Sexual degeneracy? Completely irrelevant side issues when you consider that the singles market is so screwed up that guys have to read a book by a freak wearing a stupid hat in order to figure out how to even get laid. Or that working a minimum-wage job and playing video games all day is more economically sensible then getting married and having children.

This lays out the problem pretty well, but it doesn't state the core issue at hand: conservatives and traditionalists don't understand the concept of tit-for-tat.

Have you ever wondered whether or not you should support or fight for something or someone? As Advocatus Diaboli put it, there's a simple pair of questions you should ask yourself in these situations:

Why should I care? What's in it for me?[41]

This doesn't apply to stuff like saving the whales, going vegan or any choice that won't impact your life tremendously, but to decisions that require you to invest a large portion of your life and/or resources into making them happen. What do you get out of it? How will it benefit you? If it doesn't benefit you, or it actually hurts you, you'd be a fool to bother with it.

Ask yourself this. When the U.S. entered World War II, men were so eager to fight for their country that many teenage boys lied about their age in order to join the military. A little more than two decades later when the U.S. invaded Vietnam, a new generation of young men fled the country, burned their draft cards, sought deferments, and used any other method they could think of to avoid going to war. Why the sea change in just a short amount of time? You can blame antiwar leftists all you want, but since sympathy for communism in the U.S. ran extremely high in the years preceding WWII, you'll have to explain why they had no influence then but had massive influence in the 60's.

It was because the men who came of age during Vietnam realized that they would be fighting for nothing. Nazi Germany and Imperial Japan were real, tangible threats to America, while Vietnam was just some pissant ex-colony in the middle of nowhere. When the Great Depression occurred, the U.S. government acted as a benevolent steward towards its citizens, defusing a potential communist revolution that would have been inevitable had the *Ludwig von Mises Institute* crowd gotten their way. Whether you think they were right or not, the youth of the 1960's viewed the government as antagonistic and opposed to their interests. As Muhammad Ali put it, "No Vietcong ever called me a nigger."

To summarize, young men were happy to die in battle in Europe or the Pacific because they were fighting for a country they believed in, a country worth dying for, against a foe who could destroy it. Young men refused to die in battle in Southeast Asia because they no longer believed in their country, and because their foe posed no threat to it: they would be nothing more than tools for politicians. The fact the America could lose the Vietnam War (Vietnam is flying the commie flag, so shut up you patriotic morons, *we lost*) and still remain a world power is proof of the latter.

What conservatives, traditionalists, white nationalists and their ilk don't understand is the necessity of offering something of tangible value to the people they need to make their movements successful. Most of the time, their response is to double-down on insults and shaming, finger-wagging anyone who doesn't want to hop on their train ride to oblivion. Nuh-uh, holmes. It doesn't work that way. Robert McNamara needed the dirty, smelly hippies in Haight-Ashbury way more than they needed him. It's not our place to beg *you* for a chance to join your little clique: it's *your* responsibility to entice us to join by telling us what we'll get out of it.

On the few occasions that conservatives and traditionalists aren't insulting the people they need to stay alive, they *do* explain what they have to offer them: and it happens to be less than nothing. A few months back, some clown made a comment at *Mangan's* that made my blood boil when I read it:

> "I agree the laws need to change. But, in the meantime, it makes no sense for a conservative to argue that men should stop reproducing and pursue hedonism. Life is not without risks. Yes, the paranoia spread by 'MRA' and 'PUA' types is not entirely without basis: if you get married, there's a chance your woman will cheat on you, lie about you to the police, divorce you, and take all your money. I don't care. Do it anyway. If you manage to get 2.1 kids out of her before that happens, you have done your minimum duty. The future belongs to those who show up, as they say."[42]

But that's just one random idiot on a comment thread. Surely the whole of conservative-dom doesn't think this way! Au contraire, in the above-linked *(Un)Thinking Housewife* post, Laura Wood and her commentariat bear the ugliness of their souls for all to see. Just read her response to a commenter who, trapped in holy matrimony to an obstinate wife, cautions other men to avoid marriage:

> "I cannot diagnose what has gone wrong in your marriage, but it could just be a phase, a very rocky period. If your wife has changed dramatically since the time you first married her, she may change just

as dramatically in the future. I am sure you pray for her and love her. You chose her. She is the mother of your children. I'm sure your children give you immense pleasure. Since you are a Catholic, you know that the most important marital issue for you is how you uphold your vows not how she upholds hers. Whether you are doing the right thing determines your future. There are far worse fates than an unhappy marriage. You are wrong to fear or bemoan suffering. You are committing a serious sin by telling other men not to marry. That is evil. The fact that you have freely chosen a woman who does not please you is not justification for denouncing the institution of marriage or for suggesting that men go outside their culture to marry. You are in grave error in this advice, similar to feminists who go around publicly complaining about their husbands."

While Laura's rejoinder contains the Not All Women Are Like That nonsense that we've become accustomed to, and she automatically assumes that our poor commenter is in the wrong, those aren't the most obnoxious parts of her screed. What offends me most is that her contention that the commenter is "evil" for warning men against marriage due to the risks involved. That's right: *Laura Wood wants men to suffer for her cause.*

This is the thin, watery gruel that traditionalists offer men: the chance to be cannon fodder in their culture war, another mark for their con game. They want you, knowing full well that marriage is a minefield surrounded by a piranha-filled moat, to dive in anyway. They expect you to endure pain, misery and humiliation for… for what? The continuation of the white race? The preservation of Western civilization? What *you* want, what is best for *you*: these things never enter their minds.

If that isn't enough, Jesse Powell, one of Laura's most frequent commenters, chimes in with his own brand of lunacy:

> "Speaking as a man, what bothers me the most about the men's rights movement is that it represents men rejecting their duties and moral responsibilities as men; they attack and undermine what being a man is all about. As a man it is my duty to protect women and to create a functioning order for society overall and men have roles and duties in the overall social order that they are bound to uphold. The MRA, with his blatant disregard for upholding and maintaining the overall order of society, represents a threat to the well being of the community and a danger to precisely the

populations that I as a man am bound to serve and protect; women and children."

 I hate to burst your bubble boy, but there's no such thing as an unconditional duty. Men in eons before protected and provided for women and children because they got something out of the deal, not because of some nebulous "moral responsibilities." A man protects, provides for and loves his wife because she maintains his house, sexes him, rears his children and loves him in return. A man is not required to do anything for his defiant, controlling little shrew of a wife any more than a woman is required to do anything for her layabout, philandering, absent husband.

 Essentially, Jesse Powell wants men to uphold their end of the societal bargain without any guarantee that women will uphold theirs. He wants you to sacrifice for absolutely nothing. Go ahead, you stupid, hairless, Y-chromosomed biped, get married. Bust your behind five days a week so your wife can blow it all on clothes and useless junk. Stay faithful to her so she can deny you sex because she's "not in the mood." Raise children with her so she can cuckold you with the next-door neighbor and poison the little sprogs against you when you're not around. Give up your hobbies and social life to be home constantly so she can accost you for "being gone all the time." It's your masculine *duty!* Stop whining, grow up and fulfill your "moral responsibilities," you blubbering manboy! *Ehe macht frei!*

Boy, with an unbeatable offer like that, I just *can't* see why men aren't flocking to the traditionalist cause. Just can't see it at all.

Laura Wood, you are a loathsome, repugnant, evil woman for luring men to their doom. You are a siren enticing naive men to their death with your poison song of "tradition." If there is a hell, you will surely be damned to it.

Jesse Powell, you are not a patriarch: you are a weak, pathetic momma's boy groveling for women's approval. A true patriarch would spit on you as the spineless cur that you are.

This is why the conservatives and traditionalists are doomed. They are offering men struggle without triumph, suffering without reward. They have nothing aside from appeals to "duty" and "tradition," urging men to defend a culture that no longer exists, to protect a civilization that is corrupt and deserves to die. Their attempts to shame men into taking up their banner won't work, because they have no practical way of punishing anyone who refuses to fall in line. Traditionalists simply cannot answer why anyone should care about them, and this has condemned them to defeat and dishonor.

Women get the men they deserve, and Western women are getting men who are abandoning civilization in droves, and there's not a thing that Laura Wood and her cohort can do to stop them. How they'll live their lives is up for them to decide. Some will become cads and pickup artists, preying on women for carnal pleasure and giving them nothing but a good Friday night rogering for their trouble. Some will go ghost, dying as bachelors without a day of being ensnared in marital bonds. They'll work the bare minimum they need to get by, and spend their paychecks on beer and useless baubles. They'll let doors slam in women's faces, they'll ignore them if they see them getting assaulted, and they won't shed a single tear when their choices ruin them.

And I understand, without condoning or condemning, why they will do what they do.

December 16, 2010

Night Game is Dead

It's time to pronounce the death of night game. After having its limbs hacked off and its genitals yanked out by the root for dog food, night game has finally shuffled off this mortal coil to that big swank discotheque in the sky. If you just discovered this 'sphere and are reading up on the best shotgun negs to use on a HB7.5, you're already behind the curve. The minute you step out of the cab, you're going to get slaughtered.

I myself have gradually lost interest in the game over the past year, which is why I've haven't felt motivated to write about this. Nonetheless, the fact that my nightlife observations are being backed up by men across the country is more than a little frightening. Here's is why I say night game is dead, based on my barhopping adventures over the past few months in the not-so-great American Northeast:

1. More cock than a rooster farm.

I'm not exaggerating when I say the ratio of penises to vaginas in any given bar on a weekend night is 8 to 1. It's wall-to-wall braciola parties from the Hudson to the quads. Women, being the risk-averse creatures that they are, have been frightened away from the nightlife circuit by the crummy economy. If you live in the northern U.S., Canada or any other region with a winter, you're even more screwed, because girls *really* don't like going out in the cold. And if you live in an area with a lot of snowfall, God help you. The eastern part of New York state from NYC to the Canadian border isn't so bad in this regard, but if you live west of Amsterdam, you can forget about getting laid until Easter. When the snow is falling, the gals don't come calling.

2. More douche then a supermarket feminine hygiene aisle.

A typical Friday night in the Capital Region looks like *Jersey Shore*, only this isn't Jersey and there's no shore. Ed Hardy threads, tribal tattoos, popped collars, and other markers of douchiness abound. And every single one of these 'roid-raging Doucha-Loompas is competing against you to see who can win the slut's heart and defile her in the loo. You can't win. You try, and you'll just get drowned in an ocean of gelled-haired duckfaced fist-pumping.

3. More female detritus than People of Walmart.

SEXUALITY

When the economy's bad and leaving your house entails digging your car out of four feet of snow when it's five below zero, only a certain type of woman is willing to endure the trials and tribulations of going out: the kind of woman you wouldn't fuck with your dog's dick. Fatties, fuglies, drug addicts, and dipsomaniacs puking on their own shoes are who you get the pleasure of trying to boff now. And on the off chance you do find a bangable girl, you'll have to contend with every Pauly D wannabe in the city who's trying to get in her pants before you do. All this fawning male attention won't get her any closer to anyone's bedroom, but it *will* engorge her ego until she's crushing hapless douchebags in her Roche limit.

4. Girls who are less attentive and outgoing then an autistic kindergartener bombed on Red Bull.

So you aren't intimidated by the bratwurst-swinging hordes, you can douche it up with the best of them, and you don't mind porking porkers. Even with all that in your favor, you might as well warm up your porn stash, because you are going home alone Friday night. Mr. Douchey McChubbylover, you simply cannot compete with the greatest piece of chick crack ever invented: the iPhone.

I decree Steve Jobs to be the biggest cockblocker in human history. In the good old days when cell phones were overpriced walkie-talkies, people who went out on the weekend were forced to engage with the world around them. As late as two years ago, you could introduce yourself to a girl and be assured that you could carry on a civil conversation for at least fifteen minutes. You might not get the lay or even a number, but you could put in a decent effort.

No more. The minute the girlies get to the bar, they whip out their iPhones and start texting all their friends to tell them where they are. Then the whole gang shows up and they all turn a deaf ear to everyone else save for the bartender. Try and introduce yourself? They'll give you the cold shoulder. Get talking to a girl on her own? Her fat friend will pull her away in less than five minutes. You and your pals become fast friends with her and her friends? One of 'em will suddenly get a text and announce, *"Oh, our friends are at [OTHER BAR], so we've got to go. Nice meeting you."* I've had all this and more happen to me and my friends in the past three months alone, and it's all due to those fucking smartphones.

Oh, and did I mention that half the bars and clubs out there have their music cranked up so loud it's impossible to hold a conversation without screaming at the top of your lungs? Have fun blasting through her bitch shield when your ears are bleeding from the bass.

Nope, night game is done, at least for the time being. You may be heading out looking for a good bad time, but your chances of getting any play are bad unless you're rich, famous, or lucky. I won't have to deal with the boorish girls in this city for much longer, but I pity the guys who are stuck here.

So, how is a man supposed to bust a nut in this world? Day game. I also predicted in the above-linked post that there would be an explosion of interest in day game as savvy men realized that nightlife was a useless prospect for racking up notches. Barnes & Noble, Panera Bread, and Target are the new battlefields of the mating war. It is within their walls that openers will be honed, negs will be dropped, and new love shall bloom again in the winter of our discontent. Whoever is smart enough to pounce on this market with a day game guide will become a very wealthy man.

The frontlines have shifted, gentlemen. Get with the times or get left in the dust. Your choice.

December 20, 2010

Why I Don't Respect Women

In an article at her blog, men's rights/anti-feminist writer Laura Grace Robins critiques an anti-domestic violence campaign that urges men to teach boys to respect women:

> "...There is this assumption that respect is something women are entitled to by simply being a woman. They don't have to earn it through good behavior or by being a lady. Men are to respect women no matter what. If one wants to use such a

blanket definition, then men too should be respected no matter what. Men should be respected when they behave badly and when they don't act like gentlemen. But of course, we all know that will never happen, because a man "has to earn a woman's respect"; we hear that often enough, but women never have to earn a man's respect.

"Plus, if we are applying respect equally, who is out there teaching girls/women to respect boys/men? Insert crickets playing here..."[43]

I'm very familiar with these types of campaigns. Having spent an inordinate amount of my driving time listening to hatemongering right-wing talk radio, I've heard countless PSAs to this effect. One of my least favorite is the one about teaching your son "what not to hit," in which a grave-voiced announcer reminds us that "all violence against women is wrong." No word on whether there's a self-defense clause, but I doubt it, because as we all know, only *men* are violent!

I didn't write the title of the post just to be provocative: *I really do not respect women, and I never will.* I don't respect men either, but I doubt anyone will get mad at *that.*

In our liberal humanist egalitarian happy happy joy joy world, respect is defined as something you're supposed to give to everyone, from the mightiest paragon of Galtian innovation to the lowliest bum pissing on himself on a street corner. If you *don't* respect everyone on this planet for the mere reason of being human, why then you're a horrible, terrible, very bad person, cast out of the Family of Man like an elderly flasher waving his junk in a supermarket. Nuh uh, holmes. Just because I don't want to kill you or otherwise make your existence a living hell doesn't mean I have to "respect" you. I'll tolerate the urine-soaked bum because he deserves that much as a human being, but I'm not going to give him accolades just because he had the good fortune to be squeezed out of someone's uterus.

Respect is not something that is automatically given to you, it is something you *earn*. Specifically, in the world of men, respect is a currency meted out on the basis of individual merit. If you are a man and you want to be respected, you have to prove that you *deserve* to be respected. You earn respect by excelling in something, be it in the form of a skill, interesting life experiences, or extensive knowledge in a particular field. If you can't make something of yourself in Man World, you're nothing. You're weak, deadweight, a useless cunt, and you have no right to demand *anything* from your betters aside from their contempt.

This comes down to the differences in how manhood and womanhood are perceived. Women automatically confer respect to each other because there's nothing exceptional in being a woman, aside from menstruation. If you're a female and your vagina bleeds, congratulations, you're a woman. It's a natural process, no different than farting or burping. In contrast, males have no obvious physical trait that separates the men from the boys. The reason why many traditional cultures have rites of passage for boys but none for girls is because manhood itself is something that each individual male must earn.

In my circle of friends, we all respect each other because each of us has skills or knowledge that require talent and work to master or accumulate. Can you change the oil on your car, re-assemble a computer, or run a snowblower without getting your hand cut to ribbons? How many books have you read? Can you paint, draw, compose or write? How good are you with women? How well can you cook barbecued ribs on a charcoal grill? Have you lived in another country, served in the military or done prison time for selling drugs? Are you a loyal, trustworthy person? Every group of men has something they will respect other men for, even if its something trivial like video games.

This is why I don't respect women as a group. I respect individual women who have earned my respect through their words and deeds. But feminists, as exemplified by the ad Laura commented on, don't understand this. Despite the fact that women now compete with men in the workplace and other spheres, they demand that men afford a blanket respect to the fairer sex irregardless of what they've done or who they are. Like with chivalry, they want to reap the rewards of Man World while playing by the rules of Woman World.

Well, I say no way, chica. If you're going to live like a man, you're going to be treated like a man, and that includes being judged on who you are as a person. Want my respect? Impress me. Learn a foreign language. Go on a trip. Work out at the gym and lose weight. Master a trade. Write a book. Don't cart around your 3.4 GPA and bachelor's in Latin American Studies from NYU like I'm supposed to give a damn, do something *real* with your life. *If you insist on being a worthless cunt, I will treat you like a worthless cunt;* like I would treat any man who behaved the same as you.

Oh, you say I *offend* you? That I'm a misogynist for holding you to the same standards I'm held to, both by myself and others? Well ladies, if you don't want to run with the guys, you're always welcome to go back to the old ways… and all the restrictions and responsibilities that implies. If you don't like that, then shut up and get back to work. Crawling out of your mother's vagina or having one yourself doesn't entitle you to anything in Man World. You chose this path, and now you must walk it all the way to the end.

January 14, 2011

The Rape-Supporter Quiz

Reader Alice sent me this checklist by deranged feminist (redundant, I know) Eve's Daughter on how to tell if a man supports rape.[44] I could tear Eve a new vagina on this one–Lord

SEXUALITY

knows, she probably has it coming—but my fisking talents would be wasted on this pissant little nutter, like hunting deer with a tank. So I've decided to do something different: use her checklist to create a quiz so my male readers can determine where they stand on the paramount issue of rape.

I should stress that due to the gendered nature of the list, this quiz is for *men* only. Sorry ladies, you'll have to petition Eve for your own checklist.

Here's how it works: for each statement that applies to you, give yourself one point. Some questions have multiple applicable statements and thus you can get multiple points from them. When you've finished, add up all your points to see where you stand. I've included my own answers in italics, with a running total of my points. Ready? Let's begin!

You Are a Rape-Supporter If…

1. You have ever sexually engaged with any woman while she was underage, drunk, high, physically restrained, unconscious, or subjected to psychological, physical, economic, or emotional coercion. (1 point for each statement, for 6 total)

Well, this is a mouthful. I'll work through this point by point:

Underage: Youngest girl I've ever had sex with was 16, and it was legal at the time, so no. 0 points.

Drunk: Um, like yeah. Alcohol is the lubricant greasing

the cogs of male-female relations. If you've never had sex with a drunk woman, you're either a virgin, a Mormon, or a liar. 1 point.

High: Yup. Sheesh, has this woman ever been to college? 2 points.

Physically restrained: If she asked for it, does it count? 3 points.

Unconscious: No. Contrary to the fevered fantasies of feminists, I actually DON'T get a hard-on for fornicating with inanimate objects. 3 points.

Psychological, physical, economic, or emotional coercion: Don't even think too deeply about this one. Given feminists' fast and loose definition of "coercion," if you have a penis, you're guilty by default. 4 points.

2. You defend the current legal definition of rape and/or oppose making consent a defense. (1 point each, for 2 points total)

I'm not a fan of the current definition of rape, but not for the reasons she expects. And "making consent a defense?" So we haven't drowned enough witches already? 5 points.

3) You have accused a rape victim of having "buyer's remorse" or wanting to get money from the man. (1 point each, for 2 points total)

A quick Google search turns up dozens of stories proving that there are plenty of "rape" victims whose motives are less than

SEXUALITY

pure. 7 points.

4) **You have blamed a woman for "putting herself in a situation" where she "could be" attacked.** (1 point)

Yes, namely since rape is the only crime where it's unacceptable to even suggest that victims should take measures to protect themselves instead of blaming everything on the cruel, cruel world. 8 points.

5) **You have procured a prostitute.** (1 point)

Nope… not yet, anyway. 8 points.

6) **You characterize prostitution as a "legitimate" "job" "choice" or defend men who purchase prostitutes.** (1 point each, for 2 points total)

Didn't you know that prostitutes, strippers and escorts aren't adults capable of making adult choices, but children who need to be coddled and protected from the predations of the evil, evil penis?! Omigod!!!!! 10 points.

7) **You have ever revealed you conceive of sex as fundamentally transactional.** (1 point)

Yes. 11 points.

8) **You have gone to a strip club.** (1 point)

Oui. 12 points.

9) **You are anti-abortion.** (1 point)

No. Abort away, dear! I don't enjoy the feeling of slinging a bratwurst through a train tunnel. 12 points.

10) You are pro-"choice" because you believe abortion access will make women more sexually available. (1 point)

Jesus, there's no way to win with these broads, is there? If you're against abortion, they hate you, but if you support abortion for reasons they don't approve of, they STILL hate you. 13 points.

11) You frame discussions of pornography in terms of "freedom of speech." (1 point)

No, I frame them in terms of the male sex drive. I don't think that was the answer she was looking for. 13 points.

12) You watch pornography in which women are depicted. (1 point)

There goes 95 percent of the male species. 14 points.

13) You watch any pornography in which sexual acts are depicted as a struggle for power or domination, regardless of whether women are present. (1 point)

Not into BDSM (aside from spanking), so no. 14 points.

14) You characterize the self-sexualizing behavior of some women, such as wearing make-up or high heels, as evidence of women's desire to "get" a man. (1 point)

Yeah, those girls are dressing sexy because THEY want

to. Men don't factor in at all. As evidence, look at all those lesbians who aren't fat and dress their Friday night best all the time. 15 points.

15) You tell or laugh at jokes involving women being attacked, sexually "hoodwinked," or sexually harassed. (1 point each, for 2 points total)

If only the hysterical reactions of feminists who think that rape isn't funny weren't so danged funny. 16 points.

16) You express enjoyment of movies/musicals/TV shows/plays in which women are sexually demeaned or presented as sexual objects. (1 point)

Again, like the "coercion" question, this is so vague and ill-defined it applies to you by default if you're a man. 17 points.

17) You mock women who complain about sexual attacks, sexual harassment, street cat-calls, media depictions of women, or other forms of sexual objectification. (1 point)

Since the feminist idea of sexual objectification is completely arbitrary (i.e. women only mind when certain types of men engage in it), then yes. 18 points.

18) You support sexual "liberation" and claim women would have more sex with (more) men if society did not "inhibit" them. (1 point)

Wait a minute, I thought feminism was all about sexual liberation! Now you're telling me that it's a bad thing? Oh wait, anything that benefits men in any way is bad for women. 18 points.

19) You state or imply that women who do not want to have sex with men are "inhibited," "prudes," "stuck-up," "man-haters," or psychologically ill. (1 point)

Depends on the woman. 19 points.

20) You argue that certain male behaviors towards women are "cultural" and therefore not legitimate subjects of feminist attention. (1 point)

People are different, you liberal pansies. Get over it. 20 points.

21) You ever subordinate the interests of women in a given population to the interests of the men in that population, or proceed in discussions as if the interests of the women are the same as the interests of the men. (1 point each, for 2 points total)

Erm, so the only acceptable way to discuss these sorts of things is to elevate the interests of women OVER the interests of men? 22 points.

22) You promote religious or philosophical views in which a woman's physical/psychological/emotional/sexual well-being is subordinated to a man's. (1 point)

Women have proven over and over again that they only respect men who lead them. See: patriarchy, traditionalist Christianity. 23 points.

23) You describe female anatomy in terms of penetration, or use terms referencing the supposed "emptiness" of female anatomy when describing women. (1 point each, for 2 points total)

Guilty as charged. It's a matter of SCIENCE, goils. 25 points.

24) You defend the physical abuse of women on the grounds of "consent." (1 point)

He wouldn't hit her if she didn't keep coming back to him afterwards. 26 points.

25) You defend the sexualization or sexual abuse of minor females on the grounds of "consent" or "willingness." (1 point)

Teenage girls are adults, not children, capable of making their own decisions and aware of their sexuality. It's not "sexual abuse" to shag one. Paging Schopenbecq... 27 points.

26) You promote the idea that women as a class are happier or more fulfilled if they have children, or that they "should" have children. (1 point each, 2 points each)

Not all women, but most women would be happier as wives and mothers, so yea on the first one. Not that I'm interested in telling women what to do... just reminding them that choices have consequences. 28 points.

27) You argue that people (or just "men") have sexual "needs." (1 point)

SEXUALITY

Um, yeah. Sexual beings have sexual needs. 29 points.

28) You discuss the "types" of women you finds sexually appealing and/or attempt to demean women by telling them you do not find them sexually appealing. (1 point each, for 2 points total)

So I'm not allowed to have sexual preferences? I'm supposed to find the obese, crater-faced, crabby heffalump as desirable as the 18-year old tight-twatted teen making eyes at me? Yes on both. 31 points.

29) You sexually objectify lesbians or lesbian sexual activity. (1 point)

Not a big fan of lipstick lesbos, though I do watch girl-on-girl pr0n sometimes. I suppose that counts. 32 points.

30) You defend these actions by saying that some women also engage in them. (1 point)

What was that Bible verse about taking the log out of your own eye first? 33 points.

That's it. Now add up your score. There are 43 points possible to get from this quiz. Use the handy guide below to determine if you are a rape-supporter:

0 points: Congratulations! You are *not* a rape-supporter! You are a true friend to women everywhere. You also probably talk with a lisp, listen to Linkin Park, have never been kissed, and worked as a curtain-puller for your school's production of *The*

SEXUALITY

Vagina Monologues, but hey, you can't have everything.

1–10 points: You are a moderate rape-supporter. You've probably had drunken or stoned sex, watch porn, and talk about the kinds of women you think are "hot," but you aren't totally hopeless.

11–20 points: You are a dedicated rape-supporter. You likely engage in victim blaming on a regular basis, laugh at jokes about rape, and mock women for daring to complain about being cat-called. You are a bad man, but far from the worst out there.

20–30 points: You are a hardcore rape-supporter. You're probably a traditionalist Christian, have paid for sex, or espouse an oppressive, patriarchal philosophy. You are beyond help, so try not to cut your knuckles open dragging them everywhere.

31+ points: You are a fanatical rape-supporter, and probably an actual rapist. In fact, I'll bet you were raping a woman while you took this test. Your beliefs about sex and women are so retrograde and backwards, it's a wonder you can even breathe. You should be castrated and locked up in prison for society's sake.

If you haven't figured it out, the joke of this quiz is that any normal, functioning, healthy heterosexual man will score *lots* of points. That's right; according to feminists, being a normal man is enough to make you a supporter of rape. Here I thought it meant, y'know, actually supporting rape, but watching porn and fucking while wasted on Keystone Light has been redefined into

123

pathological behavior. *Feminists want to pathologize the very things that make men, men.* Eve's Daughter herself acknowledges this by writing at the end of her post:

> "So, let's see how many women reading this know at least *one male over the age of 18* who does not fit this list. Anybody?"

Precisely. The problem is that by defining rape as a problem that needs to be "solved" is that *the endgame of any "anti-rape" movement will always be the pathologization of masculinity.* In their denial of human nature, feminists like Eve seek to remold it to conform to their twisted, lunatic prejudices.

Here are the facts: there will always be a small minority of men in any population inclined to rape women, a minority who can be policed and punished but not eliminated entirely. There will also be situations in which this small minority will be able to exercise power. And we're talking real rape here, not "date rape" or "broken condom rape" or whatever definition of rape feminists have made up this week. In this light, you can't end rape anymore than you could end murder or war or death. Attempting to criminalize masculinity while shouting down anyone who suggests women should protect themselves from rape as *BLAMING THE VICTIM OMG!!!!!!* is at best fruitless, and at worst enabling actual rapists.

It is not men, but feminists, who have the blood of raped

women on their hands.

May 24, 2011

Mammas, Don't Let Your Babies Grow Up to Be Self-Shooters

Ever feel like telling the world to fuck off and leave you alone?

I've been AWOL from the Interwebs this week largely because I don't feel like writing. I'm in one of those emotional sinkholes where I lose all motivation to do any work or even leave the house. Despite all the free time created by my twisted ankle, I'd rather thumb through the bibliography of Hunter S. Thompson or turn Nod bases into smoking craters in *Tiberian Sun* than do anything productive. You go-getter types can piss off; a man's entitled to retreat to the confines of his secret place and mope every once in a while.

But unfortunately, heading up a site like *In Mala Fide* keeps me from hanging a "Sorry, We're Closed" sign here for two weeks or so until my mood swings back and I feel like emerging from my pit of despair. So I'm going to attempt to write something worth reading. If it sucks, well, I'll live with it.

Advocatus Diaboli suggested I write something about the preponderance of self-shooters and other similar phenomena and what they say about modern women. "Self-shooter," for those of you who don't know, is slang for a girl (usually a teen) who uses her cell phone camera to photograph herself in various stages of undress, then puts it on the Internet for every man with five minutes and a box of Kleenex to beat one out to. And there's enough of 'em on the Web to fill a small city. It's one thing to sext your boyfriend with a picture of your tits, but it's another thing to sext the entire planet.

If you want a snapshot of the sheer variety of smartphone whores out there, take a look at the *Fuck Yeah Self Shooters* Tumblelog, the number one hit for "self-shooter" (without quotes) on Google.[45] (Be forewarned, it is full of nudity.) The first thing that came to me when looking at that blog is that despite the protestations in the sidebar, the mean age of the girls featured is probably 17. Yep: at least half of self-shooters are technically child pornographers. You can tell from looking at the girls' youth, the way they dress, and the fact that a goodly chunk of the pictures were taken in spacious suburban and McMansion bathrooms. No doubt most of these girls have walk-in closets that are bigger than the room I grew up in.

The second thing that came to me when looking at the self-shooters was their relative *wholesomeness*. This means more than you think. It's a truism that women who become "sex workers" (God I hate that loathsome, PC phrase) tend to be fucked up. You *have* to have a screw loose in order to have sex with strangers or even just expose your body to strange men for money without going insane. I'll bet almost all prostitutes, porn stars and strippers were molested as children and/or come from broken homes, particularly homes in which daddy was absent.

SEXUALITY

In contrast, teenage self-shooters almost all seem to come from upper middle class families. They've got well-off, doting parents, hot boyfriends, good friends, and probably are popular at school: the exact opposite of the "sex worker" demographic. They look like the girls I grew up with, and I don't doubt that had iPhones been around when I was in high school, half of the girls in my graduating class would have shot themselves and put it online not long after their Sweet Sixteen, unbeknownst to their parents. Granted, nude photography has literally been around since photography was invented, but we've never had a deluge like this.

So, we've got teenage girls all over America who were ostensibly raised right but are *still* posing nude in front of their mirrors for all the world to see. Something is rotten in the state of Dawson's Creek. Explanation, please!

Well, I've got one. The reason girls nowadays are baring it all for the camera without so much as a free hamburger in return is because they're vain, arrogant and stupid. The vanity is easily explained; how can you not take a picture of yourself in the bathroom mirror posing nude without being intoxicated with your own good looks? There are even paid erotica websites like *I Shot Myself* that consist entirely of self-shooters, though the quality is usually better and none of the girls are underage. If anything, the ubiquity of self-shooters is evidence against the feminist/conservative claim that teens are asexual angels being preyed upon by older men, because you can't get more sexually

SEXUALITY

aware than snapping your snapper and showing it off online.

The arrogance and stupidity part needs elaboration. Because our feminist world insulates girls and women from almost every consequence of their actions, girls growing up today think they are invincible. None of them understands that plastering their buck naked bodies all over the web could *possibly* have any consequences down the road, even though we live in a world in which people get fired from their jobs for mild antics on Facebook. And, it's not like they're publishing their names along with their pictures, so they're safe… right?

Wrongo. As it turns out, pictures taken with iPhones, Blackberries, Androids and other smartphones often have embedded GPS data telling where the picture was taken, when it was taken, and other information our budding phonewhores don't want publicly known. You can turn this feature off, but a lot of people have no clue it even exists, and it's not like teengrrlz are known for their technical savvy. In fact, there's now a whole online community dedicated to extracting EXIF information from self-shots to find out where these girls hail from. Just take a look at this forum thread, which not only has precise latitudes and longitudes of self-shooters' locations, but satellite pictures of their homes and neighborhoods.[46] *Ouch.*

A large percentage of the girls who upload self-shots to the Web are putting themselves in danger of being stalked, and they don't even know it. The guy who started the forum thread explicitly put a warning against this in his first post. Advocatus Diaboli wrote over a year ago on the future of self-shots and data mining:

> "I see a future, very soon, where you could use the cell-phone number of a girl to search for self-shot pictures of her at 'gray' information sites. Given the decreasing cost of data storage, access, transmission and computing power combined with the increased use of smartphones, the possibilities are mind boggling."[47]

In the future, we probably won't even have to take our own nude pictures of our girlfriends: they'll have them floating on the Interwebs already, taken in the bloom of youth, preserved forever whenever you need to do the old rub 'n' tug. Talk about a great homecoming gift! Unfortunately, it doesn't bode so well for an entire generation of phonewhores who will eventually have to grow up and enter the workforce, short of a massive realignment in the priorities of bosses nationwide, who, as I mentioned already, have no problem firing people for comparatively minor Facebook infractions. Hedotopia is all we've got left, so we might as well enjoy ourselves.

June 3, 2011

SEXUALITY

Why I Refuse to Pay for Porn

Longtime friend of *In Mala Fide* and occasional dispenser of legal advice J. DeVoy has a burning question for moi:

"So, Ferd:

"Why won't you pay for porn? Or will you pay, but just for certain subsets of it?"[48]

I was tempted to brush him off, but an earnest young lad like DeVoy who's supported my blogging efforts for so long deserves a response that isn't flippant and dismissive.

So, why won't I pay for pr0n? I have two reasons, both of them very simple:

1. I don't need it (as much).

Back in January, I took a pledge to curtail my masturbating after figuring out that it sapped my energy and will to write, read, or do anything productive. In the time since I first fell off the wagon in February, I can count the number of times I've whacked off on one hand. The sole purpose of porn is to rub one out. That's it. Forget the stories, the "acting," the staging: it's about getting hard and putting yourself up wet. It has no other purpose. Since I'm not jerking off that often, I don't need any new porn; the few gigabytes or so stashed away on my computer is more than enough.

SEXUALITY

But okay, let's assume that I didn't take the pledge and I was still beating my meat every other day like all men under the age of forty. Even then, I still wouldn't cough up any cash for the privilege. This is because...

2. Porn is not worth paying for.

Look around you. There's so much porn around us that we're drowning in it. It's on tube sites, torrent sites, and file upload sites. It's on our TVs, on the streets, everywhere we go. Even if all of the pirated studio porn was to vanish tomorrow, there'd still be enough amateur stuff to last the average man to the end of his life. His sticky, sweaty, clammy life. And most of the time, the amateur stuff, made by couples for kicks or released by vengeful boyfriends in the wake of breakups, is superior to the studio stuff.

It wasn't always like this. Some guys wistfully remember the days when porno flicks had parody plots and dialogue, but being a guy in his twenties, that era was done and gone before I was a sick, perverted thought in my father's head. The era of porn I remember fondly was the early "gonzo" era of the late 90′s/early oughts; sites that looked like crap, typo-laden descriptions, and basement-level production values. The actual videos had minimal lighting and makeup, shoddy editing, the dumbass cameramen kept making stupid jokes, were filmed in a creepily bare rooms with piss-colored walls, and were short, averaging around 10-20 minutes. But the girls were actually somewhat feminine and normal-looking compared to the glassy-eyed, fake-titted, synthetic pop tarts that are typically associated with porn. I liked those videos because their homemade quality skipped the fluff and focused on the important stuff: the big tits, the round asses, and the retarded Cuban guy fucking girls-next-door with his freakishly huge dick.

Now compare it to modern stuff. The last time I whacked off, I was watching some clip from Brazzers starring Ava Devine, a porn starlet who looks one testosterone shot shy of being a dude. For the first five minutes (the movie clocked in at 42 minutes total), she started in with this embarrassing dirty talk act, spouting out cringe-inducing lines like "even my asshole feels like a pussy" like she was a mother cooing baby talk at her newborn son. I'm not fucking kidding. When the woodsman, a bald freak who looked like he belonged on a sex offender registry, finally walked in, I breathed a sigh of relief: *"Great, now he can shove his dick in her mouth and shut her the fuck up!"* But nope, we had another five minutes of him playing with her cheeks and licking her anus, which almost made me vomit. Dude, *poop* comes out of that thing! What sort of a sick fuck *wants* to watch a man stick his tongue into a chick's Hershey Highway?

Ava *finally* started blowing him around the ten minute mark, but even then she kept pausing every other stroke to run her piehole. Then three minutes later, Baldy started squirting baby oil onto her ass and boobs. In fact, the idiot squirted so much at her that it ran onto the wood floor and they started slipping on it. After another few minutes of awkward slip 'n' slide tit-rubbing handjob action, Ava started sucking him off again. We're midway through the goddamn movie and there's been zero anal action so far, which is what the whole point is supposed to be.

Finally, penis is inserted into asshole, at the 22 minute mark. But even then, this motormouthed bitch couldn't just quiet down and pretend like she's enjoying herself, we had to have a whole running commentary on how excellently our man was sodomizing her. Plus, every inch of her body was covered in oil at this point, making her look like Arnold Schwarzenegger if he had gotten a sex change during his bodybuilding career. And even after fucking a girl in the ass, getting blown multiple times (including ass to mouth), tit-banging her, and getting a handjob from her all over the course of forty minutes, our woodsman *still* needed well over a minute of windup before he could deliver the money shot.

And I'm supposed to find this tranny-lookalike arousing? I'm supposed to jerk off to her clumsy sex talk and greased-up gams? I'm supposed to pay $39.99 a month to watch her and other molestation victims get cameras rammed up their rectums?

Nuh-uh. I don't want what the adult video conglomerates are selling. I don't want ass makeup, I don't want nonstop dirty talk, I don't want fake tits, and I sure as hell don't want HD video. (The human body was not intended to be seen on camera with that level of detail.)

In his post, J. DeVoy appeals to my selfishness in keeping the San Fernando Valley's economy going:

> "As a nihilist, it is not your duty to care about whether other people earn a living. You recognize the broad costs imposed by a coarsening of society. But, from a self-interested perspective, you can appreciate what the deluge of sex and pornography means for your personal life. By buying porn, you're supporting the arts; under an extreme view, it could be like patronage for creators you particularly support, like the Medicis of Renaissance Italy..."

I get the patronage argument; in fact, even though I pirate most of my movies and music, I still go out of my way to buy certain DVDs and CDs solely to support the people who made them, particularly if the musician/filmmaker is obscure or underground. But no website or studio is making the kind of porn I want to watch; in fact, they can't do it by definition. The only guy who can make a POV blowjob movie starring a slut-next-door with a cheap Best Buy camera is her boyfriend, and he's not getting paid to do it because she's not wearing any ass makeup. On the off-hand that a website (I don't bother with DVDs; can't have physical evidence) *does* have a scene I like, I'm not going to cough up $40 a month just to watch a handful of clips from their back catalog that they've done their damndest to obscure.

DeVoy also argues that porn helps improve mens' sex lives by opening girls up to more extreme and slutty behavior:

> "...Thanks to the lifetime oeuvre of, for example, John "Buttman" Stagliano – someone who risked a lengthy prison term to follow his principles – anal sex is not merely a reality for many men, but expected. Sure, Stagliano got wealthy in the process, but his work and that of those he influenced have ensured that north of 80% of girls in our age range are up for some Greek – and I'm not talking about gyros. This is just one example of how what happens in porn affects real life, and, from my perspective, is worth preserving."

Is this true anymore? Buttman was big in the 90's, and the whole BUG/LUG (Bisexual Until Graduation/Lesbian Until Graduation) thing is still popular at colleges. What taboo behavior is porn pushing now that guys are desperate for their girls to do? Salad tossing? Dude-dude-chick threesomes? Do people actually *like* this crap? Maybe I'm just a prude. For all my opponents painting me as being on the level of the Marquis de Sade, my sexual tastes are decidedly vanilla. I like straight p-in-v, blowjobs, facials, and spanking girls, and I'd love to have a threesome with two girls someday for the novelty. That's it. I don't even like anal anymore; yeah, I know that it's outright heresy for someone in the manosphere to *not* enjoy buggery, but there you go. If it weren't for my anti-social, anti-marriage, and generally anti-human disposition, I'd hook up with the traditionalists so I might be able to have a normal sex life again.

The big porn studios aren't doing anything to advance American sexuality. If anything, they're taking us backwards by encouraging otherwise attractive girls to ruin themselves with boob jobs and spout "dirty talk" in the bedroom that makes me want to gag them with my dirty socks. Like how the mainstream media is stifling honest intellectual discourse in this country, *Vivid*, *Brazzers* and *Naughty America* are stifling honest sexual expression.

Now, if we're talking about erotica, I *might* be willing to pay for that. But otherwise, the mainstream purveyors of sleaze have outlived their usefulness. It's time for the porn industry to be swept aside to usher in a new era, an era of narcissistic self-shooting teenage girls and braindead broskis filming their drunken sexcapades on their smartphones. All hail the amateur future!

June 22, 2011

Not All Women Are Like That, Explained

Not All Women Are Like That. A common refrain

SEXUALITY

leveled at manospherians from feminists, traditionalists and other white knights, so common it has its own abbreviation: NAWALT. But its meaning is often misconstrued by people outside the manosphere.

Save for embittered basement dwellers who haven't touched pussy since pussy touched them, no man actually believes that every single woman in the totality of human existence is Like That. Any population gets large enough, there are bound to be exceptions to the rule. The problem is that people, fond of believing that they are special little snowflakes, *think that the existence of ANY exceptions disproves the rule*. To the average modern, stereotypes and generalizations can be unmade with just *one* example that defies them.

That's not how it's supposed to work. The root of "generalization" is "general," meaning that generalizations are assumptions that you can make about something because they are true most of the time. For example, let's say we have a people called the Zigzags. 65 percent of Zigzags have chronic diarrhea, while the other 35 percent do not. However, the existence of a few Zigzags who have normal bowel movements does not change the fact that sixty-five is more than thirty-five. Therefore, we can generalize that Zigzags usually shit pure liquid when they have to go to the bathroom.

Liberals are notorious for their inability to do math in this regard. Take for example, the oft-cited HBD claim that blacks

SEXUALITY

have a lower mean IQ then whites. What will liberals respond when confronted with this (assuming they don't immediately accuse you of being racist)? They'll probably say something like, *"That's not true! I know lots of smart blacks!"* In order for liberals to accept that blacks are on average less intelligent than whites, they have to believe that every single black person on Earth is a moron, not understanding the concept of a mean. Or take the prevalence of black flash mobs and Blacks Behaving Badly. When the Vancouver hockey riot occurred a couple of months back, some idiot liberals responded to the effect of, *"Ha! The hockey riot proves that whites are just as violent and unruly as blacks!"* In the minds of these morons, one single, solitary white-instigated riot was equivalent to the literal dozens of black flash mobs that have occurred in the past year alone.

This is how Not All Women Are Like That works. We aren't saying that all women are Like That, but that enough of them are that we can safely make this generalization about their behavior. Take for example, the oft-echoed claim that country girls are more mature and feminine than city ones. Rural areas are by definition less populated than urban ones, so country girls can never be more than a small minority of a nation's womanfolk. Hence, the existence of feminine country girls doesn't mean we can't generalize that American women are typically narcissistic, childish whiners.

Another example is how Southerners like to tout that their women are more feminine that women in other parts of the country. They forget that South only comprises about 30 to 40 percent of the U.S.'s population. Even if we assume that every single Southern girl isn't Like That (which is impossible), that still leaves 60 to 70 percent of the population who *are* Like That. The stereotype still stands.

So the next time you find yourself in an argument with a white knight touting the women of his back-of-beyond town of 50 people as proof of NAWALT, remind him how basic mathematics works.

August 15, 2011

Why Cohabitation is (Generally) for Chumps

The blogger formerly known as Roissy muses on how cohabitation provides the same benefits as marriage, for men at least:

> "The reasoning is simple: the pro-marriage studies are conflating the benefit of living with someone under marital contract with freely living with someone who loves you. Sex, love and affectionate companionship don't feel any more fulfilling when a piece of paper is signed. If you really think about it, it makes no sense that a man's health would improve and his lifespan increase because he signed on the marital dotted line. Something else is

at work here, and that something else is long-term shared love, with or without the imprimatur of a marriage license."[49]

Heartiste is right in demolishing the claims about marriage being beneficial in any way to men, but recommending cohabitation as an alternative is like substituting getting shot in the head with getting stabbed in the face. Cohabitation is for young men flush with hormones and clingy beta males; it's a waste of time for everyone else. Here are my reasons why you should say no to letting your girl move in with you:

1. It's expensive.

I don't know your current housing situation, but I assume that unless you're living at home, you prefer function over form. You probably have a small apartment, not many material possessions, and you live with roommates. You don't spend more than you need: a crummy one-roomer downtown beats a spacious McMansion in the suburbs. All of this goes out the window the minute your girlfriend moves in.

For starters, you're going to need a bigger place, if not for "women are materialistic money-grubbing whores who always want *moar*" reasons, then for personal space reasons. Claustrophilia loses its allure when you've got another body sleeping in the same bed, lounging on the same couch, and crapping in the same toilet. Second, you can forget about roommates; nobody in their right mind wants to live with a couple. So either way, you're going to be spending more on rent and such each month. This isn't so bad if you and your girl make the same amount of money, but if you're making more than she does, you're going to be getting the short end of the stick.

My girlfriend asked about getting a place to move in together a few days ago, and it ain't happening both because I make way more than she does (she's in college and works part-time) and because I've spent the past year living way below my means, trying to build up a pile of Fuck You Money. I live in a tiny apartment, I don't have cable, all of my worldly belongings (sans furniture) fit in the trunk of my compact, and my only debts are student and car loans. Cohabitating, for me, entails burning more of my paycheck every month so I can experience a facsimile of married life: an incredibly dumb fucking deal.

2. You will get tired of each other that much more quickly.

Cohabitation inevitably degrades to the same level of dullness that married life does. When it comes to relationships, familiarity breeds, if not contempt, then ennui. Conversations become less substantive and more small-talky. Sharing a bed with someone slowly engenders resentment at all their bad sleeping habits, whether it's excessive farting or hogging the sheets. Lust and infatuation ebb away. Eventually, the only thing separating you from a married couple is the wedding:

GF: Oh hai honey, how was your day?

FERD: Oh, same old same old. Our deal with the Ohio people is going great; I'm heading out to Cleveland next week to seal the deal. How was class?

GF: Ugh, I *hate* my calculus professor! He doesn't even teach anything, he just writes stuff on the board and blah blah blah...

(FERD stares longingly at butcher knives, contemplating self-murder.)

Listening to women natter on and on all the time lowers your IQ. Before the haters start in with something like *"Gee, maybe you should stop fucking brainless floozies and date a Strong, Independent Woman™!"*, it has nothing to do with age or life experience: most Western women don't advance beyond the intellectual level of a teenager. I can understand putting up with it if you want to have a family, but if you're single, what's the point? Who can honestly stand this inane chick talk day in day out?

Even marriages that work decline to this level. Example: my parents are model spouses, having been married for over thirty years and never having been divorced or married before. The Thanksgiving I came home after graduating from college, my mom told me that she'd been sleeping in my bed ever since I'd moved out; she couldn't take my dad's snoring any more. If two people who've been husband and wife for more than three decades can barely tolerate each other, what hope do the rest of us have?

Furthermore, you've got the loss of independence that comes with living with someone else. Sometimes I just want to be alone to read a book, practice on the guitar or just lay on the couch and think. Solitude is golden. I can't do that if I'm sharing my abode with someone else. (And the whole concept of a "man-cave" is insulting, another example of the pussification of American society. You're the man; the entire house is your cave. Having a "man-cave" psychologically reduces you to a tenant on your own property, gives your wife/girlfriend dominion over you. Fuck that.)

3. You will be doing *all* the cooking and cleaning.

Modern Western women pride themselves on being unable to perform basic household tasks like cooking dinner or cleaning up after themselves, and the younger they are, the more inept they are. If they don't live at home, they eat out every night or eat microwavable dinners. And unless they're neat freaks, they let their homes collapse into filthy pigsties, with crumbs, dirty clothes and overflowing trash cans everywhere. If you let her move in with you, guess who'll be picking up the slack in those departments?

You, you poor, pathetic fool.

Unless you don't mind the damage to your waistline and wallet that eating out every night will wreak, you *will* be cooking all the time. And you'll also be doing the dishes, vacuuming the floors, taking out the trash, and shoveling the driveway too. You'll be a housekeeper, only you'll be getting paid in blowjobs instead of cash. And again, this isn't simple malevolence, it's usually ignorance. Girls these days are so poorly socialized that they don't realize that you're not supposed to leave your dirty clothes strewn about on the bedroom floor, and it's not like any of her sycophantic beta orbiters or catty girlfriends are going to dare criticize her in any way.

Going back to my situation, my girlfriend is decent about keeping her room clean, but she can't cook anything more complicated than a microwavable pizza. I had to show her how to freaking boil water without burning the house down. Of all the women I've ever been with, only a handful had more than rudimentary cooking skills, and shock, horror, surprise, that handful of women were at least born in other countries. I don't mind cooking for two sometimes, but I'm her boyfriend, not her father; it's not my job to teach her skills that her parents should have.

There are more reasons why cohabitation is a bad idea, but this article is long enough as it is, so I'll leave off here. Point being, cohabitating is a dumb idea that doesn't enhance your sex life enough to compensate for its downsides. You can have a real good time together without having to live together.

January 25, 2012

The Pornification of Sex and Why it's Not Entirely a Good Thing

Via Ray Sawhill, I came across this article on how the ubiquity of Internet porn is changing sex, and why that's a bad thing for teh wimmenz:

> "And what has a formative decade of self-pleasure before the soft glow of computer screens wrought? Well, I'm not the only one inadvertently attracting Seymore Butts acolytes; almost every female friend of mine has had an experience with pornified sex super-early in a relationship. A newly single friend recently started seeing a lawyer she'd met online: He hated wearing condoms, which was weird, because usually men just can't stop talking about how great prophylactics feel. So he asked if he could pull out instead and come on her chest. Considerate! And he did! Another friend hooked up with someone who tried to coax her into anal sex three times in one night. He just really thought she'd 'like it.' When the final emphatic 'NO' was issued, he wondered if he could, considering, maybe just put it between her breasts. I met one guy on Jdate—the Jewish matchmaking site that

floods your inbox with subject lines like 'Here's one to bring home to Bubbe!'–and the first time we had sex, he pulled out a ball gag from his nightstand and gingerly placed it next to me on the bed. *Just in case we want it later.*"[50]

The author, Siobhan Rosen, refers to the fact that she's in her late twenties. Let me take a wild stab and guess that *all* of the women complaining about being expected to take a jizz load in the face are either from my generation–the early Millennials–or older. We're the generation that came to free Internet porn late, having grown up in the halcyon days of AOL, Altavista and infinite redirect scams, so it's no surprise that the gals are less than enthused about having to reenact *Buttman's Bend Over Brazilian Babes* when a mere blowjob would have sufficed back in their college years.

Fortunately, the rest of America has been slowly slouching towards Gomorrah, and the younger they are, the more depraved they are. A 28-year old girl has to be coaxed into backdoor banging; a 21-year old not only is wild about anal, she acts like YOU'RE the freak if you don't bring it up first. You damn kids really have no idea how good you've got it. It's been a long hard slog, but American women have finally been molded into the perfect sluts, ready and willing to do anything.

And I don't think that's entirely positive. I've already

exceeded my self-indulgence quota for this month, so now I'm going to rant about bad bedroom habits that girls really need to stop. Because I sometimes like to delude myself into believing I'm a glass half-full kinda guy, I'm going to start with the good things that porn has done for us.

Great: Facials/Swallowing

This one always perplexed me. There's never been a shortage of girls happy to munch on my hot dog, but too many of them balked when it came to tasting the mayonnaise. It's not that I'm particularly obsessed with making girls swallow my semen, but it's the weird prudishness that always annoyed me. If you're not willing to go down on guys period, that's one thing, but telling me that cum is "gross" just before you stick the organ I pee out of into your mouth requires some serious cognitive dissonance. I always felt this aversion to baby batter was just another example of the entitlement of modern women, wanting to do whatever they want without having to face the consequences.

Those days are long gone. An increasing percentage of girls these days seem to use semen as a major source of protein, even the so-called "good girls." And on the off-chance she's not a swallower, she'll at least let you finish on her face. Or tits. Or ass. I've come to realize that I hate coming in condoms; it's like trying to spit into a balloon. There's a certain primal satisfaction in painting a woman with your seed, like how the wild cats in my neighborhood mark their territory by pissing all over everything. A big, thick pearl necklace says, *"This is mine. Back off world, or I'll bash your face in."* Just make sure she's not the type who'll scoop it into her vagina while you're in the can and you're good.

Good: Going Bald

I like baiting the bush-lovers from time to time; they're easier to wind up than granddaughter clocks. Aesthetically, I can appreciate a full, luxurious pelt on a girl… in a picture. In real life, they inspire revulsion and disgust, whether it's from the faint reek of urine they emit or the crabs that are potentially nesting in there. Few women these days are unshorn anyway, but the younger ones are more likely to get it all waxed off, while the older girls tend to be satisfied with basic shaving. I don't think this can be attributed solely to porn—all the porn actresses in the 70's had plenty of bush to go around—but it acts as nice reinforcement for the Internet Generation.

Meh: Anal

As recently as a decade ago, backdoor lovin' was still taboo, rarely acknowledged outside of Internet porn. Getting your girl to let you stick in her ass involved copious amounts of begging and crawling through broken glass. The first time I tried buttsex, way back in college, involved several weeks of pitifully pleading my then-girlfriend until she finally broke down and agreed… after I took her out to dinner at the most expensive restaurant in the city (a mid-level Italian joint). Now everyone

SEXUALITY

and their sister from Saskatchewan is going Greek, which is supposed to be fantastic! Superlative! A long awaited triumph for masculinity! Bite me.

In the manosphere—hell, among men in general—admitting to not liking sodomy is tantamount to being a Jew for Jesus, but I'm gonna get up on the cross anyway. Buttfucking's appeal, to me anyway, was two-fold:

1. **It was forbidden and exotic.** When something is frowned upon by society, that makes doing it more fun because it gives you the juvenile thrill of sticking your thumb in God's eye.

2. **It appealed to the sadist within me.** I've been nursing a theory on sex for a while now; pursuant to gender parity, if women have natural masochistic sexual desires, then men have natural sadistic sexual desires. I'm not talking about BDSM or domestic violence, but rather the vanilla fantasies that most girls have: getting spanked red raw, having their hair yanked during sex, and whatnot. *If women secretly want to be dominated, then men secretly want to be dominant.* The reason why guys want big dicks, for example, is not because they want to impress or please women, but because they want to *hurt* them.

Even back when buttlove was still taboo, I didn't really get into it. *"But it's sooooo much tighter."* Who the hell are you fucking, middle-aged ex-strippers? For most girls under the age of 25, tightness is hardly an issue. And even vaginas that are less than snug have a indescribable warmth and texture to them; they just feel right. The anus may be tight, but it ain't snug; it's muscle-y and alien and it feels like your dick is constantly on the verge of being kicked out. With the stigma surrounding anal sex deader than Don't Ask, Don't Tell, what's the motivation?

As for sating my inner sadist, I have two words for you: wooden hairbrush. If she doesn't have trouble walking after you do it, you didn't do it right.

Bad: Dirty Talk

Faking an orgasm is a subtle but simple art. According to the feminist narrative, men never cared about a woman's pleasure until the Wretched Patriarchy was overthrown fifty years ago. It's complete bullshit, but most people are morons and believe it. Therefore, fooling a guy into thinking you're having the time of your life really shouldn't be that hard.

When you immediately start shrieking, *"Oh my God yes, fuck me like a dirty whore,"* and exaggeratedly flailing your arms before I've even finished the first thrust, you completely give the game away.

My long-standing policy on the female orgasm is one even the feminasties could agree with: *"If you don't care enough to tell me what I'm doing wrong, I don't care enough to figure it out on my own."* But when I see a girl so self-consciously and blatantly putting on a show, I feel like pulling out and jerking myself off just to make a point. Gals, if your exclamations of ecstasy are any longer than two words per sentence, we can tell you're full of it: we saw some tarted-up coke whore doing the exact same thing on our laptop screens last night. You're not being sexy and you're not fooling anyone. No wonder that guy from *JDate* kept a ball gag in his nightstand.

Awful: Analingus

Not that common, but more common than it should be (which is never, ever, never). Two girls have tried to pull this on me recently, and both times I had to push their heads away while in shock. Look ladies, your devotion to my sexual pleasure is much appreciated, but don't you know that *poop* comes out of that thing?

There's a lot more I could list here, but I've had enough. One wonders how much more depraved the American sexual marketplace can get. Will breeding parties and financial domination be the new normal in ten years? I might have to join the priesthood if this keeps up.

February 13, 2012

The Necessity of Domestic Violence

I remember the first time a woman attacked me.

It was roughly a decade ago. I was having the typical beta lovers' spat: I was angry that my girlfriend didn't want to hang out

SEXUALITY

and she was disgusted by my clinginess. We yelled at each other for twenty minutes before I gave up and decided to leave. As I opened her door, I turned my head just in time for her soccer cleat to hit me full on in the face.

I was lucky. If I'd been hit a inch or so to the left, I could have been blinded for life. Instead, my right eye was swollen shut for a week.

As I collapsed screaming in pain, my girlfriend switched from raging tiger bitch to demure kitten. "Omigod Ferd, are you all right? I'm so sorry! I didn't mean to hit you!" She accompanied me to the free clinic, where the nurse gave me an icepack to bring the swelling down. For the next week, whenever someone asked me what the hell happened, I told them I was mugged; a ridiculous face-saving lie, because there was no violent crime in this placid rural town. Nobody was cruel enough to say the truth to my face.

But I couldn't tell them I'd been maimed by a woman.

***

I have absolutely zero sympathy for women who are the victims of domestic violence, for a multitude of reasons. Most notably, the constant hand-wringing about violence against women puts the lie to the feminist claim that gender is just a social construct. If women have all the same rights and responsibilities as men, if denying privileges to someone because of the shape of their genitals is morally wrong, then that means there's nothing wrong with bashing a woman's face in; or, more accurately, it's no more wrong than bashing a man's face in. *"Teach your son that all violence against women is wrong."* What if she's coming at me with a kitchen knife? Do I get to defend myself or does the code of chivalry require me to stand there and let her stab me through the heart?

But more importantly, the reason I don't care about women who are beaten by their men is *because nine times out of ten, they put themselves in that situation.* Spengler's Universal Law of Gender Parity:

> **"In every corner of the world and in every epoch of history, the men and women of every culture deserve each other."**

Women are masters of refusing to accept the consequences of their own behavior. *Girls who habitually end up in relationships with abusive men do so because they are attracted to men who abuse them.* Of course, point this out and the rationalizations will sputter forth: *"He wasn't like that when we first started dating! He only started abusing me after we got married/moved in together!"* Can it. Jekyll/Hyde transformations are impossible for anyone to pull off. People can change, but change is slow and incremental; it doesn't happen overnight, nor after a wedding. If you paid attention, you could have seen signs that your man was an abuser, but you ignored them because unconsciously, that's what turns you on, what gets you wet.

Finally, I have no sympathy for most abused women because *a great many of them deliberately incite their men into attacking them, if not by being physically abusive themselves, then by creating drama.* Extreme cases of this are diagnosed as borderline personality disorder, but a great percentage of the normal female population engages in this behavior as a matter of course. I found this out the hard way.

***

Rewind back to my first months out of college. I'd reluctantly moved back home after getting a semi-decent job loading trucks for a certain package delivery company. Not long after, I fell in with a sophomore at one of the local colleges, Constance, and she convinced me to move in with her. Constance was a little on the hirsute side and a bit chubby, but she had great tits, a nice plump ass, and most importantly, she was a demon in the sack. I'm talking nails digging into my buttcheeks, bedsheet-staining, screaming loud enough to wake the neighbors sex. Between our jobs, we could eke out a decent living in the bohemian district, right by the college and not far from downtown and its (pathetic, overhyped) nightlife.

Domestic tranquility was short-lived. Not long into autumn, I was cut from my full-time position and reduced to working part-time on the second shift (5pm-11pm). Constance had to beg her parents for an allowance so we could make ends meet. I would've rather died then gone to my parents for a handout, let alone move back in with them. She had me by the balls financially, and she knew it. Sex dropped off, replaced by increasingly heated arguments.

I'd assumed an asshole persona during my college life of casual sex and booze, but I was reverting back to beta in an relationship. I had no idea what to do, so I dealt with Constance the way my dad had dealt with my mom whenever she wanted to argue: avoidance and acquiescence, hoping she'd just shut up and leave me alone. All I did was make her angrier and more strident. Finally, things came to a head.

I was getting ready to go to work one night when Constance started unloading on me. I don't remember the exact details of how it started, but it quickly devolved into her ranting about how I was always slinking off with my friends and I wasn't spending any time with her. I tried my usual avoidance-cowardice strategy, but she would have none of it.

"Look baby, I have to go to work—"

"Oh no no no, you're *not* running off like you always do!"

"Can't this wait—"

"SHUT UP YOU ASSHOLE! LISTEN TO ME!"

I tried to turn and leave, but she ran up to me and shoved me, all the while screaming at the top of her lungs: "I am tired of this and that and yadda yadda yadda…"

I'm a calm guy, very slow to anger. But Constance's abuse snapped me. I wasn't going to become my father.

"I AM SICK OF YOU!" I bellowed.

THWAPP!

"Aaugh!"

Constance recoiled as I smacked her across the face. Both of us went silent. She stared at me, nursing her wounded cheek, her strident pose replaced with a look of terror. I just stood there, flitting between looking at my outstretched hand and her fearful gaze.

"I'm going to work," I broke the silence, turning around to leave. She said nothing.

The gravity of what I'd done didn't hit me until I was in the car. *God, I am so fucked. She's gonna call the cops. The neighbors are gonna call the cops, if they haven't already.* By the time I pulled into the parking lot, my hands were trembling.

I couldn't concentrate that night. It felt like I was having an ulcer. During my dinner break, I could barely eat, picking at my ham-and-cheese sandwich and staring into space. My co-workers sensed something was wrong, but I just brushed them off. Then, just as we were about to go back to work, the announcement boomed over the intercom.

"FERDINAND BARDAMU, PLEASE COME TO THE FRONT OFFICE ASAP. FERDINAND TO THE FRONT OFFICE ASAP."

My stomach dropped into my knees. *Here it comes.* "Mr. Bardamu, you are under arrest. You have the right to remain silent, anything you say can and will be used against you in a court of law." *My mug shot on the front page of the local paper, interviews with all my childhood friends and teachers. "Ferd was such a good kid growing up, I don't know what happened to him."* I trudged up to the front office as my stomach twisted into knots.

I entered the lobby to find Constance waiting by the front desk. There were no cops. I zeroed in on her cheek; no evidence of my assault remained on her cinnamon-colored skin.

"I think we should take this outside," she said.

"Yeah."

I followed her out to the parking lot, craning my neck to look for cops. None in sight.

"Look Ferd, I wanted to apologize—"

"Wait, what?" I stammered incredulously.

"I said I'm sorry!" she yelled, a note of humility in her voice. I shut up.

"Look, after you left, I realized that I've been a gigantic bitch to you. I've been treating you like crap, but it wasn't until now that I realized what I was doing… I'm sorry."

"Uh…" I couldn't believe what I was hearing.

"Ferd, we've… you've, I know you've been under a lot of stress lately." She bit her tongue. "I want to make this relationship work. I want to make *us* work."

"I… thanks," I gasped, still in disbelief. "You're not calling the police?"

"No," Constance replied. "Matt and Jessica [our next-door neighbors] heard us yelling and came over after you left. I talked them down."

"Connie," I came down to earth, "I shouldn't have hit you like that. I don't know what came over me."

"No, it's fine," she swatted me down, a bit of irritation in her voice. *You're off the hook, dipshit! Don't fuck this up!* "Well, you've probably got to get back to work."

"Right. Well, see ya."

I gave her a quick peck on the lips and went back inside. *Did that really just happen?*

Later that night, after I came home, we had sex for the first time in two weeks, the most intense make-up sex I've ever had in my life. I pounded her so vigorously I knocked one of the support slats loose, causing the middle part of the bed to cave in. When we were done, the sheets were so drenched with her cum they looked like they'd been through the washer. God knows everyone in the building must've heard us. *"AAAGGG, FUCK ME! OH GOD! Ferd…"*

The relationship petered out not long after, but we were on mostly amiable terms when it ended. I drifted out of contact with Constance when I moved away; not sure what she's doing now.

***

Despite all this, *I do NOT recommend you start hitting the girls in your rotation*, mainly because the risks are too great. For every one girl who'll pounce on your dick after a good backhand, there are three more who'll dial 911 without a second thought. I got lucky. But unless you exclusively fuck single moms, cougars and spinsters, you've likely had girls either try to physically hurt you or bait you into hitting them. Young women (teens to early twenties), sexually voracious girls, and high-T (check the digit ratio!) girls are all more likely to be abusive.

Ever wonder why spanking is the preferred form of corporal punishment for children? If the sole purpose of hitting a disobedient child is to inflict physical pain, why not just uppercut the little shit in the jaw (assume we lived in a society where physically beating your children was acceptable)? Or why not just

SEXUALITY

smack the brat with a two by four plank of wood? Why go to all the effort of yanking his pants down and wearing your palm out on his dirty ass-cheeks? The answer is that corporal punishment isn't merely about pain, it's about *humiliation.* Exposing a kid's bare buttocks for all the world to see is about making him feel weak and powerless, reminding him who's in charge. (By the way, this humiliation aspect is why so many women are turned on by getting spanked. Nothing says "submission" like being bent over your man's knees, totally exposed and helpless against his punishing blows…)

It's the same when it comes to disciplining women. Slapping a girl across the face isn't just about hurting her, it's a kind of neg. It says, *"I can crush you like an insect, but you aren't worth the effort."* It's a tacit acknowledgment that she's weaker than you, beneath you, and if she crosses you again, you'll put her in the hospital. You treat her like she's a child throwing a temper tantrum, not an equal.

Like I said already, *you should NOT hit women, not unless you want to end up in jail.* But the principle still stands. Women should be terrorized by their men; it's the only thing that makes them behave better than chimps.

***

A couple months back, career blogger and self-admitted Aspie Penelope Trunk posted a picture of a bruise her husband gave her during an argument:

> "I took the kids and went to a hotel so I could have time to think. I think I need to move into a hotel for a month.
>
> "The Farmer told me that he will not beat me up any more if I do not make him stay up late talking to me.
>
> "If you asked him why he is still being violent to me, he would tell you that I'm impossible to live with. That I never stop talking. That I never leave him alone. How he can't get any peace and quiet in his own house. That's what he'd tell you.
>
> "And he'd tell you that I should be medicated."[51]

Trunk's not stupid. She knows full well that she's deliberately enraging her husband, baiting him into beating the stuffing out of her. She gets off on the drama and the conflict. Just look at that picture; it should be in the dictionary next to the entry for "attention whore." The bruise is barely in frame, the emphasis being on Trunk's softening middle-aged tucus. Not only does Trunk get off on manipulating her husband into a violent rage, she gets off on manipulating her readers into sympathizing with her. Some white-knighting dorks even called the police on her behalf.

And how did Penelope reward her loyal beta orbiters and e-girlfriends? By telling them to kiss her cougar ass:

> "Blog commenters will argue against this idea by telling me not to change because it's not my fault.
>
> "But really, how do they know? We know that I grew up in a home where there was lots of violence. So it's likely that I will be in that kind of house when I'm an adult. And surely it's possible that I am contributing to the mix since I am statistically likely to create a violent household. Here's another thing: You don't know what I did leading up to the bruise in the photo."[52]

This post is the equivalent of a Bond villain's expository monologue. Penelope is thrashing her readers around like a potbellied hick thrashing his meth-head wife around the double-wide, and they just sit there and beg for more.

Did you know that Rihanna's been hooking up with Chris Brown, the man who nearly beat her into a coma, for a year now? And that Brown's got his own posse of fangirls who love him in spite of his violent predilections? Damn, it's almost like some girls like this "domestic violence" thing!

This is why I have no sympathy for battered women. Far too many of them are like Penelope Trunk: *conniving, manipulative cunts who wear their men down for the 'gina tingles, then trick innocent bystanders into squirting tears to their sob stories.* They are slapped, punched, and kicked because they inflict emotional violence on their husbands and boyfriends, fueling a never-ending cycle of drama and pain. They are just as abusive and twisted as the thugs and jerks they get wet for.

They deserve each other.

February 27, 2012

How to Be a Man

During my first semester at college, I had the misfortune of having an emo for a roommate. Everything about this guy was effeminate and despicable: he talked with a lisp, he wore his hair long with bangs, and all of his friends were girls. We clashed on almost everything, from his habit of making out with his girlfriend underneath the sheets to our fights over the thermostat (he always bitched that it was too hot, even when it was five degrees out). Living with him was like being married. I initially just tried to avoid him, spending most of my non-class time hanging out with my friends or other stuff, only coming home to sleep, but things eventually came to a head and I ended up transferring to a new room.

But despite his general obnoxiousness, Emo Roommate

had one thing over me: he got laid. All the time. With reasonably cute girls. During the short time I lived with him, he basically had a rotating harem of three or four girls at any given time, inexplicably drawn to his fey mannerisms and pissy passive-aggressive behavior. In fact, one Sunday morning I came home from a long night of drinking Keystone Light and striking out with the ladies to the sight of his girlfriend making out with a redheaded girl on his bed while he grinned. I suppose it was a violation of the bro code to cockblock him like that, but I couldn't have cared less at the time; served him right for being an unbearable prick.

As desperate as I was to remake myself, I had my limits. Emo Roommate may have been getting more pussy than I was, but he was something I didn't want to be. He was a *fag*.

I'm from the generation for whom "fag" and "gay" were common taunts, much to the consternation of our teachers and parents. To a bunch of third-graders jostling for social status on the playground, faggotry was like porn: they couldn't define it, but they knew it when they saw it. Faggotry doesn't refer specifically to homosexuality, though a lot of homos happen to be fags. Faggot, gay, girly-man, fairy, fruit: these are all terms to describe men who fail at being men. More than that, these men not only *don't* care that they've failed at being men, they revel in it and demand the world reorient itself to accommodate their failures.

SEXUALITY

I couldn't have articulated all this a decade ago, but at a certain instinctual level, I knew it. So did my friends, and so does any man who's ever used "fag" as an insult. So does society at large, never mind their claims of gender being a social construct. Look at all the mindless "man up" shaming coming from the media today. Implicit in using the phrase "man up" is that there is a fixed definition of "man" that the males of today have failed to meet. More importantly, "man up" implicitly states that *manhood is something that males must earn.* There's no equivalent phrase for women, nobody calling on them to "woman up." The reality that Bill Bennett, Kay Hymowitz and the rest acknowledge but won't say aloud is that *women are born and men are made.*

Jack Donovan's latest book, *The Way of Men*, is not a self-help guide. Reading it won't get you laid, make you money or give you bigger abs. *The Way of Men* is an attempt to answer the questions, *"What is masculinity? What does it mean to be a man? What is the essence of manliness?"* It's an articulation of what makes men men, unencumbered by ideology, philosophy or religion, the truth that we all know and have known for millennia but could not find the words for.

This is going to sound like hyperbole or ass-kissing, but *The Way of Men* is easily one of the most valuable books I've ever read. Decades from now, when the current dystopia becomes nothing but a bad memory, Donovan's book will be seen as one of the seminal works of the alt-right/manosphere canon. I hate even using this analogy because it trivializes the sheer impact of Jack's work, but it's the only way to make my point: *The Way of Men* will do for men what *The Feminine Mystique* did for women.

The Way of Men is important precisely because Jack approaches masculinity from an objective, amoral, almost mathematical standpoint, a perspective that is literally absent in the past few decades' writing on the subject. The problem with defining masculinity is that every single clique in the world wants to repurpose masculinity and men to serve their own interests.

Ask a dozen people what manliness is and you'll get a dozen different answers:

- To a traditionalist Christian, being masculine entails getting married, having children and going to church every Sunday.
- To a gamer/manospherian, being masculine entails having sex with lots of women.
- To a feminist, being masculine means serving the interests of women every minute of every day.

Donovan dispenses with all this noise and distills manliness down to its core attributes, independent of culture and morality. These are the virtues that define men throughout space and time, whether we're talking about the samurai of feudal Japan or the knights of medieval Europe:

"To understand who men are, what they have in common and why men struggle to prove their worth to each other, reduce male groups to their nucleic form. Sprawling, complex civilizations made up of millions of people are relatively new to men. For most of their time on this planet, men have organized in small survival bands, set against a hostile environment, competing for women and resources with other bands of men. Understanding the way men react to each other demands an understanding of their most basic social unit. Understanding what men want from each other requires an understanding of what men have most often needed from each other, and a sense of how these needs have shaped masculine psychology.

"Relieved of moral pretense and stripped of folk costumes, the raw masculinity that all men know in their gut has to do with being good at being a man within a small, embattled gang of men struggling to survive.

"The Way of Men is the way of that gang."

This short section should give you an idea what Jack's

writing style is like: direct and unpretentious. This isn't a dry academic work full of puff words and run-on sentences. Donovan is economical with his words and doesn't waste your time. Indeed, he actually cut a section out of the book because he felt it was a diversion; he released these chapters for free as *No Man's Land* last November.

Jack's concept of the "gang" being the way of men informs the entire book, specifically his analysis of the central traits of masculinity: strength, courage, mastery and honor. The "gang" is the basic unit of male organization going back to the caveman days. All effective male organizations, from the police to the military to the mafia, are gangs in which the four aforementioned virtues are necessary to survive and advance the group's interests. Drawing on evolutionary biology, history and philosophers from Aristotle to Hobbes, Donovan breaks it down:

> "People like to make friends. Being on the defensive all the time is stressful. Most people want to trust other people. Most people want to be able to relax. If you are smart, until you know *them*, *they* will remain *out there* on the other side of the perimeter. Even if you let your guard down to cooperate or trade with them, *they* may or may not be absorbed into *us*. As long as other men maintain separate identities, there is always the chance that

they will choose to put the interests of *their own* ahead of your interests. In hard times, agreements between groups fall apart. Competition creates animosity, and men will dehumanize each other to make the tough decisions necessary for their own group to survive."

Donovan also distinguishes between the concept of a being a good man ("good" as in moral) and being good at being a man (being masculine), noting that most people confuse the two:

"A man who is more concerned with being a good man than being good at being a man makes a very well-behaved slave."

It goes without saying that certain figures would do well to read that quote carefully.

The second half of *The Way of Men* is concerned with the state of men today, serving as a great antidote to all the "man up" articles coming out of the media today. Society has gradually crippled mens' ability to be manly by making the world safe and neutered, yet the Bennetts and Hymowitzes of the world wonder why the Millennial generation has no interest in anything aside from porn and video games. The chapter "The Bonobo Masturbation Society" drives the point home:

"If you're a good boy and you follow the rules, if

you learn how to speak passively and inoffensively, if you can convince some other poor sleepwalking sap that you are possessed with an almost unhealthy desire to provide outstanding customer service or increase operational efficiency through the improvement of internal processes and effective organizational communication, if you can say stupid shit like that without laughing, if your record checks out and your pee smells right–you can get yourself a J-O-B. Maybe you can be the guy who administers the test or authorizes the insurance policy. Maybe you can be the guy who helps make some soulless global corporation a little more money. Maybe you can get a pat on the head for coming up with the bright idea to put a bunch of other guys out of work and outsource their boring jobs to guys in some other place who are willing to work longer hours for less money. Whatever you do, no matter what people say, no matter how many team-building activities you attend or how many birthday cards you get from someone's secretary, you will know that you are a completely replaceable unit of labor in the big scheme of things."

SEXUALITY

This is a woman's world; we men are just visiting.

But it won't be a woman's world for much longer. With the slow-motion collapse of the economy and the government's impotence, it's only a matter of time before new gangs of men arise to take their place. Donovan is critical of the men's rights movement's first principles and pessimistic of their chances of success, though he does praise the work they do. The future of men is the same as their past: the Way of the Gang, good, bad or wretched.

A while back, the author of the *Danger & Play* blog commented to the effect of "this is the first generation of males who were not taught how to be men." Generation Zero is the generation of Sesame Street and Ritalin, a generation raised without any memory or first-hand knowledge of a world in which masculinity was encouraged and celebrated rather than punished. *The Way of Men* is the first complete roadmap to masculinity ever published, the truth your fathers never told you. For the men of my generation, this book is beyond invaluable.

But even if you aren't a Millennial, you have to own *The Way of Men*. There is literally nothing out there like it: a book that describes the fundamentals of manliness without getting bogged down in religion or politics. It is a guiding light out of the darkness.

But whatever you do, don't be a fag.

April 11, 2012

II

WHAT'S WRONG WITH THE WORLD

Gott ist Tot

For all my busting of libertarians' balls, I was more sympathetic towards libertarianism when I was younger. While in high school and searching for an ideological pier to tether my boat to, I happened upon my mom's collection of dog-eared paperbacks by the world's most famous female autist, Ayn Rand. Her philosophy and its ethos of capitalism, logic and reason was a refreshing change from the soft, squishy socialism that permeated the teachings of the Catholic school I attended. I glommed onto her worldview like a barnacle on an oil tanker, quickly devouring her four novels and her countless essay collections. I even cited Rand's *The Virtue of Selfishness* in an essay in my religion class on how to create a world free of war and violence. I was just a kid then; I didn't notice Rand's repetitious, Aspergery writing style, her turgid prose, the massive logical holes in her arguments, her complete lack of humor (actual Rand quote from *The Philosophy of Objectivism*: "The worst evil that you can do, psychologically, is to laugh at yourself. That means spitting in your own face."), and the fact that her writing actually got *worse* as time went on. Once I started tearing into the likes of Hayek, Mises, and Kirk, I was done with Rand for good. Objectivism is only a credible philosophy to the young and pliable of mind.

The Myth of Natural Rights and Other Essays, by L.A. Rollins, is the kind of book I wish I had had during my teenage years, as it would have saved me a whole lot of winding through bad writing. Rollins' tract takes the foundation of modern libertarianism—the concept of natural rights—and not only smashes it into teeny-tiny pieces, he makes libertarian icons like Rand, Murray Rothbard, and others look like complete and utter morons in the process. As such, it's a must-own book for anyone interested in political theory.

As Chip Smith, whose *Nine-Banded Books* has republished *The Myth* along with a collection of Rollins' other work, writes:

> "Originally published by Loompanics Unlimited in 1983, the central monograph is a two-fisted display of lib-targeted philosophical shit-stirring that holds up well after 25 years. In its previous incarnation, *The Myth* provoked a fair amount of measured praise along with entertaining fits of blustery

outrage among libertarian stalwarts and natural law votaries, with much of the tooth-gnashing playing out in the pages of the Sam Konkin's old *New Libertarian* magazine. Rollins' thesis also famously prompted movement luminary Murray Rothbard to pen a delightfully truculent head-in-the-sand essay enjoining 'The Duty of Natural Outlaws to Shut Up,' and it inspired Robert Anton Wilson to publish a lively book-length companion essay entitled *Natural Law: Or Don't Put a Rubber on Your Willy.*"

The central argument of *The Myth of Natural Rights* is that the concept of natural rights, as formulated by Enlightenment thinkers such as John Locke and serving as the foundation of libertarian theory, is a fiction, a religious idea that has zero relevance in the real, secular world. As blogger TGGP of *Entitled to an Opinion* writes in his introduction:

"Without giving the game away, it is perhaps better to start out by saying what natural rights are *not* than what they are. If one were to begin a sentence with the phrase 'natural rights are,' that sentence would already be false. Natural rights are *not*. That they do not exist is the blunt thesis of *The Myth*. Natural rights are the tooth-fairies of political philosophy, claiming no more substance than the epiphenomenal gremlins inhabiting Daniel Dennett's car engine. Despite the carefully parsed semantic rigging, a 'natural right' is to be found nowhere in nature, and unlike an actual legal or customary right, it confers no protection upon its claimant."

Rollins' monograph is less polemic than carefully researched academic argument, albeit written with a snarky undertone, free of filler (the primary text of *The Myth* clocks in at less than seventy pages), and absent the panicked defensiveness that characterizes academic writing. In the opening chapters, Rollins draws a distinction between natural rights, which are "fake or metaphorical rights," and "real rights" or "positive rights," describing the latter as "those rights that are actually conferred and enforced by the laws of a State or the customs of a social group." Contrasting the two groups, Rollins reduces natural rights to little more than wishful thinking on the part of libertarians, mocking them as "bleeding heart libertarians" who conjure up bogus rights out of thin air.

My biggest complaint with *The Myth* is that the bulk of it is focused not on proving the phoniness of natural rights but on making mincemeat of noted libertarians who base their arguments on the theory. To be sure, Rollins accomplishes his goal with aplomb, tearing Rand, Rothbard, Tibor Machan, and others to shreds, exposing the gaping holes, paradoxes, and pretzel-like mutilations of logic in their writings. In particular, his chapter on Rand rips apart her rationalist, atheist facade to reveal a deeply religious, irrational woman, amusingly dubbing her "Mrs. Illogic." By spending most of his time picking fights with other intellectuals instead of making an independent argument, Rollins limits *The Myth's* effectiveness as a standalone work. Nonetheless, for those who are looking for an airtight reason to disavow mainstream libertarianism once and for all, or those who're looking for a book on ideology that is unlike anything else out there, *The Myth of Natural Rights* is a text you should read ASAP.

    Reviewing this book without mentioning the "other essays" in the title would be dumb, considering that those "other essays" make up two-thirds of *The Myth's* pages. The middle third of the book is a trio of essays on Holocaust revisionism which displays Rollins' penchant for misanthropic iconoclasm. In "The Holocaust as Sacred Cow," he lays into "Holocaustorians" who perpetuate falsehoods about the Holocaust and who refuse to debate the subject, comparing them to religious fanatics. On the subject of the number of Jews killed in the Holocaust, he writes:

> "For many people, the six million figure is not a fact, although they call it that; rather it is an article of faith, believed in not because of compelling evidence in its support, but because of compelling

psychological reasons. For such people, the Six Million figure is a Sacred Truth, not to be doubted and, if necessary, to be defended with dogmatism, mysticism, illogic, fantasy or even downright lies."

The second essay, "Revising Holocaust Revisionism," is by far the most interesting of the bunch, because in it Rollins turns his guns on revisionists for pushing falsehoods and lies, accusing them of having hidden agendas beyond "set[ting] the record straight". At the end of the paper, he declares himself to be "skeptical of both sides", stating that "[n]either side in the Holocaust controversy claims a monopoly on falsehood." The final essay, "Deifying Dogma," is the most boring, as it's nothing more than a point-by-point refutation of the anti-revisionist tract *Denying History* by Michael Shermer and Alex Grobman, who made the fatal error of smearing Rollins in its pages. Remind me to never get on this guy's bad side, as it makes for poor writing on his part.

The remainder of *The Myth* is devoted to L.A. Rollins' satirical writings, serving as the cherry on this ice cream sundae of idol destruction. "Lucifer's Lexicon: An Updated Abridgment" is a Samuel Johnson-esque collection of witty, laugh-out-loud definitions (ex: "Blowjob, *n.* A nice job, if you can get it.") that deserve to be re-published on their own. On the other hand, "An Open Letter to Allah" is simply awful, tenth-rate anti-religious invective delivered in the voice of a Rand-drunk teenager who keeps a copy of *The God Delusion* under his pillow. "An Ode to Emperor Bush" is a moderately entertaining bit of doggerel, but it lacks the spark that makes "Lucifer's Lexicon" such a wicked read. The book would have been improved if both of these diversions had been taken out.

Aside from its few flaws, *The Myth of Natural Rights and Other Essays* is a great read, a well-crafted collection of works by a sadly-forgotten writer. Whether you're interested in shibboleth-skewering essays or satirical shots at sacred cows, you ought to pick this one up.

February 15, 2010

Anti-Anti-Semitism

About a month ago, a reader of mine asked me why I refused to label myself an anti-anti-Semite. The answer is that I think anti-anti-Semitic hysteria is a growing melanoma on the American body politic. While I'm not fond of the conspiracy-mongering on the anti-Semitic right, I'm not stupid: a group of basement-dwelling losers having a circle jerk on a blog aren't a threat to anyone but themselves. Jim Giles will not be spearheading the rise of the Fourth Reich from his trailer out in the ass-end of Mississippi. Those lunatics are marginalized and have no influence beyond their social circles, which are only populated with people as crazy as they are. The biggest problem with anti-Semitism of that variety right now is that it threatens to clip the wings of the alternative right.

Anti-anti-Semites on both the left and right, on the other hand, are very powerful and very committed to shouting and shutting down anyone who has a less-than-hagiographic view of the Jews. Anti-anti-Semitism is bolstered beyond the usual minority-loving anti-racist whinging by the semi-unique instance of the Holocaust. Liberals and neocons have spent the past sixty plus years constantly picking at that Holocaust wound in one of the biggest and most ignored examples of scar worship in Western society. The Holocaust cult is so powerful that an entire European nation is forced to self-flagellate constantly for a crime that the majority of its inhabitants had no role in. And anyone who questions the influence Jews have on modern society gets a roundhouse kick in the face from the Foxman-Schlussel-Victimologist crowd: *"OMIGOD YOU FILTHY NEO-NAZI SCUM YOU WANT TO STUFF JEWS IN OVENS YOU AWFUL PERSON YOU!"*

The logic behind anti-anti-Semitism is, on the surface, sound. If the logical conclusion of anti-Semitism is ghettos and gas chambers, then ideas and statements that could potentially go down that road must be snuffed out in the womb. But what causes anti-Semitism? The liberal explanation is the same as the ones for racism and every -ism on their hit list: ignorance, selfishness, and people not letting the *love* into their hearts and being big meanies. The Judeophobes will say that anti-Semitism exists because teh Joooos secretly rule the world and they are on to their Jewy tricks. Both sides are wrong.

The reason anti-Semitism exists can be explained with a simple quote: "proximity + diversity = war."[1] Like I explained on Tuesday, human beings are tribal, and multiple tribes in the same space will always be at each others' throats. The beauty of Roissy's equation is that it can be applied to any ethnic tension in any country on Earth, whether its the Quebecois in Canada, Chinese in Malaysia, or the Kurds in Turkey. No kooky tinfoil hat theories, no fudging facts, no insanity. Essentially, so long as the Jews remain visible minorities in gentile societies, anti-Semitism will persist. It will fluctuate in intensity, but it will never go away. If the anti-anti-Semites really wanted to accomplish their goal, they'd launch a campaign to get every Jew outside of the Holy Land to make *aliyah*, combined with a political push to get the U.S. government out of Israeli affairs.

The biggest sin of the anti-anti-Semitic crusaders is their insistence on painting all gentiles with the same broad brush. Their worldview is as Manichean as it gets, and doesn't account for the differing treatments of Jews in various countries and regions of the world. On one end of the spectrum you have Nazi Germany and the Holocaust. Moving down you find Czarist Russia, where state-sanctioned anti-Semitic mob violence was so common a word had to be invented to describe it. On the extreme other end is the U.S., the most philo-Semitic nation that doesn't have a Star of David in its flag. While Jews were legally discriminated against in the early years of America's existence (as were all immigrant groups), the U.S. was far kinder to the tribe then any pre-WWII European nation. The only Jew to ever be killed in America because of his religion was Leo Frank, an Atlanta factory manager who was framed for the murder of one of his workers. American-born evangelical churches are by and large enthusiastically Zionist, and the U.S. is home to the largest population of Jews outside of Israel. The anti-anti-Semites don't care about any of this historical nuance, though: to them, Americans, like all other goyim, are two steps away from *arbeit macht frei*.

This intolerant, inquisition-like treatment of anyone who criticizes the Jews is problematic because it turns ordinary people into frothing-at-the-mouth Jew-haters over time. You keep hitting a man, sooner or later he's gonna start hitting back. Robert Lindsay recently wrote an interesting post on the evolution of Kevin MacDonald's views of the Jews:

> "Non-Jewish critics are savagely attacked, and dirty attacks are launched on their careers, reputations, etc. A lot of Gentile critics of the Jews actually like Jews, and they try for a while to reason with their Jewish attackers. Always a futile exercise, and the Jews never give in or back off. A lot of critics just throw in the towel and give the Jews the abject, groveling apologies that they demand. Even after that, the critics are not really out of the woods, and

the Jews treat them gingerly as if they were parolees of uncertain rectitude. But at least the smears stop.

"But a lot of others won't give in. So the attacks escalate, and often the Jews issue physical threats. Physical attacks of various types are not unusual. Jews are scary people. You don't fuck with them.

"One thing you notice is that the critics who don't give in start becoming increasingly anti-Semitic with time. They're probably getting more and more enraged by the attacks, and the attacks start making them dislike Jews in general. So we see how Jews often create and increase the virulence of the very anti-Semites they claim to hate so much. But I secretly think that many Jews need anti-Semites and would go nuts if all the anti-Semites disappeared tomorrow."[2]

I don't agree with Lindsay that Jews, outside of the hyper-PC ADL types, really want anti-Semites around, but the rest of his thesis is spot on. By viciously attacking critics of Jewish behavior, Jews and their hangers-on are creating their own worst enemies.

As of right now, the anti-anti-Semites are in the seat of power. The marriage of left-wing multiculturalism and Holocaust worship ensure that anyone with an opinion of the Jews that isn't Abe Foxman-approved will spend the rest of their lives in the shadows. But multiculturalism is being exposed for the hollow sham that it is, and the death camps at Auschwitz and Birkenau will fade from memory, to be remembered only as words and pictures, as is the fate of all history. I still think that most anti-Semites are deluded and dishonest, but the actions of the anti-anti-Semites may very well swell their ranks. If Kristallnacht comes to America, the Jewish elite will have only themselves to blame for behaving like inquisitors burning heretics at the stake. I write all this not to threaten, but to warn.

May 27, 2010

Liberté, Egalité, Conformité

The old political saw about libertarians is that they're conservatives who like to smoke pot. A better description would be that libertarians are liberals who hate paying taxes. Mencius Moldbug described libertarianism as "contain[ing], at its core, a shard of pure Left," which is why it "will always fail as a revolt against progressivism." The shard of liberalism embedded in libertarianism is egalitarianism, the myth that all human beings are interchangeable irregardless of culture, class, race, national origin, or sex. This is why, when it comes to matters of cultural and tribal preservation, most libertarians, from mainstream Beltway-goers to Ron Paul-loving Austrian types, sound completely identical to liberals. For example, during the Muhammad cartoon debacle in 2006, *LewRockwell.com* contributor Eric Margolis took the side of the rioting Muslim crybabies *upset* that their hole-y prophet was satirized.[3] There are a few exceptions I can think of in my blog circle, but the overwhelming majority of libertarians are as blind as liberals when it comes to matters of race, ethnicity, and culture.

Recently, some clown named Charles Glass wrote a piece for *Taki's Magazine* opposing France's new law banning women from wearing veils. While I don't know if Glass is a libertarian, the argument he makes against the French law is essentially a libertarian one, as summed up at the end:

"...What ever happened to live and let live?"[4]

The real problem here that no one wants to address is that the French, along with the other nations of western Europe, have allowed alien tribes to settle and grow in their lands, tribes that have no interest in integrating with the majority and no respect for their traditions. Multiculturalism is the enemy of freedom. The presence of multiple tribes in a single area requires excessive coercion from the government in order to keep the peace. The Muslim riots that occurred in Paris a few years back are proof positive that "live and let live" is impossible due to inter-tribal conflict. Libertarianism is only feasible in culturally homogenous nations; in a multiethnic, multiracial society, it is suicide.

The French are one of the European peoples who have realized that if they allow the aliens in their midst to remain apart from them, their country will be destroyed. The true purpose of the anti-veil law isn't to uphold some "universal secular principle," it's to force the predominantly Muslim, non-European underclass to conform to French culture and values, since they refuse to do so on their own. It's a clumsy, half-hearted attempt, but it's a step in the right direction. But Glass doesn't like it, and he pulls out all the usual stops to inveigh against it:

> "...The young women I met in the schools of suburban Paris would have done credit to any family. They were not gum-chewing drunks like London's street urchins, and they bore little resemblance to the girl gangs of many American urban concentrations. They were thoughtful and polite and, from their polished shoes to their sometimes-covered heads, exhibited an elegant sense of style."

Reminds me of the idiotic pro-amnesty arguments that George Bush and John McCain used to make: *"Durr, these people are hard-working, good folks who just want a better life!"* Who fucking cares? Even if they were all Mother Teresas, that still wouldn't change the fact that they're *aliens*. They have a different culture, and that fact alone means they shouldn't be here. The Muslims in France are visitors, there at the pleasure of the majority. If they're unwilling to obey the majority's laws, they're perfectly welcome to leave.

> "...A few days later, I took a train to London. At Waterloo Station, where the Eurostar stopped in those days, a British Muslim woman immigration officer was standing with her male colleagues. Her head was wrapped in a demure, white scarf. She was laughing unselfconsciously with her male colleagues, one of them a Sikh whose own head was wrapped in the long scarf of his turban. It was the most natural scene imaginable. I had to ask myself, what is wrong with the French?"

I can't help but wonder if Glass' libertarian viewpoint is merely a cover to disguise his dislike of the French. Appropriately enough, according to his Wikipedia page, Glass writes for *The Spectator*, that venerable Limey rag of Tory snobbery and imperialist nostalgia. He also holds British citizenship. One would think that those grizzled old reactionaries would jump at an opportunity to shove Western civilization down the throats of foreigners once more, but apparently frogs are more hated than wogs in Old Blighty.

Here's the question I have to ask myself, Glass: *what the hell is wrong with you English?* Like the rest of western Europe, you had the genius idea of opening your doors to hordes of foreign peasants from Africa and Asia who gleefully shit all over your traditions while taking advantage of your hospitality. Outside of the Germans (who at least have the excuse of losing two world wars), no Western tribe displays as much masochistic self-hatred as you Brits. It's so bad over there, the leader of your major "conservative" party (and Prime Minister) is a preening castrati whose first move upon becoming leader was to launch a recruiting drive to get more women and minorities into the party. You love mocking the French as cowards, but unlike you geldings, they actually have the balls to do what needs to be done. The nicest thing I can say about you Limeys that you aren't nearly as pathetic as the Swedes.

> "The anti-niqab law stems from the kind of zeal for which the French used to ridicule the English. English missionaries who forced women in their tropical colonies to conceal their breasts from public view were a laughing stock in France. Here are the French doing the opposite, not letting them cover their heads. What is it in Western civilization that creates this obsession with telling women what to wear?"

There's a big huge difference between invading foreign lands and telling the inhabitants what to do and letting foreigners into *your own lands* and telling them what to do. The former is the equivalent of taking over your neighbor's house at gunpoint and banning him from wearing shoes inside his own home, and the latter is like inviting him to your place for a cup of tea and asking that he leave his loafers on the porch. The French are fully within their right to tell the people they permit to live in their country to obey their laws.

This is one of the big showdowns we will be witnessing in the next decade: Muslim minorities in Europe versus angry natives who are tired of seeing their traditions trampled on. Along with the French standing up for their culture, the Italians have been fighting back as well, and Geert Wilders could very well become the Netherlands' next prime minister; oh, the liberals will have a collective vein-popping stroke when that happens. If a peaceful solution cannot be found, the next stage will be anti-Muslim pogroms. Regardless of whatever happens, I can say for certain that the siren song of multiculturalism and diversity that has seduced the West will wither and die, whether morons like Charles Glass want it to or not.

May 31, 2010

Why Nobody Likes Nerds, and Why You're Justified in Hating Them

Two weeks ago, I mentioned that I was planning to write an essay on "why white nationalism is a doomed ideology." Said essay will come along when I'm in the mood to hammer it out. I've realized, however, that even if the philosophical issues with white nationalism were ironed out, the WNs would still be condemned to failure and obscurity, because rank-and-file WNs are disproportionately nerdy. Why is this a bad thing? Normal people despise nerds, and for good reason. Nerds are repulsive human beings and a blight on civilization. Nerds worship everything evil and heap calumny on everything good. Nerdiness is a social cancer to be fought in all its forms.

You may have read the above paragraph and think I'm off my rocker, or at the least I'm being too extreme. Well, to paraphrase Barry Goldwater, extremism in the defense of normalcy is no vice, and moderation in the pursuit of tolerating the intolerable is no virtue. You must keep in mind that nerdiness as I describe it is not a lifestyle or a superficial attribute, but a way of thinking and looking at the world. And nerdiness is a way of thinking that is destructive, for the following reasons.

1. Nerds can't understand nuance.

Nerds live in a world where everything is either/or. If you're not with them, you're with their enemies. If you aren't complimenting them, you're insulting them. In situations that run afoul of their Manichean programming (which happen constantly), nerds clam up and become disconcertingly defensive.

This is a trait shared by nerds, geeks, dorks, and all manner of social misfits and outcasts: extreme defensiveness. The nerd, being regularly picked on by his peers, eventually learns to respond to every slight by raising his fur, baring his claws, and hissing. His social intelligence is so poor that he's incapable of distinguishing between true attacks on his character and innocuous comments, bringing the hammer down whenever he perceives his honor to be assaulted. When normal guys are in a friendly social setting, the default mode is to insult and put each other down, but nothing is meant by it; in fact, you could consider it a form of bonding. The nerd can't handle these environments, responding to friendly jabs from others with a "fuck you" or something equally offensive, bringing a nuclear bomb to a pillow fight. Part of effective masculinity—hell, part of being a social creature in general—is learning to relax, know when to fight, and know when to let things go. The nerd, social retard that he is, can't grasp these nuances of human communication.

Nerds are also ignorant of context and take everything literally. It's impossible for them to tell if someone is being totally facetious or even partly facetious unless it is specifically spelled out for them. This tunnel vision makes talking to them needlessly painful because they will always, to some degree, be misinterpreting what you're saying. Udolpho further explains the nerd's problems with communicating:

> "Whereas the introduction from which I quoted asserts that geeks are inventive in their use of language – a very strange assertion – my

experience has been that the best you can expect from one of their ilk is slavish adherence to partially absorbed rules. In the worst cases they exhibit outright antipathy for expressive language.
Creativity is out of the question, and what you most often get is a retarded patois of computer references which bespeak not cleverness but a very confined lifestyle. For the geek, language is a finite array of words and phrases lifted from lowbrow entertainment and repeated, parrot-like, with the same primitive design as that of avian chirps and squawks. Many of the geek's attempts at communication seem merely to serve the purpose of announcing his physical proximity, or are otherwise unanswerable."[5]

2. Nerds are obsessive.

Whenever the nerd encounters an activity that he enjoys, he plunges into it with aplomb, spending time doing it to the exclusion of everything else, from working to bathing to having a life. This pastime is usually something geeky and stupid, but it can be anything they choose. For example, one of the legacies of the seduction community's nerdy origins is the excessive amount of time they advocate spending working your game out on the town. They substitute playing *World of WarCraft* for four hours a night with chasing tail for four hours a night, but the same pathology is present. The reason why many PUAs and seduction gurus can't keep girlfriends is because their obsession with sarging impedes their ability to improve other social skills with women.

3. Nerds are herd conformists.

The claim that nerds are iconoclastic free thinkers is a lie so huge and magnificent that Goebbels himself would be aghast at its pervasiveness. A nerd's willingness to buck the status quo is limited to which club of pariahs he joins to escape the harshness of the real world. Once safely ensconced in his chosen clique, a nerd becomes slavishly devoted to upholding the myths and pretty lies of his overlords, no matter how stupid they may be. Dissent is only permissible within a narrow range: leave it, and not only will the nerds throw you under the bus, they'll back over your body repeatedly to make sure you're dead.

Because nerds are incapable of thinking beyond their self-imposed mental ghettos, debating with them is an exercise in frustrating futility. Nerds reflexively use semantic stopsigns and thought-terminating cliches to combat their opponents while short-circuiting their own already limited capacity for critical reasoning. And nerds are pack animals at heart: if a nerd appears to be at risk of having his mental defenses penetrated, his comrades will swarm upon the offender and spew more nonsense in an attempt to get him/her to quit out of frustration. They then declare "victory" and go back to their regularly scheduled circle jerk.

4. Nerds are lazy and cowardly.

While they diligently waste their time with their chosen hobbies, be they anime, cosplay, or collecting comic books, nerds are deathly allergic to everything outside of their comfort zone, which is so small it might as well be a solid dot. Nerds won't take risks or go the extra mile, and as a result live lives of quiet mediocrity in which they never accomplish anything.

For example, the average nerd's fantasy woman behaves like a sex-starved player in her dealings with men. She is violent, vulgar, boorish, and ball-breaking. In other words, she is Lara Croft. The most obnoxious grrlpower stereotypes in the media are found in nerd-targeted media for a reason. Because most nerds refuse to do the legwork necessary to seduce women, they fantasize about beautiful girls who will fall into their lap and do all the hard work for them. This is part of the reason why most nerds rarely get any action.

5. Nerds are manginas.

Keeping in theme with the previous paragraph, a man whose ideal woman is basically a dude with breasts and a vagina is a man who will likely allow women in general to walk all over him. Afraid of confrontation and used to bowing and scraping, nerds place themselves at the mercy of women in the vain hope of getting laid. Also, male feminists are overwhelmingly nerds; see pansies like Hugo Schwyzer and Barry "Ampersand" Deutsch.

It's worth noting that nerdiness is largely unique to the male of the species. Having hung out with and dated nerdettes, I can say that there is no female nerd on Earth who can match her male counterpart in social tone-deafness.

6. Nerds aren't cool.

Nerds are rationalistic to a fault, and are rabidly opposed to anything beautiful, attractive, or otherwise representative of good taste. As Udolpho writes:

> "Where the geek becomes truly disturbing is in matters of visual aesthetics. His personal appearance, of course, is often weird, repellent, unnerving. When allowed to dress himself the results betray a lack of understanding of his own appearance. Is he fat, bald, dough-faced? You can bet that these qualities will be horrifically exaggerated by his choices in grooming and apparel."[6]

Because nerds reject aesthetics and coolness, nerd-led groups, ideologies, and movements never expand beyond the non-nerdy part of the population. How you sell your message is just as important as what your message is. Being right on everything is meaningless if no one can bear to be around you.

Women in particular demand coolness and social savvy and will not tolerate anyone or anything that doesn't have either. This is why, for instance, talented "misogynistic" bloggers like Roissy and Welmer have tons of female fans while the mere handful of women who frequent WN blogs are all frothing-at-the-mouth lunatics.

There *are* women out there who claim to prefer nerdy men. Don't be fooled: when these girls think of nerds, they envision perfectly normal guys whose "nerdiness" is limited to wearing glasses or watching *Star Trek* reruns. Matt Savage elaborates:

> "When a girl says she likes nerdy nice guys, what she really means is a guy with some minor nerd like characteristics yet has his shit together. For example, perhaps he plays a lot video games or tinkers with computers, but he's also a decent looking guy who cleans up well. He could also be a really good provider and a down to earth family man, just the right type of guy that women will go for after slutting themselves out in their early twenties. There's a reason that nice guys finish last, it's because they're the safe bet when the biological time bomb starts ticking, so long as he doesn't dress like *Tron*."[7]

Women who like genuine nerds are as representative of the female population as fat fetishists are of men. The average girl finds nerdiness as appealing as rape.

Throughout history, the physical beatdowns and social shaming of their peers taught nerds to normalize their behavior well before adulthood. There's no better way to learn that picking your nose in class isn't apropos then everyone around you calling you a disgusting loser. Because young children haven't yet been indoctrinated with the social mores and "anti-judgmental" and "tolerant" propaganda of adults, they are utterly shameless and ruthless about ostracizing nerds from the herd. Unfortunately, the rise of anti-bullying programs, zero-tolerance policies for such things as bringing anything resembling a gun onto school property, and a culture of encouraging kids to run crying to their teachers, principals, or parents whenever they get their *poor widdle feewings* hurt have allowed nerdiness to grow out of control.

I say, as a normal guy who is sick to death of nerds, that enough is enough. It is time for we, the cool kids, to descend upon the nerds and make their lives miserable once more. We guys can give them wedgies and swirlies, and you gals can wound their souls with cruel, cutting remarks about their fashion sense, hygiene and overall creepiness. The future of the world depends on your willingness to break the hearts and spirits of the socially retarded. Are you game?

June 16, 2010

How Democracy Killed Video Games

Some time ago, I came across an interview with famed game designer Roberta Williams on a now defunct website. Williams is a legend in the video game industry, one of the founders of *Sierra* and the creator of several popular game series, including *King's Quest* and *Phantasmagoria*:

> "Back when I got started, which sounds like ancient history, back then the demographics of people who were into computer games, was totally different, in my opinion, then they are today. Back then, computers were more expensive, which made them more exclusive to people who were maybe at a certain income level, or education level. So the people that played computer games 15 years ago were that type of person. They probably didn't watch television as much, and the instant gratification era hadn't quite grown the way it has lately. I think in the last 5 or 6 years, the demographics have really changed, now this is my opinion, because computers are less expensive so more people can afford them. More "average" people now feel they should own one. There's also

the influence of the game consoles as well. So most of these people have gotten used to shoot-em-up kind of games on the consoles. Now they want to get that kind of experience on their computers."

Blogger Agnostic wrote a post a year ago in which he rides one of his favorite hobbyhorses: the claim that video games are boring nowadays because they've become glorified movies due to the all-pervasive influence of egalitarianism. As evidence, he points back to what he considers the "Golden Age" of video gaming, the late 80's/early 90's, when Nintendo and Sega ruled the roost and games were mostly repetitive button-mashing exercises designed to keep sugar-bombed kids occupied and out of trouble:

> "On the plus side, home video games are selling better than ever—because they're so easy that they won't bruise anyone's ego or offend by highlighting skill differences between individuals. Video games may have been somewhat late in jumping on the egalitarian bandwagon, but there they are. If you can insert a disk into your DVD player and click your way through to the end of the movie, you can complete any video game released in the past 10

years. Conversely, if you're too used to the two most recent "generations" of self-esteem-boosting video games, you'd probably hate most of the games on Nintendo since they'll only reveal how mediocre your skill is. Just pick up Ninja Gaiden or Mega Man and see. Then again, you may learn that playing challenging games is fun, whether you win or not—much more fun than dozing through a glorified animated movie."[8]

This paragraph, along with almost everything Agnostic writes on gaming, makes me wonder if the poor, dumb bastard's ever played a computer game in his life. What he doesn't know is that there were already a class of "glorified animated movie[s]" in existence during the same time he was jumping on anthropomorphic turtles in *Super Mario Bros 3*. It's just that they were confined to the PC, away from ADD-addled little twerps who wouldn't appreciate them.

From the dawn of gaming in the late 70's to roughly the late 90's, computer and console games evolved on separate, parallel paths. While consoles were squarely targeted at kids (as evidenced by their simple premises and lame aesthetics), PC games targeted more mature, refined individuals. The reasons for this bifurcation are twofold. One, up until the early oughts, computer graphics technology was superior to consoles. Pop in the ludicrously stripped-down Super Nintendo version of *Doom* to see what I mean. Two, as Williams remarked above, the high price of computers in the pre-Windows 95 era kept them out of the hands of all but the privileged few. To give an example, the 386 my parents bought in 1990 cost *$3,000*. According to the Inflation Calculator, that's roughly $4,900 in 2009 dollars. In contrast, video game consoles like the NES and Genesis sold for only a couple hundred dollars when they were brand new.

Because computer games catered to an older, more cultured clientele, their subject matter was frequently more mature, cerebral, and story-focused then console games. In the same time period when the Genesis and Super Nintendo versions of *Mortal Kombat* had the blood and gore removed, you could buy computer games that you wouldn't want your kids to play like *Doom, Phantasmagoria,* and the *Leisure Suit Larry* series. The text-based games of the 80's like *Softporn Adventure* and *Leather Goddesses of Phobos* were basically like interactive novels, hence the snooty, pretentious phrase "interactive fiction" coined to describe them. Agnostic may complain about games these days being like movies, but when CD-ROM technology first emerged, there were a lot of games released that actually were movies: FMV titles with real people really acting, though they usually did a poor job of it.

So what changed?

Beginning in the mid-90's with the PlayStation, computer

and console technology began converging, with each new generation of consoles coming closer to replicating the graphics power that was once only available on home computers. At the same time, the price of computers dropped to the point where more people could afford them. The Windows 95 computer my parents bought in 1996 cost all of *$1,600:* a near fifty percent reduction in price in six years. Nowadays, a decent computer will set you back a few hundred dollars at the most. These twin developments democratized computers, allowing more "average" people, as Williams would call them, to infect gaming, triggering a race to the bottom in game design.

The demographic shift in gaming killed off a number of genres that were popular in the bad old elitist days, chiefly the adventure game. Adventure games are by definition inaccessible to the average moron, because you can't play them by bashing buttons like a monkey on crack. In order to win games like *Star Control II* and *King's Quest,* you've got to think! Like, with your brain! Flight/space simulators like *Wing Commander,* which also required a bit more brainpower than pointing and shooting, also fell by the wayside. Strategy games like *SimCity* and *Command & Conquer* are the only PC-centric game genre from the pre-Windows 95 that have survived, albeit in a considerably dumbed-down form.

Video game storytelling remains trapped in a rut because the plebs demand it. About 99.9 percent of video games released in the past ten years have the same damn plot: you, the protagonist, having to save the world/land/galaxy from some Big Bad Evil Dude. And while mature content is more common, it's primarily of the juvenile OMG TITS BLOOD AWESOME variety. Contrast older computer games like *Phantasmagoria* or *Ripper* with *Tomb Raider* or *Grand Theft Auto III*. I personally didn't understand what all the hubbub was about GTA3 when I first played it; I found it a repetitive, third-rate shooter with no plot, no interesting characters, and no reason to keep playing aside from the questionable thrill of slaughtering random bystanders on the street. Hell, just read *Leisure Suit Larry* creator Al Lowe's description of 2004's *Leisure Suit Larry: Magna Cum Laude*, a game he had no involvement with at all:

> **Differences:** It is not *Larry 8!* Even though VU calls it a "Leisure Suit Larry game," Leisure Suit Larry's only role is a cameo as the "help voiceover." It is not an adventure game. There are no real puzzles, no interactive dialog, no narrator, no character development, and nearly no plot. Much of the dialogue is uninspired and trite. There's more profanity in the first scene than in all the previous Larry games combined. Women cuss like sailors. The F-word is repeated so often the writers must have used a macro. The plentiful load screens show cheesy photographs of average-looking

college-aged women who don't look sexy, but rather, ill-at-ease.

"**Similarities:** The protagonist is a loser named Larry who has trouble scoring with women. The game works hard, usually too hard, to reference earlier Larry games. Like Larry Laffer, it seems to desperately want to fit in. The animation is 3D and wonderfully jiggly. (Actually, "pendulous" would be a better word; most of these breasts are too large to jiggle.) There's some humorous dialogue. And it's more than bawdy enough.

"**But...** All this ignores the glaring disaster of those damned mini-games! They're distracting, repetitive, and boring. Who wants to play lame arcade games that wouldn't be fun even on a GameBoy? Not even this game's giant breasts are worth this slog.

"MCL is definitely unlike the other Larry games."[9]

 The transition wasn't immediate. In fact, I still regard the late 90's as the golden age of video games. But I lost interest around the turn of the century, when the democratization of the industry was more or less completed. Agnostic is right that games today are boring. He's wrong on the reason. It's not because of designers making games more accessible to avoid bruising the egos of those who don't have finely honed twitch reflexes, it's because of the lumpenproles ruining everything they touch with their lumpenprole tastes.

June 18, 2010

Soccer and Multicultural Imperialism

I know there's a World Cup in soccer going on. I don't know what the fuss is all about. I don't know who's winning or losing. I don't know what a vuvuzela is or why it's such a big deal. All I know is this:

Fuck soccer.

That's right, fuck soccer. Fuck its everlasting monotony of movement. Fuck its stalemate-encouraging design. Fuck the fact that the only way to win at it is to wait for the opposing team to make a major fuck-up. Fuck it in its faggy too-long gym socks. Fuck it so hard it will never be able to fuck again.

And while I'm at it, fuck the whiny wankers who kvetch about Americans calling it soccer and not football. If you're one of those wankers and you're from England, fuck you even harder, you bloody stupid cunt. You're probably the same jack-offs who bitch about we Yanks dropping the superfluous "u" from "color" like it's still 1775 and you can still fucking tell us what to do. You lost the right to dictate to anyone how to do anything when you ceased being an ass-kicking empire and commenced being an American satrapy. I'll have no problem listening to you talk about what to call soccer all day long when you pull Uncle Sam's throbbing, meaty dick out of your arse.

And finally, fuck the phony, snooty, ignorant upper middle class white American cocksuckers who lie about liking a sport only sub-90 IQ turd worlders and alcoholic Limey lumpenproles on welfare could enjoy. Fuck you most of all, you prickish posers, you prancing pansies, you assassins of good taste. You *nouveau riche* asswipes crowd into shrines of misappropriated culture, indulging in the cuisine and pastimes of the foreign equivalent of the people you turn your noses up at at home. You revel in the symbols of other societies while taking special care to insulate yourself from the aftereffects of your maniac ideology, all the while denouncing the people who are affected most by it as intolerant evil racists. Fuck you SWPLs. Fuck you like a skinny white pothead tossed cheeks-first into the Black Guerrilla Family-dominated prison block. Fuck you like a wasted barfly cornered in a dark alley by three horny rapists. Fuck you like Barack Obama's approval numbers. Fuck you all very much, and God bless the United Fucking States of America!

Ah… that felt good.

For the record, I don't hate soccer: I just don't care about it, like I don't care about baseball, football, or any team sport except college basketball and maybe hockey. I don't hate Brits, despite loving to poke fun at the foibles of their women. I don't hate SWPLs: I laugh at them like everyone else with a clue. I'm not even that much of a nationalist anymore.

But whenever I read opinion pieces from liberals lamenting why oh why don't Americans care about soccer, I have the gut urge to wrap myself in the Stars and Stripes and waltz on down to the local indie coffeeshop blasting Rush Limbaugh on my boombox and singing "God Bless America" like some sort of patriotic wigger, or pound out chest-beating rants like the one above. Like clockwork, every four years during the World Cup, the same morons write the same editorials asking the same questions. *"Why don't Americans love soccer? Why won't they join the rest of the world in a celebration of love, peace, harmony and understanding? Are they parochial xenophobes or what?"* Of course, they forget that there is another major Western country that is aligned with the Red, White, and Blue in not caring about a bunch of prissy girly men kicking a ball around a field and treating every little scrape like a life-threatening injury: Canada.

Yep, Canada. The nation that liberals love, that magical northern wonderland of tolerance, diversity, and socialized medicine is as indifferent to the beautiful game as the evil racist rednecks to the south. In Canada like in America, "football" refers to a homegrown sport involving 'roided up freaks in padded suits manhandling a pigskin. And like the Americans, the Canadians stick to sports that originated on their continent, like baseball and hockey. The Quebecois are the only French-speaking people in the world who use "le soccer" instead of "le football." Yet, none of those whinging internationalist liberals ever take the piss out of the Canucks for behaving exactly like we ugly Americans. You'll never read an idiot like Dave Zirin of *The Nation* accusing the Canadians of being nefarious nativists:

> "Every World Cup, it arrives like clockwork. As sure as the ultimate soccer spectacle brings guaranteed adrenaline and agony to fans across the United States, it also drives the right-wing noise machine utterly insane. [...]
>
> [...] "Among adults, the sport is also growing because people from Latin America, Africa, and the West Indies have brought their love of the beautiful game to an increasingly multicultural United States. As sports journalist Simon Kuper wrote very adroitly in his book Soccer Against the Enemy, 'When we say Americans don't play soccer we are thinking of the big white people who live in the suburbs. Tens of millions of Hispanic Americans [and other nationalities] do play, and watch and read about soccer.' In other words, Beck rejects soccer because his idealized 'real America' – in all its monochromatic glory – rejects it as well. To be

clear, I know a lot of folks who can't stand soccer. It's simply a matter of taste. But for Beck it's a lot more than, 'Gee. It's kind of boring.' Instead it's, 'Look out whitey! Felipe Melo's gonna get your mama!'"[10]

Yes, yes Zirin, Americans aren't happy that their culture is being transformed by foreign invaders. And they *especially* aren't happy that people like you are accusing them of being evil for not yelling, *"Thank you sir, may I have another!"* every time the multiculti canoe paddle lands on their rear-ends.

Zirin's piece (which, I should add, was featured on NPR's website: nice use of government dollars there) made the rounds on the right-wing sites last week. It's quite amusing to watch mainstream bloggers like *Allahpundit* and *Ace of Spades HQ* squirm and wriggle out of the obvious reason why Americans don't take to soccer: it's a foreign sport being forced on us from the top-down by people who have an obvious antipathy for our way of life. Never mind that soccer's popularity is in part due to European imperialism; something tells me that a European sport wouldn't be nearly as beloved in Africa and Latin America if those places hadn't spent part of their history under the white man's boot. Never mind that people are watching the World Cup not out of some spirit of brotherly love but because they want their country to whip everyone else's asses. It's the world's sport, and those Mexican-hating Yanks (and, um, Canucks) are standing in the way of the dawning of the Age of Aquarius!

Because the mainstream right can't admit that there's nothing wrong with rejecting foreign traditions for no other reason then that they are foreign, they can't point out the big irony of left-wing multiculturalism: it purports to celebrate other cultures but in practice works to meld them together into one. The Unabomber was two decades ahead of everyone on this issue:

> "Here is an illustration of the way in which the oversocialized leftist shows his real attachment to the conventional attitudes of our society while pretending to be in rebellion against it. Many leftists push for affirmative action, for moving black people into high-prestige jobs, for improved education in black schools and more money for such schools; the way of life of the black 'underclass' they regard as a social disgrace. They want to integrate the black man into the system, make him a business executive, a lawyer, a scientist just like upper-middle-class white people. The leftists will reply that the last thing they want is to make the black man into a copy of the white man; instead, they want to preserve African American culture. But in what does this preservation of African American

culture consist? It can hardly consist in anything more than eating black-style food, listening to black-style music, wearing black-style clothing and going to a black-style church or mosque. In other words, it can express itself only in superficial matters. In all ESSENTIAL respects more leftists of the oversocialized type want to make the black man conform to white, middle-class ideals. They want to make him study technical subjects, become an executive or a scientist, spend his life climbing the status ladder to prove that black people are as good as white. They want to make black fathers "responsible." they want black gangs to become nonviolent, etc. But these are exactly the values of the industrial-technological system. The system couldn't care less what kind of music a man listens to, what kind of clothes he wears or what religion he believes in as long as he studies in school, holds a respectable job, climbs the status ladder, is a 'responsible' parent, is nonviolent and so forth. In effect, however much he may deny it, the oversocialized leftist wants to integrate the black man into the system and make him adopt its values."[11]

This is the end goal of multiculturalism: all of the cultures of the world dumped in a blender and mashed into a pulpy juice. The diversity-loving liberals want everyone to be a carbon copy of everyone else, from the food they eat to the sports they watch on TV to the way they think and the color of their skin (I once had an earnest leftist college classmate tell me in an argument that the end goal of diversity was "to get everyone to interbreed and have lovely brown kids so that the world would be at peace"). They encourage multiculturalism to destroy diversity.

In this sense, the Glenn Becks and G. Gordon Liddys (seriously, who listens to G. Gordon Liddy anymore aside from bored lefties looking for quotes to cherry-pick?) of the world have far more respect for its diverse cultures than the Dave Zirins. They and other Americans are saying that they don't want their national and ethnic identity subsumed in a global multicultural soup. They are saying that this is as far as the barbarian hordes can come and no further, where their proud waves must stop. If you truly believe in diversity and not multicultural anarchy, you will join them.

June 21, 2010

What's Wrong with White Nationalism?

As the multiculti rainbow world of peace and harmony among peoples collapses around us, a specter long thought perished re-emerges. It is tribalism, that horrific inclination that the liberals thought they had squashed decades ago, at least among the racist, imperialist palefaces of North America, Europe, and Australasia. White nationalists seek to be the new spokesmen of the white tribes, and could potentially become one of the major factions in the emerging new world order. But only a fool thinks the enemy of his enemy is automatically his friend. While white nationalists get many things right, the foundations of their ideology are flawed and thus make it inadequate for combating the liberal dystopia.

My opposition to white nationalism is not due to fear of "racism." Ethnic nationalism is inevitable in a multiracial nation, and in a country such as the U.S. in which the freedom of association is constitutionally protected, either all racial nationalisms are acceptable or none are. If we can have black and Hispanic nationalist outfits like the Nation of Islam and La Raza, then white nationalist groups are equally legitimate. My problem with white nationalism is based purely on pragmatic concerns.

While I have my doubts about the political viability of white nationalism, I'll readily admit that most of the criticisms I've made up to this point are superficial and/or ancillary and can be overcome. This doesn't change the fact that white nationalists are wrong, only that their losing is not a given. I argued a similar point last March when I wrote that the Tea Party Movement would fail to achieve their objectives even if they achieved political success. The fact that communism was wrong didn't prevent Lenin's Bolsheviks from seizing control of Russia in

1917, nor did it prevent Mao from ousting Chiang Kai-shek from Beijing. Revolutions are pointless if they end up replacing broken, unjust systems with different broken, unjust systems.

And there we run into our first problem with white nationalism: it doesn't confront the core of what is wrong with the West. White nationalists are right that multiculturalism and ethnic infighting are serious issues, but they don't recognize that the tribal soup that America, Britain and other white nations are drowning in is not the cause of those nations' decline, but a symptom. To demonstrate this, I will use the time-honored method of the Socratic dialogue:

White Nationalist: We must secure the existence of our people and a future for white children!

Ferdinand Bardamu: Tally ho, chap. I say, what are you agitating about?

WN: I want my white brothers and sisters to throw off their shackles and fight the enemies who are trying to wipe them out.

FB: I see. And just who are the enemies of the white race?

WN: The Jews! They control the government, the media, and Wall Street, and they're trying to ethnically cleanse us from our own nation by robbing us, importing foreigners to replace us, and encouraging miscegenation with lesser races. And the Negroes! They're slaughtering us in the streets and raping our women!

FB: Okay, Jews and Negroes are bad. But weren't white people responsible for letting the Jews in this country and allowing them to participate in public life to begin with?

WN: Uhhhh...

FB: And the Negroes – weren't they brought here from Africa as slaves and later emancipated by white people?

WN: Errrrr...

FB: Wouldn't this mean that these problems that white people suffer from are basically self-inflicted?

WN: Ummmm... *WHITE POWER!*

White nationalism doesn't address why all of these alien tribes have popped up in our midst. WNs like to blame these and other problems on the Jews, and while I acknowledge that they've had a disproportionate, malign influence, the fact of the matter is that the ideology that wrecked the West, liberalism, originates from whites. (Note: for the purposes of this essay only, I will regard Jews as a separate entity from whites.) The intellectual forbears of modern liberalism and its offshoot ideologies like multiculturalism and feminism were all gentiles: 17th and 18th century thinkers like John Locke, Thomas Paine, Mary Wollstonecraft, Voltaire, Jean-Jacques Rousseau, and Adam Smith. The Jewish establishment in the modern West is merely a vector for a white-created disease of the mind.

And even if we accept the premise that Jews and Jewish influence are primarily responsible for the mess we're in, that doesn't absolve whites from blame. The Jews didn't invade America, Britain or any other country en masse and forcibly take over their institutions: they were invited by the natives. Prior to their emancipation in the 19th century, Jews were despised and persecuted everywhere they went, and had little to no influence on the societies they settled in. That's why the neoconservative description of the West as "Judeo-Christian" should make educated people laugh: Jews had about as much influence on pre-Enlightenment Europe as the Gypsies.[12] Jewish emancipation was a product of liberalism, as the first European state to grant them full legal rights was revolutionary France in 1791. If Jews have fired the bullet into the head of white civilization, whites themselves are culpable for letting them touch the gun to begin with.

The fact of the matter, that white nationalists are either unwilling or unable to address, is that white people are their own worst enemy. Vijay Prozak elaborates:

> "While white power movements would like to believe that one day while the white man was asleep, a horde of Jews and Negroes stole in the back door, gangfucked his wife, indoctrinated his children with 'rap' and 'crunk' music, turned the inner city into an AIDS-ridden war zone, and took

over the country, the historical fact is different: white people invited them in; white people made profit from "authentic" music of the oppressed; white people, by fighting constantly amongst themselves, have no direction that might conflict with music profiteering, inner city rot, or even violence (violence produces a product spectrum, from pepper spray to electric gates, to deal with it and is thus profitable to many sectors of the economy, although the socialized cost affects us all). White power movements, instead of being beneficial to white people, are destructive because they deny the actual sources of white problems. You can blame Negroes, Jews and homosexuals until society ends, but the problems, whitey, are within."[13]

This is why I state that white nationalism is a doomed ideology: even if WNs succeed in their goals of creating white ethnostates, the original cause of white decline will remain. There are competing explanations for the origin of the liberal impulse in the European peoples. Julius Evola blamed America, Mencius Moldbug blames Protestantism, and European New Right figures such as Tomislav Sunic and Alain de Benoist blame Christianity and monotheistic religion in general.[14-16] All of these claims are well-argued and I haven't yet solidified my own opinion on the topic. But what I can say is that the central battle in this fight is not a return to tribalism, but the exorcism of liberalism from the white soul. How this can be done is a topic for another time.

The other major problem with white nationalism is that it is essentially an exclusionary form of multiculturalism, an ideological heresy born out of opposition to the insane, also-heretical doctrine of multiculturalism. If multiculturalism is feminism, white nationalism is the left-wing masculism of Glenn Sacks and Warren Farrell: a competing heresy that purports to be the answer to the ills caused by the former, but cannot solve them because it springs from the same flawed premises.

White nationalists want to group all whites under a united banner to face off against the dark-skinned, squid-eyed hordes. This is lunacy on multiple levels. To begin with, it is as wrong to toss white and European cultures into a blender as it is to toss all cultures into that blender. I don't want Britain, Australia, France or any other country to be swamped with American culture anymore than I want them to be swamped with Arab, Indian, or Chinese culture. If I want to see McDonald's, reality TV, and fat, white whales lumbering around in clothes that accentuate their ugliness, I can get that here in the states. The white nationalist vision will create ethnic and cultural confusion, as already exists in cities like Brussels and Montreal where white tribes interbreed and bring everyone down to the lowest common denominator.

Pragmatically, pan-Europeanism/pan-Aryanism is a nonstarter. Whites worldwide not only show no signs of racial unity, *they increasingly want nothing to do with each other:*

- In the U.S., liberal blue-state and conservative red-state whites are self-segregating into their own communities, as shown by the increase in the number of "landslide counties," counties which are won overwhelmingly by one presidential candidate.[17] Secessionist movements like the Second Vermont Republic and the League of the South are popping up everywhere.

- Canada, a polyglot construction of the British Empire, is constantly confronted with belligerence from its French-speaking minority. Independence for Quebec failed by the slimmest of margins fifteen years ago, and the Quebecois are kept placated by an avalanche of concessions from the Anglo majority. Official bilingualism is the law of the land, despite the fact that French is hardly spoken west of Ottawa; Quebec is given a disproportionate share of seats in the House of Commons; and half of the Canadian prime ministers of the past forty years, English or French-speaking, Liberal or Conservative, have hailed from Quebec.

- In Europe, the Scots and Welsh want out of the United Kingdom, as evidenced by the growth of the Scottish National Party and Plaid Cymru. Vlaams Belang campaigns in Belgium to split the country down the middle between Flemings and Walloons. The European Union, a de facto alliance of white nations, will likely collapse if the global economic crisis worsens and productive nations like Germany have to keep bailing out failed states like Greece.

It's easy to be friends in good times; the true test of friendship comes during seasons of tumult and discord, a test that whites around the planet are failing miserably. We forget that barely a century ago, the tribes of Europe sought to exterminate each other in a great war. Twenty years after they poured their lifeblood out onto the Western and Eastern Fronts, they decided to do it all over again, exhausting their power and falling under American and Russian hegemony in the process. The English, the French, and the Germans et al. will always hate each other, and no kumbaya singing on the part of white nationalists will change this. This is true of all races: if you were to drop 10,000 Zulus into Compton, for example, the throat-slitting would commence faster then you could drop the n-bomb.

And even if it weren't for these factors, whites would still be too busy trying to one-up each other to come together, as Mencius Moldbug explains:

> "In my model, there are not two sides but five.
> Three of these sides are white, two are swarthy.
> And we see no mysterious masochism at all, just
> the usual hominid struggle for factional dominance.

One of the white parties (Brahmin) is ganging up
with the two swarthy parties (Dalit, Helot) to apply a
good old-fashioned whupping to the other two white
parties (Vaisya, Optimate). Just another afternoon
of nasty on the History Channel.

"Not only does my model clarify the reality, it
clarifies the tactical options. We see immediately
that Fjordman is asking the impossible. His solution
is simply for the B faction to dump its DH allies and
unite with its OV victims. The lion will lie down with
the lamb. Yeah, right! Perhaps Fjordman could be
so kind as to inform us of the last occasion on
which this worked."[18]

I disagree with Moldbug's shunning of nationalism, and I think his self-made ideology of "formalism" is pure insanity, but his analysis of the situation is dead right. If Marx was wrong in thinking the working classes of Europe would unite across national borders to take down the capitalist pig-dogs, white nationalists are wrong in thinking the existing castes of whites will unite across class borders to fight the teeming non-white masses. White nationalism is nothing but racial Marxism.

Some of you will counter my claim of permanent white disunity by pointing to the presence of black and Hispanic unity, as exemplified by the groups I named a few paragraphs up. Comparing minority nationalisms in the U.S. to white nationalism is comparing apples and oranges. American blacks have a united culture and a united sense of brotherhood because their previous tribal identities were destroyed in the Middle Passage. As part of the process of breaking down their newly-acquired slaves, British slavers forcibly deracinated blacks, as Gary Brecher explains:

> "...The English in Jamaica, Barbados and the Southern US states made sure slaves from different tribes were mixed up, made it punishable by flogging or worse to speak African languages, and forced the blacks to find Christ or die. (Ah, you gotta love those Evangelical assholes!)"[19]

In contrast, the French didn't do this with their captives, which is part of the reason why the Haitian revolution was so successful. Brecher continues:

> "The French were sloppy. They let slaves from the same tribes stay together and speak their African languages. They let escaped slaves set up their own villages way inside the tropical forests. They let the slaves keep up African religions—that's what voodoo is. And they started up a separate mulatto

class."

As for Hispanic nationalism in the U.S., it's a misnomer: all of the major "Hispanic" nationalist groups are either *de jure* or *de facto* Mexican nationalist, with little to no input from other Latin tribes. La Raza, MEChA, LULAC, MALDEF: all Mexican groups. Like blacks, their unity is based in something real. In contrast, American whites all came to the U.S. willingly and partially retained their cultures as a result. Culture cannot be fashioned out of whole cloth, but must grow organically from generations of shared cooperation and cohabitation. In attempting to force all whites into the same tribe, white nationalists are trying to construct a skyscraper in a swamp.

With all that said, white nationalism is not a completely failed enterprise. While it is still a heresy, it is a heresy that comes close to the truth. The necessity of nationalism, of each tribe and ethnic group possessing its own state, including whites, is the most important part of WN dogma. Concomitant with the science of human biodiversity is the irrefutable fact that tribes are different and possess different ways of doing things, and trying to force every tribe into the same mold can only end disastrously. This applies to whites in relation to each other as much as it applies to other races. The Dutch can handle drug decriminalization: the English can't. The Swedish can handle cradle-to-grave socialism: the Americans can't. The Liechtensteiners can handle laissez-faire capitalism: the French can't. The Swiss can handle multiple tribes swearing allegiance to a single flag: the Italians can't. The only logical position is to support nationalism of all stripes, in which each tribe gets its own nation and is allowed to maintain its own culture, traditions, and ways of doing things, maintaining the diverse tapestry that is the human race. I'm a convert to parallelism, the philosophy espoused by the *American Nihilist Underground Society*, who explain how it works here:

> "One area where this can be seen is homosexuality. For most heterosexuals, having homosexual behavior occur in neighborhoods or other areas where children are present is not positive; they would rather raise their children according to heterosexual role models and behavioral examples. However, homosexuality occurs, and the best data available suggests that in most cases it is inborn; obviously, some are induced into homosexuality much as many heterosexuals are brought into forms of deviant sexual behavior, through sexual abuse or conditioning in youth (hence the desire for normal, heterosexual role models; most heterosexuals also do not want promiscuity, coprophagia, BDSM, etc. occurring around their children even if solely in a

heterosexual context). So what to do with homosexuals, for whom being raised in a heterosexual society can be oppressive, and heterosexuals, for whom having homosexual behavior around can be equally oppressive and deleterious? We think in parallel: some communities will choose to be heterosexual, and others homosexual, and when they meet on neutral ground, it is likely that neither will assert its morality as a dominant, inviolate rigid code. Morality after all is not something we can prove exists, but something we derive from natural structure in order to establish a civilization of the type we desire. Some civilizations will endorse promiscuity and coprophagia, but in doing so, they miss out on some opportunities granted to civilizations with a more disciplined moral code. The converse is also true. There is no one law for the ox and the raven; to do so is to commit tyranny."[20]

    This may sound a bit like multiculturalism, but there's a crucial difference. Multiculturalism is like dumping all of the animals in the zoo into the same pen and watching them devour each other: the parallelist vision of nationalism is like maintaining each species in its separate habitat where it belongs. This is the case that nationalists need to make to the aliens in their midst. We don't hate them, we don't wish them harm, and we don't want to enslave or rule over them: we simply believe they don't belong in our countries any more then we belong in theirs. This goes for all foreign tribes, including white ones. Englishmen don't belong in Scotland any more than Tunisians belong in France, Koreans belong in Japan, or Arabs belong in Israel. We're seeking an amicable divorce now that the marriage has been proven to be an utter failure. The alternative is a slow deterioration to anarchy and ethnic cleansing, as we saw during the Holocaust, the massacre at Srebrenica, and now the ongoing genocide of whites in Zimbabwe and South Africa.

Instead of fighting for a united white nationalism that would be disastrous if it ever came to fruition, white advocates should be fighting for individual white nationalisms, wherever they are. In the case of the U.S. and Canada, that means acknowledging the desires of the increasingly disparate white tribes to go their own separate ways. Southern nationalism, Vermonter nationalism, Texan nationalism, Cascadian nationalism, Quebecois nationalism, and so on. Keep in mind that turning back the virus of liberalism, however that might be done, is the key to success: otherwise, history will simply repeat itself. I don't have a definitive plan for sorting out all these issues, including dealing with the presence of blacks who've been in the U.S. as long as whites have: that sort of thing is above my pay grade.

In closing, I should advise that there are no simple, clean solutions to the problems that plague us. Much like how memorizing a couple of pick-up lines isn't sufficient to turn a Poindexter into a player, simply throwing out everyone with a shade of skin darker than yourself or a hooked nose isn't going to make the pathologies in your own culture magically disappear. If white nationalists persist in substituting hate and transferal for self-reflection and proper advocacy and myopically reducing everything down to race, their movement won't evolve beyond a 21st century version of a racist lynch mob. And that's something no one with half a brain, even those turned on to racism, will support. No my white brothers, the problem isn't the blacks. The problem isn't the Jews. The problem is *you*.

June 28, 2010

Bardamu for Governor

Hi, I'm Ferdinand Bardamu, and I'm running for Governor of New York in 2010.

Why have I decided to toss my hat into the ring? I could give the same reasons that every candidate running for public office in this cesspit of a state gives, all relating to how I'm tired of how Albany is running things and how I'm an outsider who's going to overhaul everything and take out the trash. And while I *do* think I can do a better job than the other idiots running, I have another motivation.

It was during the election four years ago when I discovered that Jimmy McMillan, an illiterate black guy with Civil War-era facial hair, was not only running for Governor on the Rent is Too Damn High line, he'd managed to get enough signatures to get onto the ballot. And he's going to be on the ballot again this year, complete with a website that's straight out of 1998, an endlessly looping rap song, and a new platform promising rent reduction (obviously), massive property tax cuts, and free college tuition. No word on where he plans to get the money to finance the latter.

McMillan also has a part of his campaign website dedicated to what he thinks about transsexuals [sic'd]:

"Transgender

(pronounced /trænz ' dʒɛndər)

Born with a chemical imbalance they are not;

GAY

And neither are they

HOMOSEXUALS

From the species of Homo sapiens they are. They

should be given a separate identity within the species of Homo sapiens.

They are normal human beings just like me and you they were just born different.

Chromosome

xx – Female

y – Male

THE MEDICAL COMMUNITY FOR YEARS HAS BEEN / HAVE BEEN MAKING THE DECISION WHO IS TO BE MALE AND WHO IS TO BE FEMALE IT'S TIME FOR THIS ATTITUDE IN THE MEDICAL COMMUNITY TO COME TO AN END."

I'm not making any of this up. You thought Alvin Greene was bad? At least he's running a multi-issue campaign.

I've got nothing against McMillan. I'm sure he's a nice guy, and I like his style. But if he can run for Governor, why can't I? I can write complete sentences, I have a better looking website, and my proposals will benefit *all* New Yorkers. If elected, here is what I will do to make the Empire State a better place.

Independence: Secede from the United States of America, in association with other separatist groups like the Second Vermont Republic and the League of the South. It's plainly obvious that the constituent peoples of the U.S. no longer want to be in the same country, so why force them to remain under one roof? Individual state governments are much better equipped to deal with the problems of our society than the clowns in Washington. And if you're worried about a long and punishing civil war, fuhgeddaboudit: the troops that D.C. needs to crush our uprising are all stuck in Iraq and Afghanistan. It'll be like the collapse of the Soviet Union! Besides, you liberal pussies made a lot of noise about seceding from the Union when Bush was re-elected... now you can get *exactly* what you wanted.

Crime: Bring back capital punishment to include white collar criminals. Arrest, try, and execute if found guilty the entire boards of Goldman Sachs, Fannie Mae, Freddie Mac, Sallie Mae and other parasitic corporations. Remove Bernie Madoff from prison for a public hanging in Times Square. Limit appeals for criminals sentenced to death to one, and require that they be executed within one year of their sentencing to cut down on the cost of imprisonment. False rape accusations become punishable with the same sentences that the accused would have received if found guilty. Frivolous lawsuits outlawed, with fines for those who file them.

Government: State senators will no longer be popularly elected, but be appointed by county governments for six-year terms however they see fit, the way the upper house in a bicameral legislature is supposed to work. Institute a two-term limit for the governor and senators and a six-term limit for assemblymen. Lobbyists and "riders" on bills banned. Electoral district redrawing and corruption cases will be handled by external agencies that do not report to elected officials.

Voting: Prospective voters must pass a literacy test in order to vote. If you can't read, write, or don't know what's going on in the news, you have no business having a say in how the government operates.

Economics: "Too-big-to-fail" banks dismantled Standard Oil-style, with laws preventing the formation of large banks who can tank the economy if they fail.

Bureaucracy: Repeal the law requiring public sector workers to join a union as a condition of employment. Gradually fire all state employees not working in a field vital to government operation, such as the police, education, or healthcare.

Welfare: Replace social welfare programs with a basic income guarantee.

Education: Reorient grade school education to teach students at their level, with less gifted ones being steered towards vocational training and retards put in separate schools. Provide free college education for all students with a track record of academic success. Announce a jubilee for all student loan debt.

Marriage: Marriage is recognized as an economic contract for the purposes of raising children in a stable environment with a mother and father. Abolish no-fault divorce, alimony and child support. Child custody always goes to the father except in extreme circumstances.

Affirmative Action: Abolished in all forms.

Immigration: Restore the National Origins Formula, restricting immigration to 3% of foreign-born persons of each nationality resident in the state according to the 1960 Census. English becomes the official language; legal citizens who don't like this will be paid to emigrate to their ancestral lands. Only immigrants with necessary skills are considered for admittance; no more refugees or unskilled laborers. End birthright citizenship. Illegal aliens are deported to their country of origin, no exceptions. Business owners that knowingly employ illegals will be fined heavily; repeat offenders will have their assets seized by the government and auctioned off to the highest bidder.

Transportation: Turn all Interstates and other highways into toll roads, with tolls doubled for highways that go into urban areas (such as I-81 in Syracuse and I-787 in Albany) to encourage people to live closer to their workplaces. End the I-86 construction project: it's an incredible waste of money. Create a new passenger rail service and fund it to implement high-speed rail service throughout the entire state.

Conservation: All previously shuttered public parks

reopened and more created across the state; littering on public property and other violations of conservation law become felonies.

Foreign Relations: Declare official neutrality.

Military: Retain a small National Guard for defense.

Trade: End all free trade agreements. Reinvigorate local manufacturing by implementing a sliding system of tariffs, adjusted based on the GDP of the nation in question. Products from backwards, low-wage shitholes like China or Mexico will receive punishing tariffs; labor-friendly countries like Germany or France will receive comparatively smaller ones. De facto free trade and open transit with neighboring countries like the People's Republic of Vermont, the République du Québec, and the Commonwealth of Guidostan (formerly New Jersey). End all farming subsidies.

Vice: Legalize prostitution and all drugs, and repeal all blue laws as well as open container laws. Allow individual municipalities to regulate these vices as they see fit. Lower the age of consent to 14 for girls and keep it at 17 for boys. Replace statutory rape laws with age of impregnation laws.

Royalty: Bring back the monarchy. North America is in need of a true, cultured aristocracy with a sense of *noblesse oblige*, as opposed to the vulgar burghers who currently constitute our ruling class. Monarchs would serve in a capacity similar to the Queen of England: no real power, but nonetheless playing an important role as symbols of nobility and arbiters of good taste, and holding reserve powers in the event a Mussolini-type gets into power and screws everything up. I personally recommend Princess Madeleine of Sweden to be crowned Queen, and not merely because I'd like to put my scepter in her Royal Court.

Destruction: Demolish the Empire State Plaza; it's a fucking eyesore. Sell it back to the city of Albany to be developed into Italian restaurants and kosher delis.

My plan, radical as it may seem, is the best way to restore peace, progress, and prosperity to America, or at least the best slice of it. So on November 2nd, don't waste your vote on establishment hacks like Andrew Cuomo or Rick Lazio, or phony populists like Carl Paladino who'll betray you as soon as they get inaugurated. Vote for me, Ferdinand Bardamu, your favoritest blogger in the whole wide world!

September 14, 2010

Carl Paladino vs. the Gay Mafia

After having laid into the Gadfly from Buffalo for his political incompetence, I am now compelled to defend him for daring to speak the truth that we all know but are afraid to say aloud. Read these remarks that Carl Paladino made to a group of Orthodox Jews last Sunday and tell me if you think they're offensive:

"I didn't march in a gay pride parade this year. My opponent did. And that's not the example we should be showing our children – and certainly not in their schools.

"And don't misquote me as wanting to hurt homosexual people in any way. That would be a dastardly lie. My approach is live and let live. I just think my children – and your children – would be much better off, and much more successful, getting married and raising a family. And I don't want them to be brainwashed into thinking that homosexuality is an equally valid or successful option – it isn't."[21]

Aside from the fact that this was an incredibly stupid thing for a Republican running in a heavily Democratic state to say, I really don't see what the problem is. Paladino simply said what most of us normal straight people believe: while we don't want to persecute gays or tell them how to live their lives, we don't want them shoving their lunacy in our faces either. Hell, he specifically said that he didn't want to hurt homosexuals. In a normal, functioning world, Paladino's speech wouldn't be the least bit controversial.

But of course, everything is upside down in the America of 2010, and everyone and their brother from Ithaca has rushed to pile on Paladino for pointing out the emperor's nudity. He's been condemned by a motley crew of freaks from the Cuomo campaign to the Republican candidate for attorney general. Even the butt-hurt loser Rick Lazio felt the need to join in.

The coup de grace is a piece by some self-righteous liberal wanker named Michael Boyajian. Writing at *Room Eight*, Mikey's article boils down to a long accusation of lèse majesté against Paladino:

> "The trials and tribulations of Republican gubernatorial candidate Carl Paladino continue now with his hateful homophobic remarks against the gay community that end with a statement by him which in effect he says do not dare call me a homophobe for that would be untrue. Yeah sure, so long as gays are kept down much in the same way blacks were in South Africa during Apartheid."[22]

The left's overreaction to Carl Paladino's gaffe is a massive obfuscation of the underlying issue: the average American's growing distaste for the antics of gays. Straight people have more or less made their peace with the concept of homosexuality. Paladino basically said as much. What *is* the problem is the retarded pomp and circumstance that compromises "gay culture" in America, and the way gays insist on forcing their idiocy down the throats of everyone. To put it another way, we're fine with homosexuals: it's *faggots* we can't stand.

Gay pride types are lying when they claim they're fighting for tolerance. The fact that a bunch of oiled-up, leather-clad fruitloops can strut down the main street of every major city in the U.S. rubbing their bits on each other and singing "It's Raining Men" without being killed by a torch-wielding mob is proof that gays are tolerated plenty in this country. The fact that a chorus of condemnations fall upon the head of every public figure who ever mutters something that isn't totally complementary of gays is proof that they are tolerated plenty. Whether it's those stupid pride parades or gay guys aggressively hitting on straight men, the narcissistic gay mafia isn't satisfied with any of what they have: they want every man, woman and child to rubber-stamp their insanity, without a thought to what any of them want.

Much like with other leftist victimologist groups like blacks and women, the gay mafia has been insulated from criticism by their opponents fear of being labeled as bigots, homophobes in this case. As Paladino's speech and minimal backpedaling showed, this shtick isn't working anymore. The irony is that by aggressively, obnoxiously pushing their dysfunctional behavior, homosexuals are creating a massive anti-gay backlash that would never have happened had they simply shut their mouths and acted like normal people. If gays don't want this to happen, they and their liberal comrades are going to have to get a few things straight:

1. Homosexuals are deviants by definition.

Spare me your ignorant accusations of "bigotry" and read a dictionary definition of "deviant": it is defined as "departing from the norm" or "a person or thing that deviates or departs markedly from the accepted norm."[23] Opposite-sex attraction is the default, normal orientation of all sexually reproducing animal species, including humans. Same-sex attraction is different, therefore it is deviant. It's deviant in the same way that being born with autism or an eleventh toe is deviant, because it is a trait that the majority of humans don't possess. It doesn't mean you are less of a human, but it doesn't make you the same as a straight person. Shut up.

2. Nobody cares what you do in the bedroom; it's when you take it into the streets that it becomes an issue.

You don't have the right to force your beliefs and behaviors on people who don't want to deal with them. You can do what you like in your own communities and where like-minded straight people live, but don't take your perversion where it doesn't belong. If a conservative Catholic like Carl Paladino is willing to "live and let live," you should be as well.

3. You are a *minority* and will always be a minority.

You are better served trying to get on the side of the straight majority instead of trying to piss them off.

4. Your "struggle" is in no way analogous to the civil

rights movement.

There have never been any "straights only" drinking fountains and restaurants or "gays need not apply" signs hung by employers. Gays were never regularly lynched by angry mobs while law enforcement looked the other way, and no gay pride parade has ever been set upon by firehoses and attack dogs by a sadistic police chief. Not having the "right" to marry each other is not the same as living under Jim Crow. Grow up.

5. Most parents want their children to be straight.

People don't want their children to be gay for the same reason they don't want their children to have autism or an eleventh toe. They may not love their gay children any less than their straight ones, but they would still prefer them to be straight. Anyone who claims otherwise is lying. Parents especially don't want their children to be bombarded with gay propaganda in schools. Save it for when the kids are grown-up and can make these decisions with an adult mind.

6. If you incite someone to attack you, you're just as guilty as they are if you end up injured or dead.

If a black man beat up a white guy who shouted "you fucking nigger" in his face, no one would consider the latter the victim of racism. If you aggressively hit on a straight guy and he puts you in the hospital, you aren't the victim of homophobia, you're a narcissistic jackass who thinks the world should revolve around you. Respect us, and we'll respect you.

While I have less of a problem with "gay culture" then most on the right and I've been critical of conservatives for wasting so much time and energy fighting gay marriage and ignoring the actual threats to the institution, I recognize that I'm in the minority on this. For the past few decades, the gay mafia has been treating the straight majority in America with contempt and derision, assaulting decency and common sense from on high and having the chutzpah to cry persecution and victimhood when their opponents respond. They've basically been kicking a chained elephant in the side thinking it would never hit back. Well, the elephant is getting fed up, and he can stomp you like a tube of lube without breaking a sweat.

October 12, 2010

The Tea Party and the Rise of American Gerontocracy

Some time ago, I saw a picture of a sign from a Tea Party rally that read "Keep Your Government Hands Off My Medicare." It dovetails nicely into an expose Matt Taibbi wrote for *Rolling Stone* in which he described the hoards of anti-government protesters rather uncharitably, to say the least:

> "Vast forests have already been sacrificed to the public debate about the Tea Party: what it is, what it means, where it's going. But after lengthy study of the phenomenon, I've concluded that the whole miserable narrative boils down to one stark fact:

> They're full of shit. All of them. At the voter level, the Tea Party is a movement that purports to be furious about government spending—only the reality is that the vast majority of its members are former Bush supporters who yawned through two terms of record deficits and spent the past two electoral cycles frothing not about spending but about John Kerry's medals and Barack Obama's Sixties associations. The average Tea Partier is sincerely against government spending—with the exception of the money spent on them. In fact, their lack of embarrassment when it comes to collecting government largesse is key to understanding what this movement is all about—and nowhere do we see that dynamic as clearly as here in Kentucky, where Rand Paul is barreling toward the Senate with the aid of conservative icons like Palin."[24]

He goes on to write how Rand Paul opposes eliminating the one government program that enriches him personally:

> "Early in his campaign, Dr. Paul, the son of the uncompromising libertarian hero Ron Paul, denounced Medicare as 'socialized medicine.' But this spring, when confronted with the idea of

reducing Medicare payments to doctors like himself—half of his patients are on Medicare—he balked. This candidate, a man ostensibly so against government power in all its forms that he wants to gut the Americans With Disabilities Act and abolish the departments of Education and Energy, was unwilling to reduce his own government compensation, for a very logical reason. 'Physicians,' he said, 'should be allowed to make a comfortable living.'"

A while back, the *New York Times* reported on a poll of Tea Partiers that backs up Taibbi's observations:

"When talking about the Tea Party movement, the largest number of respondents said that the movement's goal should be reducing the size of government, more than cutting the budget deficit or lowering taxes.

"And nearly three-quarters of those who favor smaller government said they would prefer it even if it meant spending on domestic programs would be cut.

> But in follow-up interviews, Tea Party supporters said they did not want to cut Medicare or Social Security–the biggest domestic programs, suggesting instead a focus on 'waste.'
>
> "Some defended being on Social Security while fighting big government by saying that since they had paid into the system, they deserved the benefits."[25]

The lesser mind will look at the above excerpts and proclaim, *"Aha! The Tea Party is a bunch of hypocrites!"* And yes, they may be hypocritical, but there's a method to their madness.

Liberals like to attack the Tea Party as racist, and some on the far right embrace them as an evolving expression of "implicit whiteness" in America, but race is not what defines them. The Tea Party is fighting to transform America into a *gerontocracy:* a government of the old people, by the old people, and for the old people. More specifically, the old people who will be ruling are the Baby Boomers, the most narcissistic and avaricious generation in American history. The above-mentioned NYT report identifies the demographics of the Tea Party as being primarily old and white:

> "Tea Party supporters are wealthier and more well-

educated than the general public, and are no more or less afraid of falling into a lower socioeconomic class, according to the latest New York Times/CBS News poll.

"The 18 percent of Americans who identify themselves as Tea Party supporters tend to be Republican, white, male, married and older than 45."

The more cynical among you might argue that America is already a gerontocracy, what with the levers of power held by dried-up old prunes like Nancy Pelosi, Harry Reid and Mitch McConnell. But just like how having white men in government doesn't mean that white or male interests are represented, Congress being an old folks' home doesn't mean that elderly interests are represented. When then-President Bush proposed privatizing Social Security in 2005, the old farts in this country had a collective anal prolapse.

Ever wonder why Social Security is the third rail of American politics? It's an obvious scam that is slowly dragging down the economy, but it just happens to benefit the fastest growing and most politically influential voter bloc in this country. Government pension programs by nature are Ponzi schemes because they require an ever-increasing number of citizens paying into the system to stay solvent. This leads into the primary reason why Social Security is in danger: the Baby Boomers didn't have enough kids to keep the Ponzi scheme going. Unlike their frisky parents, the Boomers preferred to have smaller families of three, two or just one kid, and in some cases none at all. No kids means no taxpayers to keep you from having to eat Alpo when you're 75 and can't work because of your bum hip. To make matters worse, Social Security was designed merely to keep seniors out of poverty, not to fund the big, expensive cars and trips to Bermuda that the Boomers are used to.

    There are only two ways to save Social Security. The first is to drastically increase the number of workers paying into the system. The government's preferred way of doing this is with immigration, legal and illegal. The negative effects of legal and illegal immigration have been hashed out so many times by so many different writers that I don't need to repeat them. Suffice it to say, importing large numbers of foreigners isn't an option, either practically or politically. This leaves our other choice: liquidate all parts of the government save for Social Security, Medicare and other programs that benefit seniors.

    That is the true purpose of the Tea Party. For all of their anti-government bluster, they're just another interest group clamoring for their slice of the entitlement pie. They are the final expression of Boomer vanity, narcissism and greed before they skedaddle on up to that spirit in the sky. If you doubt me, find me a Tea Party politician who is even considering talking about cutting Social Security or Medicare. Sharron Angle? Rand Paul? Marco Rubio? Not a chance. They are all part and parcel of the Gray Mafia, who will appropriate all of the ducats to their vampiric constituents while denying you so much as crumbs from the table. The young must die so that the old may live.

And make no mistake, the Baby Boomers are nothing more than a generation of vampires seeking to suck the blood out of their children to prolong their own wretched lives. They're also a vile gang of hypocrites. After they spent their youths in the sixties and seventies taking every illicit substance known to man, they got Puritan pious and instituted the War on Drugs in the eighties to ass-rape anyone else who did the same. After voting themselves massive entitlement programs in the form of the Great Society, they foisted neoliberal capitalism and "free trade" on America to denude blue-collar work and make getting into tens of thousand of dollars in debt a requirement just to enter the middle class. After dodging the draft during the Vietnam War when they were young enough to die for their country, they conjured up some "Support the Troops" bullshit as a salve to their corrupt souls and to browbeat everyone into becoming sunshine patriots. Every joy they indulged in they seek to deny to the rest of us, every ladder that they used to climb to the top they kicked away. And now that their lives are finally coming to a close and the scam they were hoping to cash in on is about to collapse, they're scheming to hoard the government's bullion all for themselves.

Fortunately, being the selfless Samaritan that I am, I've devised another, foolproof way to save Social Security from collapse. In fact, seniors can use it themselves! I call it the Elderly Cranial Evacuation Boomstick:

It's easy to operate. Here's how it works:

1. Load the provided Elderly Cranial Evacuation Pellets into the Boomstick.

2. Insert the end of the Boomstick into your mouth, aiming towards your medulla oblongata at the back of your head.

3. Pull the trigger.

WARNING: Don't use out-of-doors, in public places or anywhere large amounts of people will see you, because you're gonna leave behind a real mess!

Get your own Elderly Cranial Evacuation Boomstick now

by calling 1-800-OLD-FART! Only $19.99 plus shipping and handling. Order in the next ten minutes and you'll receive a bonus Boomstick for your spouse or next-door neighbor. Supplies are limited, so call now!

November 16, 2010

Why I Hate the Day After Thanksgiving

I don't shop on Black Friday.

I don't even go to *any* stores on Black Friday.

In fact, I spent this Black Friday, as well as the one before, sleeping in. I want nothing to do with you miserly, two-legged buffalo.

My abstention from joining the herd on the day after Thanksgiving, the biggest shopping day of the year, is rooted in pragmatism and protest. If you're standing in the freezing cold all night to buy a video game console that goes on sale at five in the morning, do the world a favor and kill yourself. As for the protest, it comes from having spent many a Black Friday in the store, but on the *other* side of the garage door you filthy animals smashed in so you could get your fucking $299.99 HP laptop (that will break on you in a year after you load it up with malware from all those shady porn sites you visit).

Yes, once upon a time, I was a retail wage-slave. I was the guy who said, *"Thank you for shopping at FuckMart! Have a nice night, please come again,"* as I handed you your receipt. I was the guy who lugged the four bags of soil into the SUV you bought because you didn't want the hot guy at Dunkin Donuts to think you were a mom or married or anything unsexy like that. I was the guy who grabbed the carts you let drift all the way into the Staples parking lot because you were too lazy to put them in the corral where they belonged. I was the guy who got the mop and bucket after your precious little munchkin pissed himself on aisle six.

For years, I trudged into the back of one of America's most mismanaged big box stores, punched the clock, and tried to act like I cared. I was young, still in school, and I needed beer money, and where better to get it then from one of America's exalted shrines to Mammon? It *seemed* easy enough on paper. Work the register, organize the shelves, clean up spills, help customers find stuff. At the minimum wage plus a quarter per hour, it was a decent job for someone working towards an education. So I put on the golf shirt and the name tag, the black khaki pants and the $20 dress shoes, and trudged out to the floor to experience first-hand what it's like to have your soul sucked out, one greasy puff at a time.

There's something about big box stores that encourages people to make worthless scumbags out of themselves. I remember every freak who passed through the doors of FuckMart with an eye to give me hell. The smelly middle-aged Romanians who didn't know how to use soap and water. The mean old lady with the oxygen tank who went batshit crazy because the scanner wouldn't accept her out-of-date coupons. The surly black guys who behaved like extras from *Idiocracy*, right down to starting a fight because one of 'em had called the other a "pussy ass nigga." Had to call the cops for that one.

This and more, for twenty to forty hours a week. You want to lose your faith in humanity, work a retail store on Black Friday. Deal with the soccer mom cunts who are screaming at you in the line for the latest video game to pacify their Ritalin-bombed sons. Deal with the venal morons who make in excess of $100,000 a year haggling with you over a two dollar discount. Deal with your idiot managers always afraid of a mystery shopper or a snap inspection from the regional headquarters to grade them on how well everyone is sucking the customers' dicks. And deal with it all for minimum wage (plus a quarter) per hour.

The only reason a disgruntled Kmart, Walmart or Target employee hasn't gone postal yet is because they don't pay them enough to afford guns.

That's why I don't shop on Black Friday. I don't want to inconvenience myself over a couple of measly deals, and I don't need to add to the already obscene workload that the poor schmucks working on that day already have. It's the same reason why I always tip waitresses, pizza deliverymen, and cab drivers generously (unless they do a really bad job). I've been there, working that shitty job, and I know how it feels. I know what it's like to stumble outside into your car at one in the morning, your feet aching from being on them for ten hours straight. I know what it's like to have to mop some brat's urine off the floor. I know what it's like to be treated like a dirty dishrag by the scum of the earth and not being allowed to respond with anything other than feigned politeness.

Last week, blogger Xamuel wrote on the moral duty employers have to pay their employees well:

> "We hear a lot about the work ethic, the notion that hard work is inherently virtuous. We don't hear nearly so much about its dual, the Pay Ethic. The Pay Ethic is the idea that paying generously is a virtue. There's no question that we *practice* it: we value peoples' fashion, their taste in art, their furniture, based largely on how much they payed for it. Paying more for a work of art is more virtuous, and it imparts a higher value into the art itself. Where the ethic is really most important is in paying wages. If my servant has a moral obligation to work hard for me, then I have a moral obligation to pay him generously. Not just pay him what I can get away with. Not argue with his union about contracts. If he is obligated to work more than the bare minimum to avoid being fired, then I am

obligated to pay more than the bare minimum to avoid a strike."²⁶

If you want to see where the pay ethic is being violated the most egregiously and insultingly, visit one of America's big box stores. Thanks to Sam Walton or some other penny-pinching creep deciding that "the customer is always right," the average idiot in this country thinks he has a human right to piss on cashiers, sales associates, and other retail workers who are just doing their jobs. And for all their trials and tribulations, their wonderful employers don't give them much more than the government-mandated minimum, while the top cats award themselves bigger and bigger bonuses and wonder why their workers put in the bare minimum of work.

Everyone knows that Black Friday is called that because it's the day most retailers and chain stores get into the black; in other words, start turning a profit. I can't believe no one has thought about the implications of this. *It means that the average store is so valueless, it LOSES money for eleven months out of the year.* Even with the Christmas shopping season, Walmart, Kmart et al have extremely slim profit margins, and are highly vulnerable to slight tremors in the economy.

Xamuel is right. Businesses that can't afford to pay their workers decently are businesses that don't deserve to survive. The entire model of American retail is unsustainable and teetering on the brink. Those low, low prices you enjoy at FuckMart only exist because someone else is getting shafted, whether it's the cashier who's being paid minimum wage and a quarter to take your bullshit or the factory worker who got laid off when the factory got moved to China. Something's going to give.

Not that I care too much. Like I said, I slept in on Black Friday. And I'll keep sleeping in and ordering my gifts from Amazon. Meanwhile, you roaring, furless bison can continue forming human stampedes over cheap crap while thinking you're an advanced form of life. I'm just here to watch this freak show until the curtain drops.

November 29, 2010

How Julian Assange Broke the World

Why is the emergence of *Wikileaks*—an organization capable of disseminating leaked government documents at little to no cost to itself—so significant? Blogger Advocatus Diaboli has the answer:

> "We never had anything comparable to WikiLeaks in recorded history. Imagine a decentralized, inexpensive, easy to setup/update/maintain system which can disseminate leaked digital information to anybody who has the curiosity to find out. While there have been whistleblower websites and blogs for years, they were largely individual efforts with a

very ephemeral existence and limited readership."[27]

Let me illustrate why Advocatus is right with a historical comparison.

For over a thousand years, from the fall of the Roman Empire in the west to the Protestant Reformation, the Catholic Church was the most powerful entity in Europe. Then, in the span of a hundred years, they lost almost everything. Half of Europe converted to Protestantism, breaking the political and economic grip that popes possessed over them. The Church's land holdings were gradually eaten away until today, where the Catholic Church's temporal power extends to an area the size of Central Park guarded by a bunch of Swiss mercenaries who gallivant about in Renaissance-era clothing wielding pikes. How could an organization that held so much power for so long collapse so swiftly?

While it is true that by the time of the Renaissance, the Church was a sclerotic, ineffective, corrupt empire that existed only to enrich itself and screw over the peons, that's only one half of the answer. The other half is that *technology had advanced to the point where critics of Catholic policies could not only cheaply and efficiently spread their ideas, the Church's ability to suppress those ideas was greatly diminished.* The technology in question? The printing press.

Think about it. The time cost of writing and producing

books prior to the invention of the printing press kept them out of the hands but a few, the educated clergy and nobility. With the printing press, books, pamphlets and other writings could be cheaply and easily mass-produced. Less than a hundred years after Johannes Gutenberg invented the printing press, Martin Luther nailed his *Ninety-Five Theses* to the door of Wittenberg Church. It was this combination of information-spreading technology and the Catholic Church's own record of behaving in bad faith towards its subjects that enabled Luther and his Reformation successors to crush the Church in such a short amount of time.

Every so often, leftists make noise about reestablishing the Fairness Doctrine in the U.S., a defunct FCC policy that requires radio and TV broadcasters to give equal time to opposing political viewpoints. They usually claim that right-wing talk hosts like Rush Limbaugh and Sean Hannity exhibit a malign influence on American public discourse, and the domination of corporate media conglomerates like Clear Channel prevents alternative (leftist) viewpoints from being aired. The problem with this viewpoint is that the ease of distributing information on the Internet makes radio and TV increasingly irrelevant, meaning the Fairness Doctrine would have a minimal impact at best. The exact same ease of information dissemination that makes it possible for me to write this blog also enables websites like *Wikileaks* to exist. If the Internet is our printing press, Julian Assange is our Martin Luther, in terms of impact on the world.

Like Luther, Assange is capitalizing on both a technology

that enables him to spread ideas and info quickly and cheaply and a massive disillusionment with modern society. One or the other is not sufficient for instigating social change, but the two combined are a deadly brew that can wreak serious havoc. And once the engine of revolution starts going, it perpetuates itself, no longer needing the person who gassed it up. *The people who are calling for Julian Assange to be incarcerated or assassinated are the equivalent of the radicals who wanted the Catholic Church to arrest and execute Martin Luther for "heresy."*

No matter what action the U.S. government takes against Assange, they can't stop him or the movement he's created. If they ignore him, he'll keep on publishing leaks, embarrassing them even further. If they up their internal security, they'll hinder their own operations, playing right into his hands:

> "The leak, in other words, is only the catalyst for the desired counter-overreaction; Wikileaks wants to provoke the conspiracy into turning off its own brain in response to the threat. As it tries to plug its own holes and find the leakers, he reasons, its component elements will de-synchronize from and turn against each other, de-link from the central processing network, and come undone. Even if all the elements of the conspiracy still *exist*, in this sense, depriving themselves of a vigorous flow of

information to connect them all together as a conspiracy prevents them from *acting* as a conspiracy..."[28]

If the government imprisons Assange, he'll become a living symbol of oppression and tyranny, the Nelson Mandela of the anarchist set. And if by chance a corporate hitman puts one right between his eyes, Assange will become a martyr to millions of would-be techno-jihadists around the world.

Some people will say to the previous sentences, *"Why should the government care if some anti-establishment losers hate them? Jailing or killing Assange will strike fear into their hearts and make them think twice before they mess with Uncle Sam!"* Except that you're forgetting that the government can't suppress dissidents or information on the Internet. Advocatus Diaboli explains:

> "Some techy morons, including a retard from MIT, predict that they can stop such leaks. However these clever morons don't get one property of information (as opposed to content). If someone can read it, see it, transfer it, back it up or send it to someone–it can be copied and unlike entertainment related content, low quality copies are as valuable and useful as high fidelity copies."

Attempting to fight the spread of information on the Internet is like trying to play Whack-a-Mole with one mallet and a trillion moles. No matter how many times *Wikileaks* gets taken offline, they'll simply set up shop somewhere else. And even if *Wikileaks* goes down for good, the concept and information they publicized will continue to exist. Men may die and organizations may disband, but ideas live on. Hell, there are probably already plenty of people who, inspired by Assange's efforts, will set up their own *Wikileaks-like* websites. You think Interpol's going to be able to arrest them all? You think Bank of America and the CIA will be able to recruit enough hackers to shut them all down?

Put simply, *if you oppose Julian Assange and Wikileaks, there is no way for you to win against him.* You can only choose how you will lose. The cat is out of the bag, the toothpaste is out of the tube, insert your favorite metaphor here. Arguing over things like whether Assange has the right to play God with state secrets is missing the point entirely. Short of mankind shutting down the Internet entirely and returning to a pre-computer existence, the revolution will stay alive.

Martin Luther could not have predicted that his followers in Wittenberg would proclaim a violent revolt against Catholicism in his absence, or that even more radical Protestant theologians would rise in his stead. Likewise, neither Assange nor we have any idea where the Wikileaks revolution will take us. We can only wait and watch.

WHAT'S WRONG WITH THE WORLD

December 6, 2010

How Jared Loughner Has Pushed the West Closer to Armageddon

Another day, and another crazy bastard has opened fire on innocents, albeit in a semi-targeted attack instead of a random spree. I come not to discuss Jared Loughner's politics or motives, but the greater significance of his shootings. This slobbering lunatic has kicked us one step down the road to revolution.

And make no mistake, Loughner is a lunatic. All the attempts by the left and the right to foist him on each others' side of the fence are completely fruitless. If you doubt me, here's a selection from his ravings:

> "If there's no flag in the constitution then the flag in the film is unknown.
> There's no flag in the constitution.
> Therefore, the flag in the film is unknown.
> Burn every new and old flag that you see.
> Burn your flag!
> I bet you can imagine this in your mind with a faster speed.
> Watch this protest in reverse!
> Ask the local police; "What's your illegal activity on duty?".

If you protest the government then there's a new
government from protesting.
There's not a new government from protesting.
Thus, you aren't protesting the government.
There's something important in this video: There's
no communication to anyone in this location.
You shouldn't be afraid of the stars."[29]

See what happens when you give mind-altering drugs to schizos? Loughner's completely off his rocker, and anyone trying to argue that he's a radical leftist or right-wing nutjob is reading their own preoccupations into the chaos of his brain.

It amuses me when I see people scrambling to shove everyone into a pre-defined category and going bonkers when they encounter folks who don't fit into their rigid molds. If you're not a conservative, you must be a liberal. If you're critical of capitalism, you can't *not* be a pinko commie. If you reject one ideology's dogma, people expect you to swallow their opponents' whole. How dare you think for yourself! Stop using that cerebrum-thingy and get in line with the rest of the Crowd, you pointy-headed postmodern prankster!

I've become increasingly convinced over the course of my life that political ideology is nothing more than tribalism for clever dimwits. People don't declare themselves liberal, conservative, or libertarian because they genuinely believe in a set of ideas, they do it because they want to join a club with others whom they find agreeable. They're looking to forge an individual identity to distinguish themselves from the mass of morons around them. It's no more real than rooting for the Yankees over the Red Sox or preferring Lady Gaga over Taylor Swift. So long as the club hits certain emotional buttons, the leadership can push whatever stupidity they want, even if it runs counter to the club's supposed identity. Liberals are anti-liberty. Conservatives have no interest in conserving anything. Traditionalists don't understand how their own traditions work. Libertarians are mentally identical to communists.

 The ideologues who are dabbing their hands in Gabrielle Giffords' gore are doing nothing but cherry-picking evidence about Loughner's insanity in their war against the other tribes. Loughner liked *Mein Kampf*, so he must be a right-winger! But wait, he was also a fan of *The Communist Manifesto*, so he's a liberal! Hold on there, Ludwig von Mises was one of his inspirations, so he's clearly a libertarian! If you claim to be able to discern a coherent set of beliefs out of these conflicting influences, you're an idiot, a liar, or both.

 More to the point, Jared Loughner's significance lies not in the mess that was his belief system, but his actions and how they affect the unfolding drama of our dying world. Spree shooters are common, but this wasn't just some chance attack, but a political assassination of sorts. I say "of sorts" because a true assassin would have just killed Giffords instead of shooting up the entire supermarket. Loughner wasn't just looking to end her life, he was looking to strike terror into peoples' hearts. Not only that, but a congresswoman is a target of importance. Gym-going women and school board members are expendable, and even IRS flunkies aren't that important. But a politician: we haven't seen an attempted political assassination on this scale since Hinckley tried to impress Jodie.

Unlike with Timothy McVeigh and the Oklahoma City bombings, I don't think the government-media complex is going to be successful in slapping the right-wing extremist label on Loughner. While this sort of thing has been par for the course ever since Lee Harvey Oswald blew JFK's brains out, now the freedom of information access provided by the Internet allows us to circumvent the mainstream media's carefully constructed narrative. The only people who will take the official story seriously are panicky SWPL liberals who need to constantly fantasize about right-wing Republican fascists coming to murder them in their sleep.

However, the risk that the government will act to regulate "hate speech" on the Internet to keep lunatics like Loughner from being "inspired" to kill people is high. An Unmarried Man expresses this view at his blog:

> "There will be a cyber 9/11 in our near future which will shift the paradigm and accelerate the prying eyes of government.

"The Internet is the last Wild West, it is the free-for-all mode of expression the oligarchs cannot control. Yet.

"Wait for the cyber 9/11.

"It will happen..."[30]

I agree that the cyber 9/11 is coming. Hell, this may *be* the cyber 9/11. But I don't think the government will be able to implement an online TSA to grope our minds.

One of my biggest problems with conspiracy theorists is their insistence that the government possesses an ungodly amount of power, enough to control the media, drug our drinking water, and kidnap our children for their gruesome Satanist pedophile sex slavery rings. If the Illuminati reptile aliens were as powerful as the tinfoil hat-wearers claim they are, they would have already taken over the Internet and murdered all the people who were spreading the truth about their insidious plans. The mere fact that you are still sitting in front of your laptop in your mom's basement and not being tortured in a secret military prison is a refutation of everything you paranoiacs believe in.

Don't believe me? So, how have the Powers That Be fared in trying to shut down *Wikileaks?* Last I checked, they were not only still up after being repeatedly taken down by hackers and blacklisted by major corporations, but their data is being mirrored and copied in a million different places on the Internet. Their dickhead leader is even out on bail. If the combined efforts of corporate and government forces can't keep one solitary site off the web, what makes you think they can censor the entire net?

Oh sure, the masses may surrender their freedom of speech to maintain the illusion of security, but so what? In response to my contention that Julian Assange is an agent of a new Reformation, the Social Pathologist claimed I was "still deep in the Matrix":

> "The proles don't care.
>
> "If I were the CIA, I wouldn't liquidate him. I'd simply compete against him. Free to air lesbian porn, midget wrestling and Justin Bieber on Facebook would probably do the trick. Why make him a martyr when after 15 mins he'll be yesterday's news? Democracy has failed."

The proles don't matter. When the proles rise up in revolt, that does not signify a revolution's beginning, but its end. The true beginning of a revolution is when young, intelligent bourgeois intellectuals become sufficiently alienated from their society to begin working towards its destruction. Change only comes to the streets after it has been hashed out in the back parlors of the middle-classes. And once the ranks of the disillusioned swell to a critical mass, no one can stop what they unleash.

As an example, the American Revolution was not a popular revolt initially. At the outset of fighting in 1776, less than a third of the American colonists supported the rebels, with the rest either remaining loyal to the British crown or staying out of the conflict. The Revolution was birthed in the writings and actions of a select group of men—George Washington, Sam Adams, Thomas Jefferson, Paul Revere etc.—who built on the philosophies of thinkers who came before them. Their efforts snowballed and subsequently changed the world.

A revolution is already underway in the West, and if you are reading this blog and similar ones, you are already part of it. Game blogs, human biodiversity blogs, alt-right blogs, white nationalist blogs, men's rights blogs and the like: for all their quirks, they draw a readership that is more intelligent, more educated, and in many cases younger than the general population. According to *Quantcast*, 38 percent of *In Mala Fide* readers are aged 18-34, the next largest age group being 35-49 with 29 percent. 55 percent of my readers have an annual income of more than $100,000 a year, and 50 percent are college graduates, with another 26 percent being grad students.

These numbers are all well above the Internet averages, if *Quantcast* is to be believed. That's a lot of young, educated, wealthy people who are not happy with the state of things. Now add in all the readers from all the blogs in this sphere of the Internet.

Get the picture?

Even if the government could censor the Internet, they're not going to make all the alienated people who read and are influenced by these blogs magically disappear or become un-alienated. They—and you—will find a way to make their lives miserable. No amount of censorship or coercion can stop a critical mass of intellectuals who are committed to taking down the society in which they live. And of course, the government-media complex is not going to suddenly see the light and start addressing the underlying problems. They're just going to double-down on their shaming, intimidation and totalitarianism until their empire crumbles to pieces. Those tactics didn't save the Soviet Union or East Germany, and they won't save Barack Obama and Goldman Sachs.

So, to those who want to use Jared Loughner to destroy the freedom of the Internet, I say *molon labe!* We are the new counter-culture, the tsunami that will cleanse our nations of your lies, scams and deceit. Armageddon is inevitable and you've already lost the war; all you can do is choose how your world will end.

January 10, 2011

The Rise of Generation Zero, Part One: Everything You Know is Wrong

"Man, I see in Fight Club the strongest and smartest men who've ever lived. I see all this potential, and I see squandering. God damn it, an entire generation pumping gas, waiting tables; slaves with white collars. Advertising has us chasing cars and clothes, working jobs we hate so we can buy shit we don't need. We're the middle children of history, man. No purpose or place. We have no Great War, no Great Depression. Our Great War's a spiritual war... our Great Depression is our lives. We've all been raised on television to believe that one day we'd all be millionaires, and movie gods, and rock stars. But we won't. And we're slowly learning that fact. And we're very, very pissed off."

Fight Club

Another young man has figured out that the American Dream is fiction. Willy Wonka writes on the truth of success in "the land of the free":

"My brother is an Engineering major with a high

GPA. He's about to graduate, and doesn't have a job offer.

Everybody else he knows in Engineering – is in Engineering because their dad is an Engineer.

Seriously.

They have a network in the field by association. Before they even go to school.

It makes me wonder what suburbia is really like.

It makes me wonder if a college degree is really worth anything. [...]

[...] "I was told a degree from the school I got it from was 'gold.'

Literally.

That's what I was told.

Well, I graduated 2.5 years ago and haven't seen any gold yet.

> I haven't seen any money yet either for that matter.
>
> I have friends with college degrees waitressing at restaurants, working at call centers making $10 an hour."[31]

Gee, isn't the USA the land of freedom and opportunity? A country where anyone can be what they want to be so long as they work hard and achieve? And yet, intelligent and capable American men languish in obscurity and poverty every day while dullards and morons get promoted to prominence based on their family connections and friends in high places. Horatio Alger *lied* to us!

America is no different than European countries where success is determined by your last name and your class. Except that while Europeans acknowledge their reality, Americans cover theirs in a blanket of pious Puritan lies. If you succeed in America, it's not because you were born rich, you got lucky or you cheated and stole from people, it's because you "pulled yourself up by your bootstraps." And if you fail, it's not because you were hamstrung by con men and scam artists, it's because you're just too stupid and lazy to make the grade. Get a job, slob! Nobody owes you anything! America is the land of the free and the home of the brave, and if you don't like it, you can get out of my country!

To be deemed a loser in America is to sign your own

death warrant. God may be dead, but the cubicle jockeys and castrated middle-class drones of this land still think of themselves as part of a warped Calvinist elect. To them, their willingness to have their humanity stripped away day by day sucking at Mammon's teat is proof that they are God's chosen people. Anyone who questions the presuppositions of the American cult of "hard work" and "self-reliance" is ostracized from polite society. Hippies, commies, degenerates, bums they're called. The U.S. may not have any gulags or KGB torture chambers, but Americans are still frighteningly Soviet in their treatment of anyone who dissents from the party line. Both of the major political factions in America worship the myth of the American Dream, whether its conservatives preaching about the "bootstrap" bullshit or liberals encouraging illegal immigration because Mexican aliens "do the jobs Americans don't want to do."

The only way to escape is to leave.

**

Last Christmas, I went home to see my family. Over dinner, I told them that I was quitting my job and moving. Their reaction was collective shock. Here's the CliffsNotes version of the conversation:

Mom: You *quit?*

Ferdinand Bardamu: Yeah. I couldn't take it anymore. I…just…couldn't take it. I got a new job in [NEW TOWN]. I'm going to start living the way I want now.

M: So, how much does it pay?

FB: [Figure notably smaller than what I made at my old job]

Dad: So what sparked this crisis of conscience?

FB: I can't *take* those idiots any more. If I put up with that job any longer, I'd go insane.

Cécile (sanctimoniously): You're so *stupid*, Ferd. Why would you throw away a high-paying job in the middle of a recession?

FB (deadpan): Because I would have gone postal if I stayed there any longer.

Cécile: So you like being poor? God, you're just... ugh... (to Mom) I always said you were too soft on him...

Mom: Ferd's a grown man, he can make his own decisions.

A bit of background: my little sis Cécile is studying to be a speech therapist, an occupation that requires a master's degree at the bare minimum to get a job in the greater New York area. By the time she graduates, she'll be in her mid-20's and have in the neighborhood of $100,000 worth of student loans to pay off.

Later that night, I was talking with my dad when he mentioned his quest to find an owner's manual for his ancient, hand-me-down snowmobile.

FB: Why can't you just search for one on Ebay at work?

D: Ferd, our supervisors monitor our Internet usage. The company fired a whole bunch of people after examining the cookies on their browser and seeing that they were visiting sites they weren't supposed to be visiting.

FB: They check your *cookies?*

D: Oh yeah. They've got a whole IT department who gets paid to read our emails and do things like that.

FB: They read your emails? And you let them do that?

D: Their equipment, their time. It's even spelled out in our contracts. They're allowed to fire us for misusing our Internet access and we can't do anything about it.

It's rather sickening that conservative and libertarian assholes who spend their time inveighing against the evils of communism (even arguing that Soviet Russia was a greater evil than Nazi Germany and claiming we should have fought them instead) excuse and defend the exact same behavior at home, so long as its committed by the sainted private sector. After all, if you don't like being spied on by the corporate Stasi, you can just get another job. Don't let things like a mortgage to pay, student loans, kids to feed, or the fact that *every single employer* in the country is equally inhumane to its workers get in the way of the neo-Calvinist cult's lies.

Just get back in the cotton field, you dumb nigger. It's where you belong.

***

They call my generation the Millennials. It's a somewhat appropriate term, though not for the reasons most think. A far better name, too close to reality for mainstream mediocrities to handle, would be Generation Zero. Zero not only in the eyes of American secular Calvinism, but zero in terms of philosophy and beliefs. We are the first generation fully baptized in the holy waters of nihilism, the first to experience the full force of an entire civilization's supporting pillars being torn down.

Generation Zero was born into a world in which white people were totally deracinated, the heroes and icons of old libeled and shoved aside for new phony saints deified by multiculturalist dogma. We came of age when the feminist project reached its apogee, drugging bright boys with Ritalin and crushing men with laws that denied their very humanity. We were thrust into a nation that had made "greed is good" into its national motto, empowering corporate sociopaths and destroying labor protections according to the lies of the Chicago School and its prophet Milton Friedman. We were made the heirs of a society that had replaced authentic culture with ersatz pop drivel, community with atomization, refinement and education with boorishness and indoctrination.

And the very people who were responsible for all of this have the sheer unadulterated *balls* to blame *us* for the decline of civilization! They call us "entitled" for demanding that our government and employers treat us with a modicum of dignity. They call us "lazy" for not wanting to slave away like starving peasants even though we live in a world of plenty. They call us "immature" for delaying adulthood due to the financial pressures they forced on US as a requirement to get a decent job. They call us "narcissistic" for putting ourselves first in a world where naked self-interest is the state religion. They call us "degenerate" for not believing that venial sins like drug use mandate a stay in a federal rape camp.

It's like the gluttonous condemning the lustful for being immoral.

Generation Zero is the Omega Generation, omega not in a game sense, but in a Revelation sense. We are the end of your civilization, the chickens of your poisonous gestalt coming home to roost. Like the East Germans who tore down the Berlin Wall, we are the ones who will expose your pious myths and your pretty lies, who will push your decrepit, corrupt empire into its grave. Thanks to the Internet, your fabrications and narratives are dying like worms in a rain storm. Like the man said, we're very, very pissed off.

Generation Zero is not innocent and is far from being comprised of saints, but their detractors aren't any better. This is a war that no one can win, but it is the Zeroes who will lose the least. You can't lose what you never had to begin with.

January 19, 2011

The Rise of Generation Zero, Part Two: Jenseits von Links und Rechts

"Solid Snake: So, the Genome Soldiers mean that the experiments were a success?

Liquid Snake: SUCCESS? Don't be a fool! They're a complete failure! We are on the verge of extinction.

SS: What?

LS: Have you ever heard of the Asymmetry Theory?

SS: ?

LS: Nature tends to favor asymmetry. Those species which have gone extinct all show signs of symmetry. The Genome Soldiers suffer from the same problem...signs of symmetry. So do I, as do you.

SS: !!

LS: That's right. We are all on the verge of death at the genetic level. We don't know when or what type of disease will occur..."

Metal Gear Solid

    I've always preferred to listen to news/talk radio when I'm in the car. Music radio is a waste, re-playing the same five songs over and over again. NPR is faux-intellectual drivel for SWPLs who want their friends to think they're cultured and smart. And I never really cared for sports. There's nothing like a good screaming rant from some middle-aged white guy to keep you awake during those long drives.

    Anyway, I was tuned into a distant New York station a few days ago when the local news came on. The top story was about how Governor Cuomo was going to launch his own advertising campaign to sell his plan of downsizing state government directly to the public, bypassing the public unions entirely. A Democrat making fiscal austerity the central focus of his time in office: who'd have thought we'd see the day?

    Wanna know who the majority of public sector workers in the Empire State supported for governor last year? You've got three guesses, and the first two don't count. My then-co-workers were ebullient the day after the election. A particularly loathsome forty-something woman who worked across the way from me, an overweight fatass who loved to brag to her girlfriends about how she was dating two men at the same time (neither knowing of each other's existence, of course), snidely referred to Carl Paladino as a "homophobic fascist." I told her that Cuomo would ensure that we'd all be out of a job in four years, especially since the Republicans had all but retaken the State Senate. She thought her seniority and PEF would protect her, as it had under Pataki, Spitzer and Paterson.

Given the choice between two candidates who would both fuck them in the ass, the tax-sucking makework parasites of New York went with the "lesser of two evils." They didn't sit out the election, they didn't vote for a third-party candidate, they voted for their own anal violation. And now that Sonny Cuomo is whipping out his dick and telling his loyal constituents to grease up, what is their response?

Candlelight vigils.

I shit you not. These losers think a seasoned political narcissist is going to be dissuaded by something sappy liberals use to mourn gay bashing victims.

For all their bravado and chest-thumping, Americans are the most cowardly chickenshits in the Western world, far more gutless than the "Eurotrash" they love to mock. You suckers mocked the French as "surrender monkeys" and had a good laugh with your "Freedom Fries" jokes, but the average Frenchman has more courage in his pinky then an entire Tea Party rally has in their whole bodies. Why? He's passionate about what *matters*. When public sector workers and university students in Europe have their livelihoods threatened by government spending cuts, they get *angry*. They hit the streets, they protest, they block traffic, they set cars on fire, they attack police. Their governments *fear* them because they don't respond to threats to their lifestyles by vegging out in the soft glow of the flat-screen watching fucking *Glee*. Even if you think they're a bunch of worthless moochers, you have to admire their resolve.

 You, Mr. Tea Party Patriot, you strut around with your hunting rifle pretending you're John Fucking Wayne, you wear a powdered wig to rallies demanding to see Obama's birth certificate, you think you're manly because you "support" braver men than you going to kill foreigners for you in lands you can't even point out on a map. But when the owner of the factory you worked at outsourced the whole shebang to China so he could buy a new yacht, you did *nothing*. After all, he owned the place; he can do what he wants. He *earned* his wealth! Now you're out of work and McDonald's and Walmart are the only places hiring, but Sean Hannity says you're a Great American for supporting your own impoverishment, so it's all good.

 And you left-of-center public workers, you're even worse. Your behavior towards the Democratic Party, your supposed benefactors, is like a battered wife towards her abusive husband. He comes home late at night, drunk and looking to stab a bitch. You beg him to be merciful, no please honey don't hurt me, as he readies his hairy palm for a backhand across your cheek. POW! BAM! SMACK! Now you've got a pair of shiners and three of your teeth are lying on the floor. But it's okay, because he starts crying afterwards, he says he's sorry and he loves you, and he'll never do it again. You have make-up sex in your bedroom, the power of your orgasms threatening to melt your brain.

You won't get fooled again.

But you do. And you do and you do and you do. Until finally one day, you fall to the kitchen floor, your lifeblood oozing out of the slash in your throat. The slash he made with the broken Bud Light bottle. You stare at his hateful face, mouthing shock with the last of your strength. You were stupid, and now you're dead.

God damn you all.

***

Last week, an article entitled "The Blindspot" made the rounds around the blogosphere. The author posited a radical thesis; that leftism is basically dead:

> "There are many myths within the political blogosphere, but none is so deeply troubling or so highly treasured by mainstream political bloggers

than this: that the political blogosphere contains within it the whole range of respectable political opinion, and that once an issue has been thoroughly debated therein, it has had a full and fair hearing. The truth is that almost anything resembling an actual left wing has been systematically written out of the conversation within the political blogosphere, both intentionally and not, while those writing within it congratulate themselves for having answered all left-wing criticism."[32]

The post lead me to my own equally radical realization: *he's right.*

Before the usual suspects start spluttering, *"ARE YOU NUTS OBAMMUNIST DEATH PANELS PALIN/BACHMANN 2012!!!"*, let me qualify that statement. It is *socialism* specifically that is dead. All of the other various hobbyhorses of the left—gay rights, multiculturalism, feminism—they're alive and kicking. But economic Marxism, the historic core of the Western left-wing, is as dead as Marx himself. The only people who take it seriously anymore are high-IQ cranks like Robert Lindsay and recalcitrant old hippies like Alexander Cockburn. Most so-called leftists and liberals spout a softer version of neoliberal capitalism, and even supposedly socialist states like Sweden are functionally capitalist, albeit with more robust welfare states.

There's a reason for this: *economic leftism was totally discredited by the collapse of the Soviet Union twenty years ago.* The fruits of Marxism were laid bare for all the world to see, and what they saw was rampant shortages of basic goods, widespread poverty, and the Gulag Archipelago. From Poland to Cuba, Hungary to Cambodia, socialists and communists utterly failed in providing a decent standard of living or basic freedom to the people they ruled. I don't care what phony statistics you dredge up claiming that Cubans have a marginally higher life expectancy than Americans, that still doesn't change the fact that they live in squalor and backwardness. And Venezuela is only buoyed by the high price of oil; once that gravy train runs out, people will respond to the question *"Who is Hugo Chavez?"* with *"Uh, wasn't he that migrant worker guy?"*

Leftism has been dead in the U.S. and the rest of the West ever since Nixon resigned. Jimmy Carter made no meaningful additions to the welfare state during his tenure, and Bill Clinton was a neoliberal triangulator who carried on Reagan's legacy by championing welfare reform and helping deliver the single biggest kick to the American middle class' balls ever: NAFTA. The Jackass Party abandoned any pretensions of being socialist or pro-worker when a Democratic Congress passed that bill and a Democratic president signed it into law. Aside from the healthcare bill, President Obama's economic policies are identical to Bush's, with bailouts for the wealthy and useless spending on the military and already extant social programs like Medicare. (And don't you dare try to claim that Obamacare, fucked up as it is, is socialism. The government forcing you to buy a product from a private company is not socialism, it's *fascism*. Socialism would be banning the private companies and forcing you to go to the government directly.)

Being an economic Marxist in 2010 is like being a Nazi in 1946. You lost. Get over it already.

***

But just because the left was wrong doesn't make the right right. Fukuyama's "End of History" merged the left and the right in America into offering different flavors of the same shit, neither of which serves Generation Zero's interests.

Think about it; what divides liberals and conservatives, Democrats and Republicans? One side is pro-gay, pro-weed, and pro-choice, while the other is pro-God, pro-prohibition and pro-life. In other words, the only discernible differences between the two are on wedge issues that don't matter. Who the fuck cares about Don't Ask, Don't Tell? Who the fuck cares about Roe v. Wade? I'd love to live in a country where I can screw 16-year olds while dropping acid without getting tossed in the slammer, but I'm not stupid. I know what's really important.

Right now, an entire generation is condemned to debt slavery because of crippling college loan debt, working menial jobs for pitiful wages, assuming they can get a job in a nation with at least 20 percent unemployment. (Don't believe the official government statistics. They're lies. My first-hand experience suggests we are slowly reaching Great Depression levels of unemployment.) Those who don't have that debt will never rise above asking *"Paper or plastic?"* for a living or sucking off the dole. The former group will marry and have children late in life, assuming they do at all, and the latter group will swell the ranks of the underclass with their careless breeding. Meanwhile, the Democrats and Republicans haven't found a bankster they won't bail out, or a stimulus package they won't pass.

My grandfather was able to marry my grandmother at age 18 and support a family of three on a factory job that didn't require so much as a high school degree. My father could support my stay-at-home mother, me and my two sisters making less than $35,000 a year in the Army possessing only a high school degree, a job he got in his twenties. It wasn't until *my* twenties that I could get a job anywhere that paid enough to allow me to live on my own, a job I basically lucked into. Even with the salary from my previous job, I couldn't get married and have kids even if I wanted to, thanks to the tens of thousands of dollars worth of loans that were a prerequisite to *get* the job to begin with. And consider that I'm one of the lucky ones. Many of my friends are still stuck pumping gas and waiting tables, and a few can't find work at all.

Generation Zero is the first generation in eons that will

have a lower standard of living then the generation preceding them.

Some of you are going to respond to this along the lines of, *"Stop whining you crybaby, your life is pretty good, you aren't entitled to anything."* Unfortunately, you've forgotten that *the U.S. economy is dependent on each generation being wealthier and more "entitled" than the last.* Think about it; who's going to fuel the engine of consumerism? Who's going to buy all that stuff the Chinese are making? Who's going to pay for your Social Security? Who's going to make sure the beauty of the white Aryan woman does not perish from the earth?

By scamming your children for a few lousy bucks, you have effectively doomed your entire civilization.

***

Is it any wonder why young people don't vote? There's no one in politics who gives a crap about their interests! Neither Republicans nor Democrats, conservatives nor liberals are different on issues that matter. Mainstream libertarians like Megan McArdle and Will Wilkinson are even bigger jokes, professional whores who've built their careers on wringing every last drop of cum out of the corporatists' cocks. The *Ludwig von Mises Institute* crowd are no different: they're the nerdy, pimply, four-eyed fat girl of the ideological world, mad because she didn't get picked to be the banksters' bottom bitch. The paleocons are a pathetic bunch of defeatists still whining about how they got screwed over by Bill Buckley two decades ago. The people who make the most sense to me nowadays are the *soi-disant* nihilists, whether they're on the right (Vijay Prozak, Brett Stevens) or the left (Mark Ames, Matt Taibbi).

What's the difference between a rapist who fucks you in the ass and runs off versus one who fucks you in the ass and cuddles you to sleep? Either way, you still have a bleeding asshole and a wad on your back.

Unbridled socialism doesn't serve Generation Zero's interests, but neither does unbridled capitalism. America has become a mirror image of the Soviet Union.

***

This is one of the ways that Generation Zero's inaction will prove more effective than action. A critical mass of people, particularly young people, who cannot or will not participate in a system will cause it to collapse. This is what happened behind the Iron Curtain in the seventies and eighties, as eastern Europe's own Generation Zero lost faith in their societies, grinding them to a halt. If the only choice is between a Turd Sandwich and a Giant Douche, fewer and fewer people will be stupid enough to play the game.

The future of the world will not be socialist, but it will not be capitalist either. We are on the verge of a great ideological shift that will upend our entire conception of the political spectrum. While I have described myself as a conservative in the past and I still sympathize with the alternative and reactionary right, my own beliefs have shifted far enough off the plantation that it doesn't make any sense for me to wear the label anymore. From now on, I'll consider each issue as it pertains to *my* best interests. I'm not going to swallow a Turd Sandwich just so I can fit in with a certain club.

And if history is any guide, the most intelligent of Generation Zero will do the same.

January 24, 2011

How Multiculturalism Killed the Socialist Dream

In the "Generation Zero" series of posts I wrote a couple months back, I recounted America's descent into a dystopia of "elementary particles" seeking to rip each other off, laying the blame at the feet of laissez-faire capitalism and cultural Marxism as enforced by the U.S.' cadre of hate-filled, zero-sum-thinking white Calvinist drones. This secular Calvinism is what separates the U.S. from the rest of the developed world, and part of why we lag in just about every quality of life indicator imaginable. It's why America still doesn't have universal healthcare (no, Obama's fascistic, souped-up version of RomneyCare doesn't count), whereas Canada implemented universal healthcare in the 1960's and Britain managed it in *the late 40's.*

Why has Calvinist go-fuck-yourself capitalism retained so much popularity in the U.S., whereas its been rejected everywhere else in the West? I've figured out the answer: it's because of black people. Latinos and Asians have played their roles too, but it's primarily because of blacks that Americans fervently oppose their own economic interests. Let me explain...

A while back, some blogger did a study showing that the whitest U.S. states were also the most left-wing. The epicenters of liberal insanity aren't multiracial states like New York, California or Florida (though they're plenty liberal), they're monoracial enclaves like Washington, Oregon and Vermont. The Green Mountain State, in particular, is the state that elected the first-ever democratic socialist to the Senate (Bernie Sanders, a lisping Brooklynite Jew with the charisma of a child molester) and the state that brought us the farce known as "gay marriage," among other things. And Vermont happens to be a pretty good place to live, with low crime rates, a high quality of life and a genial (if obnoxiously SWPL) populace.[33-34]

Meanwhile, the beating heart of American conservatism is the South, which has always had a substantial black population and now has a growing Latino population. What gives?

Up until recently in America, democratic socialism, progressivism and populism were championed by the whitest of white-bread locales: the frontier West, today's Middle America. "Prairie populism" could just as easily be called "white populism," because the prairie states and territories were overwhelmingly monoracial, characterized by high levels of social trust and community. Minnesota, Iowa, Kansas, the Dakotas: all whiter than white, all characterized by their inhabitants' politeness, friendliness, and community-oriented nature. It was in the West that progressivism flourished in the late 19th century and the West that gave us fiery populists like William Jennings Bryan, who opposed imperialism, Darwinism and the gold standard, a far cry from the hordes of pasty, obese, diabetic Tea Party protesters of today.

The same pattern holds in the rest of the West. The countries of Europe most famed for their extensive welfare states are Sweden, Norway and the other Scandinavian countries; homogeneous, conformist, high-trust societies. Canada had its own brand of prairie populism, with Medicare being the brainchild of Tommy Douglas, a preacher-turned-politician who hailed from the Western province of Saskatchewan and served as the first leader of the federal New Democratic Party.

The evidence is overwhelming: *societies with high levels of trust, openness and homogeneity—the conservative ideal—gravitate towards socialism.* Why shouldn't they? Implementing a generous social safety net is nothing more than an extension of the feeling of community that the residents of those areas already possess.

That's why universal healthcare and other socialist

bugaboos never caught on in America. The U.S. is distinguished from other Western nations by having a visible racial minority that has been a part of it since its founding: blacks. Mutual animosity between whites and blacks is why the majority whites, particularly in multiracial cities and states, are hardcore Calvinists who support in-duh-vid-you-al-izm and duh-three-mark-it; they don't want their tax dollars going to people they think they have nothing in common with and who don't like them at all. Tribalism uber alles. Massive non-white immigration has only pushed whites further into the conservative column. So if you're a conservative or libertarian, the next time you see a black person, shake their hand and thank them for (indirectly) ensuring that you'll never have to suffer the indignity of getting free healthcare.

So how has multiculturalism wrecked the electoral fortunes of socialism? *By eroding the community bonds that made socialism possible to begin with.* The minute the majority racial group realizes that they're being taxed primarily to support newcomers who are ambivalent at best to their country's traditions (and hostile at worst) is the minute they'll throw their support behind whoever promises to shut the spigot off. The more multiracial Canada, Britain and other Western nations become, the greater support right-wing parties will garner from their (white, European) natives, provided they get with the program and start opposing immigration and denouncing multiculturalism.

Tommy Douglas is dead, and the current head of the

NDP, Jack Layton, has thrown his party's white, working-class base under the bus by supporting even more non-white immigration to Canada. American middle-class white conservatives masochistically fellate vermin like the Koch brothers and other modern day robber barons, and vote for Republicans who give tax breaks to the rich and empower corporate crooks to steal even more, not that the supposedly "socialist" Democrats are any better. The American Protestant tradition that once lead William Jennings Bryan to decry the government's crucifixion of mankind on a cross of gold now belches out corpulent hypocrites like Pat Robertson who've made virtues out of usury and gluttony. Pro-white populists like Joe Bageant are the exception rather than the rule, and now he's dead too.

A cutthroat capitalist society, in which making moar monies is the only thing that matters, will inexorably become racially and ethnically heterogeneous, because there's nothing to hold the people together aside from the almighty dollar. Those business owners empowered by your libertarian economics are the ones agitating for more illegal (and legal) immigration from Latin America, you idiots! Anything to depress wages, anything to make them richer at *your* expense. And like good little piggies, you squeal on command and suck the sour milk from Mammon's teat thinking it's nectar from the gods. *Squeeeeeel!*

It's time to choose, conservatives. You can have neoliberal, free market capitalism, or you can have racial homogeneity and community. You can't have both. You'll either have to make your peace with the concept of social welfare or get used to pressing 1 for English.

Last year, I outlined a hypothetical political platform that combined liberal (a guaranteed minimum income, laws cracking down on bankster rentierism), conservative (limiting immigration, economic protectionism), and libertarian (legalized prostitution and drugs) ideas. I stand by most of it, but what does it make me? I'm not a conservative anymore, and I'm definitely not a liberal or a libertarian. Third Positionist maybe, but I don't think they're big on hookers and cocaine. Falangist? Franco's long gone, man. If your political system doesn't outlast your death, you have failed at life.

The way I increasingly see it, one side of the political spectrum is offering me a shit sandwich with a glass of Yuengling, while the other is offering up a tasty reuben with a pitcher of piss. No "lesser of two evils" drivel is going to convince me that eating shit or drinking piss is a good idea.

And if that makes me a "nihilist" or an "anarchist," then I wear the labels with pride.

April 18, 2011

The Death Rattle of the American Empire

May 1, 2011 will go down as one of the great turning points of history. One of the defining moments of a nation. Why?

It was the day that the American Empire was revealed to be completely and utterly full of shit.

Yes, I realize I'm late with this news. No, I don't care that I'm ruining everyone's patriotic buzz. America is finished as a world power. There's absolutely zero reason why anyone in the world should take us seriously anymore. In his death, Osama bin Laden showed the rest of the world that the American emperor is not only naked, but his dick is the size of a thimble.

I already commented on the absurdity of the government taking nearly a decade to kill bin Laden. That's not the worst part. I didn't bring up how bin Laden was being sheltered in a compound within spitting distance of the Pakistan Military Academy. And we already know the Pakistani government knew he was there. Pakistan, India's dirty ashtray and our supposed ally, has been playing us for fools for close to a decade, sheltering one of our greatest enemies in secret while pretending to be our best buddy and accepting our money all the time.

The government's failure to realize Osama bin Laden was chilling in a compound just outside the Pakistani equivalent of West Point is not a simple failure, nor is it a partisan failure. You can't blame Obama or Bush for this. It's a failure at every conceivable level of the American government. It's a failure of American diplomacy, a failure of American intelligence, and a failure of American military might. It's a failure from the CIA to the Pentagon to the State Department. It's an indictment of the very way America does business.

And we're supposed to be the sole remaining superpower. A light unto the world. And our government has their collective head buried so far up their ass they can see daylight out the other end. Did I mention how they keep changing the official story? We can't even get honesty from them on something as simple as the end of our country's supposed nemesis.

Oh, and now that the head of al-Qaida is dead, you think we'll be pulling out of Afghanistan now that our ostensible reason for going in has been accomplished? You think the government will recall the TSA twerps who strip-search us every time we want to fly somewhere? Yeah, right.

And none of you idiots are mad about this. Some people are uneasy about the giddy nature of Americans celebrating bin Laden's death. I say you people shouldn't be giddy, you should be *angry*. You shouldn't be celebrating, you should be *rioting*. You should be demanding accountability, demanding answers, demanding firings and investigations and commissions, demanding Obama make some heads roll in the CIA, the Pentagon, and the State Department. *You should be demanding to know the reason why your government has fucked up so badly.*

I was in high school when the towers fell. I was in my second period computer class, playing Tetris under the auspices of learning how to format tables in Microsoft Excel 2000, when the announcement came over the intercom. I don't remember the exact words, but I remember how they felt, like a knife being twisted in my stomach. The nun monitoring us scrambled to turn on the TV and set it to CNN to the sight of the towers smoking. Like millions of Americans, that image was permanently seared into my brain. The rest of the day, my teachers didn't even bother teaching; we just watched CNN, shuffling from class to class in stunned silence.

I didn't have any personal connection to September 11th: no relatives or friends who died in the attack, though there were a couple of kids in my school who did have relatives who were killed that day. If I actually did know someone who was killed on 9/11, I would be *screaming* for accountability right now. I would be *screaming* for an explanation as to why no one in the government did their fucking jobs.

As it stands, I'm sick to my stomach. Sick because of the government's clusterfuck, and sick because of *you*, my erstwhile countrymen, for not being angry at the government's clusterfuck. My fellow Americans, you make me want to vomit, for your lack of both curiosity and righteous rage.

In *The Decline of the West*, Oswald Spengler argued that the Roman Empire was not a great achievement because the Romans faced little to no resistance in their expansion. On the few occasions that they did face a power of equal strength, such as Carthage, they were almost wiped out. Indeed, Rome came within a hair's width of extermination during the Second Punic War, and was saved solely by Hannibal's screw-ups rather than their own genius or might. Rome was basically an "accidental empire."

So is America. We became the world's dominant power not because of superior military or technological power, like our predecessors the British and French did, but by virtue of being the only industrial power not reduced to cinders during World War II. We won the equivalent of the imperialist lottery. But no one wants to admit he lucked into his current position, but would rather delude himself into thinking he *earned* it through what he did. And that's what the American establishment has done: fool themselves into thinking their way of doing things earned them the title of "leader of the free world." And this mentality is the cause of every American fuck-up from Vietnam to the present day.

So don't fool yourself into thinking bin Laden's death is a triumph, because it is in fact America's greatest, most humiliating defeat. Our luck has run out.

May 5, 2011

How Capitalism *and* Socialism Became Obsolete

I've mentioned before that the defunct Moscow muckraking journal/gutter rag *the eXile* was one of my earliest intellectual influences. I'm still not sure whether I should be proud of that. I ran across *the eXile* sometime in high school under forgotten circumstances–probably just browsing the Internet aimlessly some school night–and it became my number one guilty pleasure. When nobody was looking, I was pouring across the site's articles with deer-in-headlights awe, amazed at the world that existed outside my safe and neutered America. Mark Ames' descriptions of the non-stop orgy of Russian nightlife, Matt Taibbi's exposure of the ruthless plutocrats plundering the country, John Dolan's hilariously vicious book reviews, and later, Gary Brecher's war analyses; it was beyond merely taking the red pill. It was like getting a injection of pure red, right in the main vein.

Mark Ames and Matt Taibbi were one of the greatest duos in the history of literary journalism. They complemented each other perfectly; Ames was always the superior polemicist and social critic, while Taibbi was the superior reporter and journalist. You can see this most clearly in *The eXile: Sex, Drugs and Libel in the New Russia*, the book they authored together: Taibbi's chapters are exposes on the nefarious neoliberal Westerners that were colluding with the Kremlin to loot and rape Russia in the late nineties, while Ames' chapters are about the piles of drugs he blew through and the piles of teenage girls who blew him. Ironically, ever since each left the eXile, they've each been trying to be like the other; Mark Ames has been trying to reinvent himself as a hard-hitting journalist with his imagining a Koch-led conspiracy around every corner, and Taibbi has been trying to position himself as the new Hunter Thompson with books like *The Great Derangement* taking aim at American society.

Which hasn't worked. Being a writer in the Thompsonian vein requires a certain detachment from the world, the ability to closely observe others and mock them without pity or remorse. Ames can pull this off because he's a deranged lunatic who doesn't care about anyone but himself. If you doubt this, consider how he knocked up a teenage girl and threatened to kill her if she didn't get an abortion, then wrote this about it:

> "Katya. For some reason, she still calls me. She tried pulling the oldest stunt in the book last spring. When a woman claims she can't have an abortion because her alleged doctor allegedly told her that if she does, she'll never have children again, call her bluff. Tell her you'll fly to France, pick up an RU-486 pill, fly back, and pop it in her mouth over a nice dinner at Horse and Hound. You'll accompany her to the toilet when Junior squirts out like a bowl of borscht; you'll even flick Junior's sardine eyes off her thighs, because U care.
>
> "That's when she changes her tact–she tells you she can't kill a living baby. 'Kill what?!' you demand. 'It's not a baby–it's a fucking larva!'

"'But at two months, it already has hands and feet,' she protests.

"'And a tail!' you reply. 'And sardine eyes!'

"But she won't give, so you're left with no choice: you threaten to kill her. That's what I did. And it worked. At 5:30 the next morning, Katya quietly got out of bed and left my apartment, acting like a martyr."

In contrast, Taibbi is too human and too easily empathizes with his subjects. He lacks the ability to separate himself from his surroundings and pitilessly heap on the morons he so frequently surrounds himself with. This is what makes him a talented reporter, but it makes his social commentary weak compared to Ames'. Even during the darkest segments of *The Great Derangement*, where he infiltrated groups like the Cornerstone Church (the church of televangelist and George Bush butt-buddy John Hagee) and 9/11 Truther circles, he always kept from unloading his entire clip on the idiots.

But that was in the past. With the advent of the ongoing global financial crisis, Matt Taibbi has finally hit his stride. His reports in *Rolling Stone* have been the absolute best on the Second Great Depression, the banksters driving it, and the politicians earnestly helping them rob us all. Now, he's released a new book, *Griftopia*, summarizing the "bubble economy" in just over 250 pages of reporting and analysis with a simple conclusion; *we are all completely and utterly fucked.*

I bought *Griftopia* back in January, but despite its short length, I've only been able to read it in fits and spurts because it's an utterly infuriating book. It's one thing to say that the world is fucked up beyond all repair. But to read page after page detailing, in non-technical, workmanlike prose why the world is fucked up, covering every angle conceivable, every obscure piece of legislation going back decades; it's a recipe for alcoholism and puking on your shoes. Taibbi's book demonstrates that the rot in American society and government is so deep, so entrenched within the system, that *nothing short of a revolution will get it out.* And the fact that the closest thing we can muster to a revolution is the Tea Party movement—a collection of corporate cocksuckers and mean old farts trying to steal all the gubmint bullion before they die—makes me sick.

And part of the reason why *Griftopia* is required reading is because Taibbi articulates what few have: our political ideologies are effectively obsolete. For all of conservatives hysteria' about how Obama is trying to destroy the American capitalist way of life, the fact of the matter is that *America is already a post-capitalist society.* While conservatives and liberals engage in an endless war over whether corporations or the government is more evil, at the highest echelons, the two have merged into a horrific monster busy stealing everything, including the kitchen sink, from everyone in the country. And to keep their scam going, they've created a two-tiered regime; one for themselves, and one for the little people (i.e. us):

> "There are really two Americas, one for the grifter class, and one for everybody else. In everybody-else land, the world of small businesses and wage-earning employees, the government is something to be avoided, an overwhelming, all-powerful entity whose attentions usually presage some kind of financial setback, if not complete ruin. In the grifter world, however, the government is a slavish lapdog that the financial companies that will be the major players in this book use as a tool for *making* money.
>
> "The grifter class depends on these two positions getting confused in the minds of everybody else. They want the average American to believe that what government is to him, it is also to JPMorgan Chase and Goldman Sachs. To sustain this confusion, predatory banks launch expensive lobbying campaigns against even the mildest laws reining in their behavior and rely on carefully cultivated allies in that effort, like the Rick Santellis

> on networks like CNBC. In the narrative pushed by the Santellis, bankers are decent businessmen-citizens just trying to make an honest buck who are being chiseled by an overweening state, just like the small-town hardware-store owner forced to pay a fine for a crack in the sidewalk outside his shop."

Although Taibbi never uses the term, what he's talking about is "anarcho-tyranny": anarchy for the people at the top, tyranny for everyone else. Free-market capitalism for the unwashed masses, welfare state socialism for the rich. Who actually runs the government is irrelevant: whether it's Democrats or Republicans in Congress or the White House, the true power rests with the bankers and their bootlickers, unelected star chambers like the Federal Reserve. The confusion this has engendered in the minds of ordinary Americans lies at the heart of the Tea Party, which Taibbi summarizes in his opening chapter as "fifteen million pissed-off white people sent chasing after Mexicans on Medicaid by the small handful of banks and investment companies who advertise on Fox and CNBC."

Like most leftists, Matt Taibbi is not a fan of the Tea Partiers—in a now-famous article for *Rolling Stone* published around the time *Griftopia* came out, he described them as being "full of shit"—but unlike most leftists, he empathizes with the Tea Partiers to a certain extent, describing the frustration with the government that many harbor as a result of what they've personally experienced. In the opening chapter, titled "The Grifter Archipelago; or, Why the Tea Party Doesn't Matter," he reports on the formation of a Tea Party chapter in Westchester County after the county was sued by the Obama administration for purportedly violating a mandate that municipalities receiving federal housing dollars to ensure that their populations were racially integrated:

> "This is how you get middle-class Americans pushing deregulation for rich bankers. Your average working American looks around and sees evidence of government power over his life everywhere. He pays high taxes and can't sell a house or buy a car without paying all sorts of fees. If he owns a business, inspectors come to his workplace once a year to gouge him for something whether he's in compliance or not. If he wants to build a shed in his backyard, he needs a permit from some local thief in the city clerk's office.
>
> "And, who knows, he might live in a sleepy suburb like Greenburgh where the federal government has decided to install a halfway house and a bus route leading to it, so that newly released prisoners can

have all their old accomplices come visit them from the city, leave condom wrappers on lawns and sidewalks, maybe commit the odd B and E or rape/murder."

This failure to acknowledge the "anarcho-" part of anarcho-tyranny is why the Tea Party is at best a distraction from the real issues, and at worst part of the problem. They all live in a fantasy world where it's still 1920 and America's movers and shakers are industrialists and business owners who create actual value. Conservatives and libertarians put on powdered wigs and paint Ayn Rand quotes on their protest signs, but they don't realize that the players in the bubble economy are already hardcore Randroids, most notably Alan Greenspan, who Taibbi cheerfully labels "The Biggest Asshole in the Universe" and in an entire chapter, blames him for "[making] America the dissembling mess that it is today."

Unlike *The Great Derangement*, Taibbi's previous book, *Griftopia* is light on expository narrative and heavy on reporting and research, which suits both his writing style and the subject matter. Being an outsider to economics (he freely admits in the first chapter that "[he didn't] know a damn thing about high finance" prior to the economic meltdown in 2008), his prose is direct, clear and low on jargon, meaning anyone with a college education can pick this book up and understand it from beginning to end. Taibbi swears a lot, but if you can stand *me*, you'll be able to take his dirty mouth just fine. And frankly, the sheer depth of the chicanery going on on Wall Street should be making *everyone* angry enough to curse out the gods.

Take chapter four, on the commodities bubble. The sudden spike in oil prices in mid-2008 fit perfectly into the narratives of the left and right; the left's belief that Americans consume too much, and the right's belief that environmentalist whackos are obstructing the supply of oil by blocking drilling for more oil offshore and in ANWR. Peak Oil cultists were having a field day, with their all-knowing swami Jim Kunstler furiously beating himself off to the collapse of American suburbia. Sino-supremacists were pounding their usual drum of *"oh well, the Chinese are consuming more oil, so the rest of us will have to live with higher prices."* All of them were completely wrong: as Taibbi writes, the high price of gas and oil has *nothing* to do with supply or demand and *everything* to do with the deregulation of commodities markets in the nineties, enabling Wall Street speculators to drive up prices:

> "...the whole concept of taking money from pension funds and dumping it long-term into the commodities market went completely against the spirit of the delicate physical hedger/speculator balance as envisioned by the 1936 law [the Commodity Exchange Act]. The speculator was there, remember, to serve traders on both sides. He

was supposed to buy corn from the grower when the cereal company wasn't buying that day and sell corn to the cereal company when the farmer lost his crop to bugs or drought or whatever. In market language, he was supposed to 'provide liquidity.'

"The one thing he was not supposed to do was buy buttloads of corn and sit on it for twenty years at a time. This is not 'providing liquidity.' This is actually the opposite of that. It's hoarding. [...]

[...] "What this all means is that when money from index speculators pours into the commodities markets, it makes prices go up. In the stock markets, where again there is betting both for and against stocks (long and short betting), this would probably be a good thing. But in commodities, where almost all speculative money is betting long, betting on prices to go up, this is not a good thing – unless you're one of the speculators..."

Do you conservatives and libertarians still think that financial deregulation is a good thing? You think it's perfectly acceptable for the Koch brothers to hoard massive amounts of oil to drive up prices? Hope you suckers enjoy paying $5.00 for a gallon of gas!

But we aren't even halfway to America's heart of darkness. The following chapter, "The Outsourced Highway," reveals a truly sickening consequence of high commodities prices: the sale of America itself to "sovereign wealth funds," most of which are based in Middle Eastern countries. The pattern goes like this:

1. Commodities speculators like the Koch brothers artificially inflate the price of oil to make more monies.

2. Joe Sixpack, hit with increasing gas and energy prices as a result, makes less money over the course of a year and subsequently pays less in taxes.

3. Joe's local and state governments, reliant on his tax dollars, are hit with budget shortfalls.

4. To patch the holes in their budgets, said governments sell off vital parts of their infrastructure, such as highways, to sovereign wealth funds controlled by the same people laughing to the bank with Joe Sixpack's gas money.

This is not a fucking joke. It's happening all around you. In a notable example, several years ago, the city of Chicago sold off its parking meters to one of these sovereign wealth funds, giving up a guaranteed, continuous source of income for a paltry one-time lump sum that only lasted one budget year. Not long after, meter rates skyrocketed from $0.25 an hour to $1.20 an hour, and the meter schedule went from 9am – 6pm Monday through Saturday to 8am – 9pm seven days a week. The Pennsylvania Turnpike was also very nearly sold to another sovereign wealth fund, but the deal died in the state legislature. *Conservatives and libertarians, who love to remind us of how much they love America, are defending people partially responsible for the stripping of America's sovereignty one stretch of interstate at a time.*

    And this isn't even a quarter of the territory that Taibbi covers in *Griftopia*. Did you know, for instance, that Goldman Sachs almost intentionally caused a global economic meltdown three years ago during the infamous collapse of insurance giant AIG? That the bailout organized by the Bush administration was basically blood money offered after Goldman CEO Lloyd Blankfein threw a shit fit demanding back the money Goldman was owed by AIG? (By the way, Taibbi has offered up the best description of Goldman in the universe: "a great vampire squid wrapped around the face of humanity, relentlessly jamming its blood funnel into anything that smells like money.")

    Or that Goldman was largely responsible for the dotcom bubble in the late 90's, by knowingly taking worthless Internet startups public in violation of federal law, but got off with only a slap on the wrist?

    Or that Obamacare did nothing to touch an obscure law passed in the 1940's that allows insurance companies to screw over their clients with impunity, to the extent that when the houses of former Republican Senate Majority Leader Trent Lott and former Democratic Congressman Gene Taylor were destroyed by Hurricane Katrina, their insurance claims were denied because their houses were destroyed by winds and *not* flooding? And that they had literally no recourse aside from crying about it to Congress?

There's more like that in *Griftopia*, way more. Have a bottle of Wild Turkey and a barf bucket close by when you read.

If you doubt Matt Taibbi's prognosis that things are totally hopeless, ask yourself these questions: where do we go from here, and how do we get there? It's obvious from *Griftopia's* facts that conservatism and libertarianism are utterly worthless ideologies, whose proponents preach outdated solutions, oblivious to the ground that has shifted beneath their feet. But the flipside of conservatism, liberalism, is just as equally worthless, as Taibbi shows that so-called progressives have been effectively cowed by the Obama administration into rubber-stamping every corporate giveaway he's done so far. It's not unlike what Joe Bageant wrote in 2009: "one party has no heart, the other no spine."

But there's more to it than that. Capitalists and socialists purport to be polar opposites, but the relationship between them is more like a pair of combative siblings; they claim to hate each other, but they live under the same roof and came from the same parents. Both capitalism and socialism are products of the

Industrial Revolution, predicated on the economic assumptions of that era. Socialism cannot exist without capitalism, as it feeds off of it like a barnacle, flooding in to solve the problems of poverty and suffering that it creates but its proponents refuse to acknowledge. Neither can be effectively adapted to a post-industrial age, where the bulk of wealth is not held by value creators but by glorified gamblers who play a never-ending game of roulette with peoples' piggybanks, when even the proles are visibly divorced from the products of their labor.

For that matter, how are we supposed to fix the problem when *everyone* from Wall Street to Washington is in on the scam? When the people who are being fucked up the ass everyday either don't care or actually worship their rapists? What's the point of pushing for more regulation when the supposed regulators are in bed with the people they're supposed to be regulating? Who is the bigger degenerate, the cad doing the fucking, or the whore who lets herself be fucked?

There is no hope. America is beyond redemption. The only option is to cut your ties and get out before the excrement hits the oscillating blades. Or start learning how to work a guillotine, for the inevitable mass executions. If you haven't already washed your hands of America, your life should be dedicated to freeing yourself before the end comes. And believe you me, it's coming.

In the meantime, buy this book, *now*.

August 2, 2011

In Defense of Juggalos

The alt-right has met the Juggalo phenomenon and the results have been predictably ugly. In response to the mini-documentary *American Juggalo*, Dennis Mangan writes:

> "The video on the Juggalos shows us a motley, highly unappealing collection of the most idiotic, most pierced morons that one could imagine. None of them seem to be able to use any other adjective but f**kin' or m*****f**kin', nor to say anything that makes much sense. All of them appear to be on massive quantities of drugs and/or alcohol. (One scene shows a bunch of them sniffing whipped cream propellant. [I forget what that's called.]) Virtually all them are fat and don't mind displaying their mounds of flesh. One of the most repellant aspects of the Juggalos is the way they have themselves convinced that they comprise some sort of brotherhood, that they receive a form of acceptance from each other that 'normal' society has somehow denied them, when in reality, if push came to shove, they look like they'd be running for the hills to save their sorry asses.[35-36]

WHAT'S WRONG WITH THE WORLD

Picking on retards is so much fun! Next up for the alt-right: tripping blind people, pushing old ladies down staircases and playing 52-card pickup with Down syndrome kids.

Yes, I'm defending the Juggalos. I'm defending them because I admire them, in a way. In a dying world full of moronic subcultures, from color-blind couch-surfers gentrifying poor neighborhoods with Daddy's bank account to revolting nerd shut-ins obsessing over a little girls' cartoon, Juggalos are one of the more positive and wholesome cliques out there. In sneering at them for their apparent stupidity, Mangan and his cohorts are no better than the SWPLs they claim to hate.

Before I get into the heart of the matter though, I want to state that I am *not* defending the Juggalos' lack of aesthetics or the quality of Insane Clown Posse's songs. Even by the basement-level standards of rap, ICP is terrible. Their lyrics are stupid and poorly written, their delivery is amateurish, and their stage presence is underwhelming (which is part of why they have such elaborate live concerts). And of course, Mangan is right in pointing out that the Juggalos themselves look like *Idiocracy* extras with their piercings, tats, spiked hair and general dumbness. That's not the point.

I have something of a different perspective on this issue, as I'm not too far removed from the cultural milieu from which Juggalos spring. I and my sisters are decadent urbanites, but my dad is a true redneck from a long line of rednecks: country music lovin', small-town, working class rednecks. Uneducated and uncouth, but hardworking and dependable. And, up until about forty years ago, being a uneducated redneck wasn't so bad. You could make a respectable living without a college degree, and while you weren't necessarily respected by the culture at large, you weren't endlessly denigrated either. A couple of my cousins are Juggalos (although they aren't freaks), and while I didn't mock them for it, I didn't understand ICP's appeal either; until now.

One of the recurring motifs of the alt-right is that whiteness and white people are shamed and shunned by the government and by society at large. And no subset of whites has gotten the level of hatred and disdain from society that the working class and underclass get every day. While the black and white underclasses have many similar problems, there are also many palpable differences between them, and this is frequently forgotten by folks who lump them together so they can criticize black misbehavior while dodging the "racist" label (I include myself in that group).

The black underclass is exalted and defended by both the black intelligentsia and white liberals. Their virtues are blown out of proportion by the media while their vices are ignored or excused. They have various interest groups and political caucuses dedicated to representing their interests. They are constantly told that their problems are not their fault, that they are being wronged and oppressed by forces outside their control, and they are entitled to everything they're getting and more. As a result of all this, underclass blacks have a very high opinion of themselves, which is constantly borne out by studies showing that blacks have higher self-esteem than all other American racial groups.[37]

This is a big part of why I can't take seriously anyone who tries to excuse flash mobs and Blacks Behaving Badly as purely a response to black economic impoverishment. Yes, economic impoverishment is part of it, but if it was the sole reason, we'd be seeing blacks target hedge fund managers and looting rich suburbs. Instead, they're beating and robbing random white people who've done nothing to them. Liberals have imputed poor blacks with an unwarranted sense of entitlement, and *the flash mobbers view themselves as enforcers beating down whites who are insufficiently obeisant to their new masters.* (Note that flash mobs were nonexistent before a black man was elected president.)

The white underclass doesn't have any of this. Nobody praises their virtues or downplays their sins, and no one fights for their interests in the halls of power. On the contrary, poor whites are the most hated group in America. They are depicted as ignorant, racist bigots who are the root of all the country's ills. The wholesale destruction of blue-collar work by free trade and illegal immigration has made it near-impossible for most of them to make a respectable living. Entertainers who wouldn't dare criticize black people feel free to whale on white trash. Phonyfuck SWPLs will pay double for "fair trade" coffee that benefits some poor brown subsistence farmer halfway across the world, but they don't give so much as a thought to poor people in their own country who actually look like them. Conservatives and libertarians are equally callous because of their Calvinist capitalist creed that preaches that if you're suffering in poverty, It's Always Your Fault. The white underclass truly are America's untouchables.

And apparently, even the people who consider themselves "pro-white" are eager to join in on the bash-fest.

This is why I sympathize with Juggalos: because beneath the creepy makeup, the cussing and the buckets of blood, Insane Clown Posse preach a message of morality and hope that poor whites desperately need. The alt-right, like all conservatives, are seemingly incapable of digging past the surface to see this message. Let's take the lyrics of ICP's earlier songs, "Halls of Illusions."

> "Back to reality, your son's on crack
> And your daughter's got nut stains on her back
> And they both fuckin' smell like shit
> And live in the gutter and sell crack to each other
> When they were kids, you'd beat 'em and leave 'em home
> And even whip 'em with the cord of a telephone
> And that reminds me man hey ya gotta call
> Watch your step to Hell... it's a long fall!"

Get past the swearing and the violence and what's this song about? It's a denunciation of domestic violence and child abuse! Not exactly the sort of thing you'd expect a couple of evil clowns to rap about.

Or let's talk about "Miracles." All the snobs who pointed and laughed at that song–admittedly much of it deserved–failed to notice that it was a rap song about family, enjoying nature, and being a good person. Considering that the popular conception of rap is that's a negative music genre about death, murder, crime and sex, and that most "positive" rap songs are tributes to black victimology, this isn't something to scoff at.

Or consider that the members of ICP, Violent J and Shaggy 2 Dope, have explicitly stated that the hidden message of their music is to follow God, and that *their albums are parables warning against the consequences of immoral behavior.* Granted, they consider "racism" part of that immoral behavior, but so does almost everyone else.

For that matter, when you're watching the *American Juggalo* video, take note of what you *don't* see. You don't see any cops. You don't see any fighting. You don't see bloodied, beaten revelers being hauled into ambulances. For all their partying and drug use, the Juggalos are a well-behaved and peaceable group. Contrast this to black hip-hop festivals and expos, which always seem to end in a full-scale riot. Hell, in one scene you can even see these "worthless human beings" cleaning up after themselves, scooping up their trash and putting it into trash bags.

"*But Ferd,*" you may protest, "*everyone is against child abuse! How is that some kind of great moral message? Herp derp!*" Well, of course it's not a great moral message to *you*, Mr. Middle Class Intact Family. ICP's music isn't intended for *you*. The Juggalo subculture is not intended for *you* (though they wouldn't turn you down either). It's for the kid who grew up in a trailer park living on food stamps with his single mom. It's for the unemployed high school grad who joined the army and served a tour in Iraq because she couldn't get a decent-paying job anywhere else. It's for the kid who got beaten every day by his alcoholic father. *ICP is a voice for America's most ignored and scapegoated social group: the white underclass.*

That's why I sympathize with the Juggalos. Yes, they are idiots. Yes, they are slovenly and look like freaks. Yes, the music they like is eardrum rape. But while they may be dopes, they're sincere and kindhearted dopes. And for a group that's been disowned and screwed over by society at large and left to their own devices, they've done surprisingly well for themselves.

And arguably, they've doing better than the frauds who shit on them.

October 3, 2011

#OccupyWallStreet and the Revolt Against American Gerontocracy

It was five o'clock on a rainy afternoon when I showed up to help stick it to Wall Street.

Befitting the Salt City's nature as an inland knockoff of New York City, #OccupySyracuse was being held at Perseverance Park, a little spit of green resting on the front yard of the local Chase bank. I would have loved to have seen the real thing, but a business trip demanded I spend the next week in the Central New York area, so I took what I could get. I parked two blocks away from the protest, paid up for an hour's worth of parking, and hoofed it to join the march.

It wasn't hard to find #OccupySyracuse: about a hundred some-odd protesters were gathered at the corner of West Fayette and South Salina, wielding anti-war and anti-corporate signs. The actual encampment was by a bus stop, a half-dozen Coleman tents guarded by three ramshackle stalls, their occupants handing out surplus protest signs. The crowd was divided 50-50 between twentysomething college students and middle-aged agitators from the Syracuse Peace Council, the local leftist protest group. You could tell the people who were camping out from those who had just showed up for the march from the smell; the campers were edging towards that peculiar mix of B.O., urine and feces that homeless people have. God knows where they were going to the bathroom.

I had come prepared, wielding a poster not much larger than a piece of printer paper reading "WE ARE THE 99%" scratched out with a Sharpie, using a spare ruler as a handle. As I joined the hubbub, a woman my mom's age holding up a banner reading "THE ONLY WAY FORWARD IS SOCIALISM" complimented me on my sign, saying "We need every one we can get!" Even with my rejection of libertarian economics, being around this crowd made me feel like a black man at a KKK rally. In the back of my mind, my long-repressed paranoia bubbled up: *"They're gonna find out who you are! 'FASCIST! RACIST! MISOGYNIST! STONE HIM!'"*

Then I heard a roar from off to the right: "MIC CHECK!"

With that, the crowd moved to assemble in front of a bunch of steps, presumably where the organizers of this whole thing were gathering. A pierced-lipped fruit with a Daffy Duck lisp took center stage.

"THANK YOU ALL–"

"THANK YOU ALL–" the crowd responded. So this was the idiotic "human mic" that everyone with a clue was making fun of.

"–FOR COMING TO–"

"–FOR COMING TO–"

"–OCCUPY SYRACUSE!"

"–OCCUPY SYRACUSE!"

Barely five minutes in and already I was resisting the urge to burst into laughter. After about another minute of call-and-response shouting, the fruit yielded the stage to a guy with a name tag that read "Igor," who looked straight out of Central Casting–"hairy, ursine, menacing Russian"–to explain that we would be marching down Jefferson St. to Columbus Circle, up Montgomery to City Hall, and back to the park on Washington. Then a cute chick wearing a fur-lined jacket and a *tres chic* Castro army cap took the stage to give us important safety instructions–"STAY ON THE SIDEWALKS! STAY OFF THE STREETS!"–as the lemming crowd repeated everything they were told in unison. In between each speaker, a long-haired pasty Rastafarian-type belted out "MIC CHECK!" to the audience.

After the chick was done talking, we filed into procession as the march got underway. As did the chanting.

"WE ARE–"

"–THE 99%!"

Swept up by the fervor, I joined in the chanting, waving my sign with one hand and pumping my other fist.

"BANKS GOT BAILED OUT–"

"–WE GOT SOLD OUT!"

"GET UP, GET DOWN–"

"–THERE'S REVOLUTION IN THIS TOWN!"

By the time we got to "HEY HEY, HO HO, CORPORATE GREED HAS GOT TO GO!" I was too consumed by what Mark Twain called "the inborn human instinct to imitate" to even snicker at the cliched nature of it all.

We rounded the corner at Columbus Circle and passed the cathedral and soup kitchen, trailed by onlookers filming everything on their cell phones and flip cams. As I goose-stepped with the marchers, I could feel my socks sliding down my feet. My boots chafed the hair on my ankles with every step. Overhead, the rain's subtle plinking intensified, the swollen storm clouds blotting out the setting sun. The rain was weakening the cheap packing tape attaching the handle to the sign, which was taking on the consistency of a used tissue.

At the corner of Montgomery and Washington, with City Hall across the street, we stopped suddenly. Igor, who'd been leading the march alongside the pierced-lipped fruit, suddenly yelled out:

"LET'S SEND THE MAYOR A MESSAGE!"

The "human mic" repeated that one, but everyone was audibly winded from bellowing out every hackneyed protest line in existence for the past half-hour. Igor was nonplussed. "I CAN'T HEAR YOU!"

"LET'S SEND THE MAYOR A MESSAGE!"

"NO HYDROFRACKING!"

With this one, I was snapped out of my mob-induced stupor. For those who don't know, hydrofracking (hydraulic fracturing) is a big issue in the Northeast, as the presence of untapped natural gas veins could potentially jump start the stalled local economy. It's facing stiff opposition due to fears that the fracking process pollutes drinking water, as well as fears that hydrofracking increases the prevalence of earthquakes, among other things. Neighboring GOP-dominated Pennsylvania has gone crazy for hydrofracking, but it's more or less stalled in New York, with the Republican state Senate and Democrat governor Andrew Cuomo in favor and the Democratic Assembly against it.

In other words, the hydrofracking issue has jack-all to do with Wall Street or banksters. I wasn't wholly unsurprised about this hijacking, but it still annoyed me.

The march started up again, and I resumed chanting with the rest of the crowd, albeit less enthusiastically. Returning to Perseverance Park, we filed back over to the steps for a post-march assembly, where anyone who wanted to make a speech could. Igor declared, "I CAME HERE... ALL THE WAY FROM RUSSIA... ON VACATION!", the fruit held a moment of silence for that marine who'd been smacked in the head with a flashbang at #OccupyOakland, and another neo-hippie headcase gave an impassioned anti-war speech that seemed quaintly dated. "ANN MARIE BUERKLE [local Republican

Congresswoman] ONLY CARES ABOUT YOU BEFORE YOU'RE BORN... ONCE YOU'RE BORN, YOU'RE SCREWED!" In between each speaker, the white Rasta repeated "MIC CHECK!" as the rain poured down. Was this really necessary?

Finally, after every deadbeat and trust-fund case in the city was done pounding the pulpit, the fruit came on to thank us all for coming and invited us to the general assembly at 6:30. I had planned to stick around and ask some questions, but I was already sick of these idiots, tired of the crummy weather, and my parking time was almost up. I trudged back to my car, waterlogged sign in hand, seriously contemplating a donation to Ann Marie Buerkle's reelection campaign.

***

#OccupyWallStreet is stupid, annoying and insufficient. It's also necessary.

I hate protests and I hate the people who go them. Before I marched through the streets of Syracuse with a couple hundred smelly leftists, the last protest I'd ever gone to was way back in college, and that was only to appease my then-girlfriend, who was an anti-globalization activist. The easiest way to turn Boobus Americanus into a frothing-at-the-mouth conservative is to take him to a leftist march. The people who go to protests are so inherently contemptible that it's impossible to side with them even if you agree with them on some things. I wasn't too surprised, for example, to hear that some idiot at #OccupyBurlington decided to off himself in public.

But #OccupyWallStreet is different. The various copycat Occupy protests notwithstanding, the original protest at Zuccotti Park is a genuine unplanned, organic outpouring of populist anger, *not* a Soros/Obama Astroturfing operation as the Glenn Beck conspiracy types claim. More importantly, #OccupyWallStreet is part of the rise of Generation Zero, the Millennials. And while I'm not going to claim that America is the same as Mubarak's Egypt, the fundamental problem facing both Western and Middle Eastern youth is the same: their future has been stolen from them by their parents and grandparents. Take a look at this *Pew* study showing that young people have been disproportionately hurt by the current recession if you don't believe me.[38]

And by the way, all those people who are browbeating Occupiers for believing themselves to be above flipping burgers and doing manual labor? Ever wonder where they got that idea from? It was from *you:*

> "But here's the thing: Those Baby Boomers who started this 'you don't want to flip burgers' bullshit *did flip burgers.* Or roof houses, or mine coal, or wax porn stars' assholes. And that wasn't something to be ashamed of back then — that was

322

the era before you needed a bachelor's degree to get a job waiting tables (but more on that in a moment). But at some point between my grandfather's time and now, getting your hands dirty became something to be ashamed of. My generation perpetuated that. We made it socially unacceptable to:

"A) Do any job that requires sweat and/or a uniform.

"B) Work 70-hour weeks to get ahead.

"So if you don't do either of those things, what's left? Getting an education and waiting for a good job in your field. But now, when we catch you doing that, we mock you and tell you to go flip burgers. And that's bullshit. We told you your whole lives that those jobs were for idiots and failures. You think you're too good for those jobs *because that's what we've been fucking telling you since birth.*"[39]

Hey oldsters, you going senile? Forget things easily? *The #OccupyWallStreet folks are mad because we did everything you fucking told us to do and we got NOTHING out of it.* And now that it's obvious that you were force-feeding us lies all the way from the crib, you think you can get on your pulpit and scold us like you had nothing to do with it. *"Um, um, it was those big government lib-ruls who said all that! Now get off my lawn kids, I have to cash my Social Security check!"*

Or maybe you'll claim that you had it rough and we're just a bunch of whiners. *"Back when I was your age, I worked five jobs to get through college and I turned out fine!"* But I'll bet you didn't have to deal with illegal Mexicans competing with you for those jobs, making whole sectors of the economy off-limits to white Americans. Or affirmative action. Or outsourcing, or downsizing, or any other of the retarded economic policies fostered and facilitated by both the Republicans and Democrats.

A few people around the 'sphere have chastised #OccupyWallStreet for focusing like a laser on the crimes of Wall Street and not enough on the crimes of Washington. I agree to a certain extent. The problem isn't the banks or the government, it's the people running them: the Baby Boomers, the most narcissistic generation in American history. Our ultimate enemy isn't socialism, capitalism or democracy, but *gerontocracy*. I've already covered how the Tea Party is nothing but a Boomer advocacy group designed to protect senior entitlements like Social Security by liquidating every other part of the government, but a recent report from *Yahoo!* articulates just how avaricious and amoral the Boomers are:

"Don't expect a big inheritance from your boomer parents — even if they are rich. Less than half of millionaire boomers say that leaving money for their kids is a priority for them, according to a 2011 U.S. Trust study. But 64% of boomers say they plan to use their money to travel and more than one in three say they want to use it to 'have fun.'

"Boomers didn't get this idea from their elders: Older retirees are seven times more likely than boomers to believe they owe their children an inheritance, according to a survey of high net worth individuals published in the Journal of Financial Planning. By contrast, "boomers are more concerned with leaving behind things like values and keepsakes," says Katie Libbe, the vice president of consumer insights for Allianz Life, the company that conducted the survey."[40]

Yep, this generation of self-centered vampires thinks they can attack the kids at #OccupyWallStreet for being self-centered. I don't think "chutzpah" is a strong enough word to describe the wretchedness of the Baby Boomers, so I'll settle for a visual metaphor instead; a mad old fart eating his own children to prolong his pathetic life.

This is why #OccupyWallStreet is necessary: it's the first major backlash against every scam the Gray Mafia have pulled in the past fifty years. An inarticulate and idiotic backlash, but a backlash nonetheless. It's the Baby Boomers' chickens come home to roost. After lying, cheating and stealing their way through life, they thought they could sit back and expect their children to selflessly sacrifice for them like nothing had changed. It doesn't work that way, gramps. Bad faith begets bad faith, and people who've been wronged have long memories.

This isn't uncritical praise of Generation Zero. Me and my compadres really are a bunch of selfish layabouts. But as with most of human history, this isn't a case of good vs. evil: it's bad vs. worse. The underemployed left-wing dolts occupying Wall Street are bad, but the old farts running Goldman Sachs and the U.S. government are worse, far worse. And in a gunfight between a young'un and an oldster, put your money on the one that doesn't have arthritis.

The clock is ticking, Boomers. Your time is almost up.

November 14, 2011

America's Four Hundred Year War Against the Catholic Church

At the new *Orthosphere* blog, Proph muses on liberals' sudden seething hatred of the Church, as shown by Obama's failed attempt to force Catholic institutions to provide free birth control to their employees:

"Things are a little worse than that, though. I've noticed a pronounced radicalization among my leftist friends since the start of Obama's war on the Church. They *really* want it beaten, subjugated, and destroyed, and they don't care what absurd and evil lies they have to manufacture. Perhaps it's just that their latent insanity has been stirred to action by an opportunity to express it with social approval; more likely, it's that people of average intellect are basically sheep and that the nature of American identity politics is such that they will *always* be radicalized by the leaders of the parties they follow. (Remember the remorseless, unprincipled shriveling of nearly every mainstream "conservative" in America during the Bush administration?) The fangs have come out. Give it another four years and they may well be dripping with blood."[41]

To this I ask, *"Where have YOU been, man?"* Americans and the American government have *always* been hostile to the Church. Obama and his supporters are just the latest manifestation of a centuries-long trend. Anti-Catholicism in America predates this country's founding because anti-Catholicism is a fundamental plank of America's ruling ideology: Calvinism, or more accurately, Puritanism.

A few people have critiqued my description of Calvinism as the source of America's ills, even though I'm far from the first person to argue this: I figured it out from reading Mencius Moldbug, who famously characterized modern America as a "Puritan theocracy."[42] Moldbug himself cobbled this thesis together from a couple dozen sources, including George McKenna's *The Puritan Origins of American Patriotism*, an excellent summation of the whole problem. McKenna writes in the Introduction:

> "In the eighteenth century, the heirs of the Puritans played a key role in the American Revolution. 'Puritanism,' notes the religious historian Mark Noll, 'is the only colonial religious system that modern historians take seriously as a major religious influence on the Revolution.' In the generations following the Revolution, Congregationalists and Presbyterians from New England carried their campaigns of evangelical Calvinism into the upper Midwest and other areas of the Puritan diaspora, and by the 1830s their voluntary organizations of evangelization and moral reform had combined budgets larger than that of the federal government. They brought with them their distinctive brand of 'moralistically inflected republicanism.' 'Wherever

you go, you will be a polis': the watchword of the ancient Greek city-states as they created new colonies could also apply to the Puritan polis, whose people brought with them their own matter-of-fact assumptions of moral rectitude and cultural superiority. A writer in the proslavery United States Democratic Review in 1855 paid rueful tribute to the Puritans in language that almost mirrored the motto of the ancient Greeks. Referring to what he called 'the New-England hive' established by the Puritans, he wrote, 'No class of people are so prone to emigration... But wherever they go they are sure to combine together, and act in concert for the furtherance of their own peculiar opinions and interests.' Harriet Beecher Stowe said the same thing but more admiringly: 'New England has been to these United States what the Dorian hive was to Greece. It has always been a capital country to emigrate from, and North, South, East, and West have been populated largely from New England, so that the seed-bed of New England was the seed-bed of this great American Republic, and of all that is likely to come of it.' Despite sometimes fierce resistance from Catholics and Midwesterners, by the outset of the Civil War 'the Puritanization of the United States' had become a fact of life throughout most of the North, and the war itself marked the beginning of its century-long march into the heart of the South."

This next statement is going to blow your mind, so make sure you're sitting down. Ready? Sure? Here we go:

Puritanism is inherently progressive.

This is important, so I'll repeat it:

Puritanism is inherently progressive.

One of the Great Lies of our time is that Puritanism and Calvinism were right-wing or conservative in any way, shape or form. It betrays a basic ignorance of American history. The Puritans were the free-love, hippie-dippie pinko commies of their day. The whole reason they settled in America was not because of "religious persecution," as the revisionists would argue, but because they felt that the Protestant Reformation had not gone far enough in England. The Puritans recognized that Anglicanism was (and is) nothing more than ersatz Catholicism, with the Queen replacing the Pope, and they sought to extirpate all Catholic influences from their lives. Even after formal Puritanism faded away, the attitudes and beliefs it inculcated stayed behind, and define America as we know it. The American Revolution was birthed in Calvinist New England; virtually every progressive social movement in American history, from abolitionism to the temperance movement to the civil rights movement, either began in New England or had significant support there. Which state was the first to legalize gay marriage again? Oh, that's right, *Massachusetts*.

America's history is the history of Calvinists exterminating everyone who posed a threat to them. The first major example of this is the Civil War, as McKenna notes above. Aside from their mutual hatred of Catholics, the neo-Roman, Anglican South always stood in opposition to the Calvinist North, always seeking out new lands to colonize. The Civil War was a decades-long cultural conflict coming to a head, a war the Confederacy had lost long before Fort Sumter; the Northerners had greater numbers and a superior, industrial economy, which is how abolitionist Abraham Lincoln was able to win election without carrying a single Southern state. The civil rights movement was the culmination of this process. The Calvinization of the South that began under Reconstruction ended when *it* ended, leaving Southerners only half-assimilated. The end of Jim Crow and the Civil Rights Act of 1964 was the final bullet in the head of Old Dixie. While the origins of the movement were with Southern blacks, anyone who thinks that Martin Luther King et al. would have gotten anywhere without massive support from Northern whites is insane. The South won't rise again because there *is* no South anymore, just a neutered extension of Yankeedom impotently waving around the Stars and Bars every April 12th.

Anti-Catholic hysteria is an ever-present reality of American history; just check any textbook. The Puritans historically painted themselves as victims of Papist oppression, always on watch for a Jesuit army invading and dragging them all back into the fold. It was totally ridiculous—nobody in the Vatican cared about a bunch of Protestant weirdos eking out a miserable existence in a godforsaken spit of mud like Massachusetts—but since when did rationality stop the Crowd? If you examine anti-Catholic prejudice in the U.S. throughout the ages, you'll notice a common thread: the Protestants always wrapped themselves in the cloak of victimhood. The Know-Nothings and other anti-immigrant movements of the 19th century claimed Catholics would be a fifth column; John F. Kennedy was savaged in the 1960's because it was feared that he'd be taking marching orders from the Pope. No matter how weak, divided or nonexistent Catholics were, American Calvinists have always lived in fear of the big bad Catholic Church coming to oppress them. This Calvinist cult of victimhood continues all the way to the present, as shown in an anti-Catholic poster Proph dredged up that reads "NO, YOU CAN'T DENY WOMEN THEIR BASIC RIGHTS AND PRETEND IT'S ABOUT YOUR 'RELIGIOUS FREEDOM.'"

No matter how you feel about the birth control issue, you have to agree that this is ridiculous. The Catholic Church resisted a government-enforced mandate to violate their religious beliefs, and *they're* the boogeyman here? Am I just out of touch? Did

Catholics gain a monopoly on the job market when I wasn't looking? Are there legions of women who have no choice but to work for Catholic institutions if they don't want to starve?

Up until relatively recently, anti-Catholic sentiment on the left was suppressed for two reasons:

1. Catholic immigrant groups, mainly the Irish and Italians, formed an integral part of FDR's New Deal Coalition.
2. Catholics themselves are largely left-wing on economic issues.

Recently though, as the descendants of Catholic immigrants have assimilated into the white middle class, Catholics have progressed from being a reliable Democratic constituency to a swing bloc; Bush won the majority of Catholics in 2004.[43] As liberals abandoned their commitment to the working class back in the early 90's with the rise of libertarians like Bill Clinton and Mario Cuomo, social progressivism (abortion, gay marriage etc.) is now the organizing principle of the American left, and the Catholic Church stands against this. Much has been written about how Obama's reelection strategy explicitly involves disregarding the middle- and working-class whites in favor of wealthy SWPLs, blacks and Latinos (for whom race trumps religion), and his throwing Catholics under the bus is part of this.[44] Liberals tolerated the Papists only so long as they were useful; now that they're no longer willing to shut up and blindly vote blue, they're out of the club.

No, there's nothing new about the left's hatred of Catholics; this is just a new battle in an old war. The liberals frothing at the mouth over the contraception issue are the heirs of the Know-Nothings and every anti-Catholic movement in American history going back to the Mayflower. Instead of stereotyping Catholics as dirty degenerates with too many kids (read: they have sex more than once a month), lazy (read: they enjoy life and don't want to slave all day for a pittance), idol-worshipping (read: they appreciate beauty), and disloyal (read: they have greater principles then mindlessly worshipping the state), they rage about how Catholics violate today's orthodoxy of pseudohedonism and non-judgmentalism. I say "pseudohedonism" because liberals only tolerate hedonism along certain approved paths. They claim to be for freedom until you want to have a cigarette, buy a handgun, or be a man and not a wussy, feminized doormat. *"Do what you want, until you make choices I personally disapprove of."*

Evangelical Christians don't inspire the deranged, manic hatred in leftists that Catholics do because evangelicalism is the moderate wing of American Calvinism; America has no conservatives, just liberals and libertarians (right-liberals). Evangelicals have the gall to call themselves "conservative" when they bend to every whim of secular society, whether it's their Mammonite worship of capitalism (*"God helps those who help themselves"*) or their chosen art form, Christian "rock." To liberals, "conservative" Protestants are the equivalent of annoying cousins; they may not like them, but they're still family. Catholics are foreigners, outsiders, the enemy, good only to be leashed or shot.

That's the sick joke here: liberals may praise rationality to the skies and profess their atheism, but they are nothing more than Puritans, working to turn America and the world into Calvin's fabled "city of glass." God may be dead, but Christianity lives on.

February 21, 2012

III

THE TAO OF FERD

When Rebellion is the Only Option

It's been a month since I started this blog, and a few people have remarked on my chosen name for it, *In Mala Fide*, and the fact that "mala fide" translates into English as "bad faith." None of them seem to think very highly of my choice. *In Mala Fide* has a deeper meaning beyond being a snappy blog title: I didn't choose it at random, but after a considerable bit of thought.

Recently, the blogger Kamal S. posted an essay entitled "You Can't Survive Without Being A Rebel." An excerpt:

> "Just the other day, a really fine example of the Contemporary American Illiterate (Illiteratus Americanus Contemperaneous) accused me of being a natural born rebel.

"While this accusation didn't exactly strike at the center of my sense of self worth nor drive me to contemplate suicide – it did cause me to begin thinking about what causes individuals to rebel against society at large.

"What immediately struck me is how difficult it would be to survive *without* being a rebel. If one were to attempt to survive by following the rules of society as officially stated, the natural evolutionary laws would give the offender quite a punishment."[1]

The essay goes on to describe how the rules of contemporary American society effectively force people to break them in order to stay afloat, using college sexual harassment codes, our Kafka-esque tax laws, and violent crime statistics as examples. It concludes with this:

"If you want to reproduce, succeed economically, or merely stay alive in modern America, you *must* become a rebel. Your other option is to be a meek virgin who spends all of his or her time indoors (afraid to go out, for fear of being robbed, raped, assaulted or murdered) filling out those 4,000 pages of IRS forms and sending your money away

> to a government which can't protect you from anyone but yourself."

We all know that society is sick and civilization is waning, but how is an individual supposed to react to this? Once you've learned that following the rules is a sure way to get screwed over, you can't go back to being Boobus Americanus (to borrow from Mencken). Western civilization, in its politically correct, feminized state, demands that you bend over and grab your ankles in order to be a good citizen, and breaking the rules will earn you the contempt of society at large: and yet, breaking the rules is the only way to survive. There's no proper ethical code in existence that requires people to submit to tyrants who seek to bind them in chains. Much like how the Christians of the Roman Empire refused to worship the emperor, sane Westerners are refusing to worship the various false idols that comprise our dying culture. Running on the corporate hamster wheel to pay off six figures of student loans that you racked up so you could get that job on the hamster wheel to begin with, spending what little discretionary income you have left on pointless objects you don't need, and working towards being unhappily married to an irritable sow who will divorce you at the drop of a doughnut and move halfway across the country with the kids out of spite: no one would call that a sane or sensible way to spend your life.

When the pseudonymous *Asia Times Online* columnist Spengler unmasked himself last April, he stated his reason for choosing that nom de plume was as a joke: the name of the German scholar who wrote *The Decline of the West* appropriated for a column in an Asian newspaper. A bad joke, but it has a point. The name of this blog, *In Mala Fide*, can be thought of as a jab in that vein. The moral configuration of Western society, as chronicled on this blog and others, requires its best citizens to rebel, to go against the grain, to behave *in mala fide* in order to secure their own fortunes.

Take the concept of game, for instance. Conventional wisdom holds that women want nice guys who will respect them, dote on them, and treat them like princesses. Any guy who tries this, however, will end up getting LJBF'ed by every girl he wants to bang. On the other hand, complete assholes often find themselves up to their chins in vaj. The conventional wisdom of dating and courtship is wrong, so wrong that an entire online community sprung up seeking to uncover methods of seduction that work. Boobus Americanus opposes game, denounces it as manipulative and dehumanizing, and the fact that it works doesn't cross his mind at all. If you practice game in your personal life, you are, according to the dictates of modern society, behaving *in mala fide*. Members of the MGTOW movement, who reject the values of our corrupt culture, are another group of individuals behaving *in mala fide*.

Behaving in good faith according to the principles of our degenerate civilization will inevitably lead to your demise. It is not immoral to behave in bad faith in regards to such a society;

you have no obligations to a culture that only seeks to harm you and keep you down. Rebelling is the only sane and moral option in an insane and immoral world.

August 19, 2009

The Provincialism of Modern Novelists

A few years back, I was waiting at the dentist's office, thumbing through a copy of *Time*, when I came across an article entitled "Who's the Voice of this Generation?" The author was lamenting the fact that not one of the "young novelists" writing today is representative of the attitudes and neuroses of this generation. As is the nature of modern journalism, this reporter was trained to ignore the truth in front of her face. The reason that not one of these "young novelists" can claim to be the voice of this generation is because all of them are nauseatingly parochial in thought and style.

Anyone involved in the world of literature is aware of the old cliché, "Write what you know." There's an unstated implication in that phrase; *make sure what you know is interesting*. The best novelists had no trouble grasping this concept. Ernest Hemingway only wrote what he knew, but the breadth and depth of his life experiences–fighting in World War I, living in Paris during the Roaring Twenties, reporting on the Spanish Civil War–was a large part of what made his novels compelling. Louis-Ferdinand Céline's *Journey to the End of the*

Night (as well as his other works) was a glorified retelling of his experiences during WWI and later working in colonial French West Africa and the U.S. The list of great novelists who infused their writing with their varied life experiences is endless: F. Scott Fitzgerald, George Orwell, Jack Kerouac, Hunter S. Thompson, Charles Bukowski, Tim O'Brien, etc.

No more. Today's crop of popular novelists, having missed the subtext, are "writing what they know," the likes of which is small enough to fit into a shot glass. Let's take Jhumpa Lahiri as an example. Lahiri has been widely acclaimed for her depiction of Bengali immigrants in the U.S. in her works. Beyond the fact that the "immigrant adjusting to life in a new land" trope is so burned out at this point its unbearable, Lahiri is incapable of writing anything beyond her dull life as an American of Bengali descent. Her first book, *Interpreter of Maladies*, was about Indian immigrants acclimating themselves to American culture. Lahiri's novel, *The Namesake*, beyond being poorly written and having improbable plot elements (Indians nicknaming their child "Gogol?" Uh-huh), was about the exact same thing: Indian immigrants acclimating themselves to American culture. Her most recent short story collection, *Unaccustomed Earth*, is about–you guessed it–Indian immigrants acclimating themselves to American culture. The cherry on top of Lahiri's solipsism sundae is that she has zero desire to write about anything else:

"But Tolstoy wrote about Napoleon. *Unaccustomed*

> *Earth* is, once again, about upwardly mobile South Asians from New England, and so is the novel she's working on. 'Is that all you've got in there? I get asked the question all the time,' says Lahiri. 'It baffles me. Does John Updike get asked this question? Does Alice Munro? It's the ethnic thing, that's what it is. And my answer is always, yes, I will continue to write about this world, because it inspires me to write, and there's nothing more important than that.'[2]

This narcissism affects even the good writers. Take Gary Shteyngart, one of the best satirists working today. His debut novel, *The Russian Debutante's Handbook*, was hilarious and riveting, as was his more recent *Absurdistan*. Unfortunately, Shteyngart is afflicted with the same myopia that wrecks Lahiri's writing. Shteyngart is a Jew of Russian descent who grew up in New York City. *The Russian Debutante's Handbook* is about Vladimir Girshkin, a nebbish Russian Jew living in New York who later visits a fictional ex-Soviet republic. *Absurdistan* concerns Misha Vainberg, a nebbish Russian Jew living in New York who later visits a fictional ex-Soviet republic. Shteyngart's forthcoming third novel will revolve around *Absurdistan* character Jerry Shteynfarb (har har har), a nebbish Russian Jew living in—wait for it–Albany. In the year 2040. No word on whether a fictional ex-Soviet republic will be involved, but I wouldn't doubt it.

There are other examples of unbearable self-absorption among the novelist class (I'm looking at you, Jonathan Safran Foer), but the question here is this: why are today's writers so unwilling to expand their horizons? At least part of it is outright laziness, as Robert Stacy McCain explains in this article on the fall of conservative website *Culture11:*

> "These young wannabes can't write gonzo because they're too cowardly to *live* gonzo. They want to do their internships and their fellowships and sit on seminar panels while they suck the milk from the non-profit teat. God forbid they should ever actually have to work."[3]

But that's not the whole story. The acquisition of publishing houses by larger media corporations has worked to kill innovation and make everything safe and marketable. Novelists themselves have to remain safe and marketable if they want to be published. There's no room for the characters of yesteryear who made writing interesting. If the womanizing spendthrift Lord Byron was writing today, for instance, no editor would touch him. Truly talented writers who upset popular shibboleths such as Maddox and Tucker Max had to go the indie route in order to get their books published at all. The Nobel literature prize judge

Horace Engdahl accurately described (in a London Telegraph article, link apparently lost) American writers as too "insular" and "isolated," and the controversy-free nature of modern publishing has done its best to ensure this.

Fortunately, there *are* good up-and-coming writers who understand the true meaning of "write what you know." I recently reviewed Roosh's new memoir, *A Dead Bat in Paraguay*. The book is a travelogue of a six-month trip through South America that Roosh took after becoming dissatisfied with his middle-class lifestyle. But then again, Roosh is a guy who bucked the system and expatriated to Colombia: a show of courage that the Jhumpa Lahiris, Jonathan Safran Foers, and Gary Shteyngarts are incapable of managing.

2Blowhards, September 25, 2009

Truth Snacks

Once you have rejected the existence of God and the supernatural, nihilism is the only credible philosophical path.

Atheism is reverse-theism, a petulant nerd's clandestine desire for a daddy figure to swoop down from the heavens and spank him for being a bad boy. The way to kill God is not to hate Him, but to ignore Him.

No ideology survives contact with reality.

The history of the human race can be read as one gradual

shift to extremes of belief and behavior and back again. Identifying these shifts and acting at the right time can allow you to make off with maximum profit.

A slave who successfully wheedles favors from his master is still a slave.

You will have more success converting others to your point of view if you frame your arguments in the myths that they believe in then if you try to force your mythology down their throats. If you can't figure out how to do this, your argument is not worth making.

Low-level hypocrisy is a constant of human nature. If you're constantly checking yourself to see if your behavior matches up with your moral or political code, you're a freak.

Perpetual happiness is a myth. Contentedness is the most you can ever achieve out of life. No drugs or self-help books can change this.

A misogynist is a jilted romantic.

Stability and progress are diametrically opposed. Each has their advantages, but if you have one, you cannot have the other.

It is better to be the king of one tribe and hated by the rest than to be an outsider nipping at the edges of all of them.

If you look at data points in isolation while ignoring the lines that connect them, you will always draw the wrong conclusions despite having all the right answers.

When you're in a relationship, improve your sex life by getting rid of the TV in your bedroom. Your room should only be for sleeping, fucking, and getting (un)dressed.

If you're unwilling to take the first step to improve yourself, you don't deserve sympathy, and you won't get it.

April 2, 2010

Smart Condom Disposal for Men

Entrapment pregnancies happen. They aren't common, but neither is getting struck by lightning, and you'd still be an idiot if you went kite-flying in a thunderstorm. The most popular method of disposing your condoms where baby rabies-afflicted ladies can't get them is to flush 'em down the toilet, but how do you get the bugger down without looking like a assclown in front of your girl? Having nailed my fair share of nutters and psychos, I've worked out a method for getting rid of used condoms in a smart, socially sensible way. If you don't want to risk getting your wages garnished to pay for a brat you didn't even want, pay attention to these simple steps.

1. Determine if you even need to flush the condom.

This may come as a shock to the more paranoid and misogynistic MRAs and MGTOWs, but not every woman is looking to scoop your seed into her vagina while you're freshening up in the commode. There are certain red flags to look for that should factor into your decision to swirlify your semen.

Is she over 30 and childless? Is she poor? Does she have a college degree? Is there a huge disparity between your respective sexual market values? Is she willing to get fucked by you the night you meet her? You should be asking yourself these questions and others. One flag alone may not be enough to justify flushing, but it should give you pause. Two or more, and you should definitely flush. Use your head and trust your gut; your manly instincts will never lead you astray.

Also, if you're in a long-term relationship and considering tossing your jimmies in the shitter, take a step back and think about what you're doing. If you can't trust your girlfriend to not impregnate herself with your bastard broodling, how the hell can you trust her with anything else? Unless your game sucks or you have absolutely no taste, the only time you should have to flush is in one-night stands or very short flings.

And finally, if you follow Tom Leykis' advice to pour Tabasco sauce in your cock socks, get your head checked. If you're so frightened of entrapment pregnancies that you carry a bottle of hot sauce around in your pocket, you've got bigger problems than the psycho skanks you're fucking on the weekends. This game is not one for the timid.

2. Carry concealed.

Always, and I mean *always* use your own condoms. I carry two in my wallet when I'm out and about. If you ever find yourself about to go love-tunneling with a chick who's setting off alarm bells in your head and you don't have a raincoat for your little spelunker, seriously consider ejecting and jerking off later. There's always another slut, and five minutes of mediocre sex isn't worth eighteen years of child support.

3. No money shots.

This should be obvious, but don't blast anywhere but inside the walls of your dick's latex prison. Only act out your Peter North fantasies with a girl you trust.

4. Take note of your surroundings.

There are only two places in the world where you have to flush: your place or hers. If you're banging it out anywhere else, the chance of her dabbing your baby batter in her pussy when your back is turned drops to 0%, rounded up by over a thousand decimal places. So if you're making a romance inside of your girl in the bar men's loo, rejoice! Your bank account is safe.

5. Dispose of the damn thing right.

After you've done the deed, don't spring up, rip off your rubber and dash to the toilet; you'll look like a first-class jackass. Instead, during the post-coital cleanup, tell your girl, *"'Scuse me, I'm gonna go take a piss."* You can vary up the language if you like, but never *ask* her if you can leave, because asking is begging. Take the condom with you, walking all casual like nothing's wrong, and drop in it the bowl, preferably while peeing so you can use it as a target for your mighty golden arc. Flush, and whammo! You're all done.

In my experience, nine out of ten girls won't ask about the condom in your hand. For the one that does though, you need to ward her off. I usually tell her that I have a sensitive nose and I don't like the smell of latex and sauteed mushrooms mixed with cleaning solvent. This works most of the time. When I'm at my place, I'll also sometimes tell her that I'm a bit of a neat freak. You'd think that more girls would notice the inconsistency of a neat freak having a problem with a used Trojan lying on his bedroom floor and being perfectly okay with a girl coming all over his sheets, but they don't. Remember that any excuse you give here has to concern primarily yourself and *not* her. For example, don't tell her, *"Oh, I don't want to stain your carpet."* If she says she doesn't care about that, you're up Sperm Creek without a paddle.

Most of the time, dropping a line will defuse any situation that arises. If, however, she gets pushy about your method of love-glove disposal, tell her she's being weird (girls hate it when this word is used to describe them) and proceed as normal. They won't do anything after that.

Occasionally you'll get a girl who offers to get rid of the condom for you. Red alert! Like with pushy girls, tell her how weird she's being and ignore her. Your gut should tip you off to the nature of these girls long before the clothes come off.

6. Your place or hers?

Your strategy will change slightly depending on the answer to this question.

Your place: This makes your job easier. Girls are much less likely to ask about the condom when they're the guest of honor in someone else's castle. Additionally, you may want to consider getting rid of the wastebasket in your bedroom, as it will give you a logical justification for taking your willy wrappers with you. My pad is small enough that I can get away with this, and since I only use my room for sleeping, fucking, and getting (un)dressed, it's not an issue otherwise.

Her place: This is where things get a little tricky. You're on her turf, which makes it more likely that she'll ask about your handling of your cum-catchers. Stand firm with your excuses at the ready.

So you've gone through all the steps. Great job, champ! Enjoy the afterglow, get under the covers, and don't forget that you have to be in to work by 8:30 tomorrow morning. Here's to many nights of boffing crazy bar chicks.

April 14, 2010

Why I Blog

Reader Spike writes:

"Why blog?

"Not a rhetorical question. I mean why? What's your motivation?"[4]

Short answer: To avoid getting the mental equivalent of blue balls.

Long answer: I've just gotta do it.

I've never felt like a particularly talented writer. It used to be that whenever someone in real life told me that I was a good writer, I'd joke that the real reason my writing seemed good wasn't because of any gifts I had, but because everyone else was so bad these days that my mediocre output looked golden in comparison. Think Luke Wilson's character in *Idiocracy*. The thought that my scribblings had merit on their own basis was inconceivable to me.

When I was a kid, I was a prolific reader. I was one of those restless boys who was smart enough to read books several levels above everyone else, be they novels or nonfiction, and subsequently couldn't pay attention to the dumbed-down public school curriculum that I had to endure for six hours a day, five days a week. I got yelled at by my teachers hundreds of times for not paying attention in class, and even managed to get on the bad side of one particularly nasty student teacher who repeatedly confiscated whatever book I was reading at the time, snidely reminding me that "there was a time and a place." Bitch. My parents, God bless them, resisted any and all attempts the school made to put me on Ritalin, which would have lengthened my attention span at the cost of turning me into one of the drooling zombies the American educational system caters to.

And while I was reading, I was writing. Before I'd even entered middle school, I'd managed to fill up an entire desk with every sort of writing a pre-pubescent mind could put out. Notes from science textbooks, short stories, poems, and more were scribbled on hundreds of looseleaf pages. Aside from a couple of school assignments that my mom has hung onto for posterity, none of it survived to the present day. When I got a new desk in high school, I threw out all of my papers with the old one.

As I aged and hormones started pumping through my body, my pen turned to the usual bathetic teenage drivel. Crap about love, raging against the world for some reason I couldn't articulate, half-baked philosophical musings that I thought were deep. But along with puberty came an adolescent sense of shame about what I was doing, a warped narcissistic fear about my work being discovered and used to humiliate me. I kept writing, but put it all in an unmarked notebook that I mixed in with my school stuff, which I later burned outright to slake my paranoia. It wasn't up until I got to college that I worked up the nerve to try and get one of my stories published in the student literary journal, and that was only after my friends egged me on. (I made the cut.) But no matter what happened, the drive to write never died.

In the last decade of his life, the science fiction writer

THE TAO OF FERD

Philip K. Dick kept a journal, the *Exegesis*, in which he documented the various paranormal and religious visions he had and his theories as to their purpose. He was so obsessed with the journal that he spent dozens of sleepless nights writing in it. By the time he died, the *Exegesis* was thousands of pages long. Some might call him crazy, and he may well have been, but you don't write an 8,000 page journal unless you've got a primal urge to sate. Dick was a man with an itch that he just couldn't scratch.

That's why I blog. It's not something that's fully enjoyable in the traditional sense, nor is it something that pays. The compulsion to write is an addiction I can't satisfy, a boulder that I will never roll all the way up the hill. You can't learn it and you can't fake it; you've either got the urge or you don't.

When most blogs get barely a couple dozen readers, *In Mala Fide* has over ten thousand unique visitors a month. When the average blog doesn't last two months, I've been around for well over a year. I won't deny that I get some validation from having a large amount of people enjoying my work. But as the kid with the desk full of scribblings and the bookshelf full of Beverly Cleary novels could testify, I'd still be doing this even if there was no one to read it.

And I'll keep doing it until I can't do it any more.

November 12, 2010

How Living In Mala Fide Became Mainstream

I read a lot of books, around four to six a month, but I usually don't blog about them because most of them simply aren't worth the effort. They don't inspire me, they don't make me mad, they just go onto my bookshelf where I forget about them. The last time I attempted to write a book review was last summer, when I had just finished Gary Shteyngart's *Super Sad True Love Story* and was bitterly disappointed, especially since I used to be a fan of Shteyngart's. Six paragraphs in and I realized I was blowing the whole thing out of proportion. *Super Sad True Love Story* is an awful novel, but it's awfulness is entirely ordinary, the self-licking ice cream cone of modern publishing that we've all come to expect. A book has to be extraordinarily good or bad to inspire me to write about it.

The 4-Hour Workweek by Tim Ferriss is such a book. I first found out about Ferriss a few months ago, when I was winding down at my old job and researching the burgeoning, pretentiously-named field of "lifestyle design," the art of living a life that isn't confined by a 9 to 5 work existence. I began reading Ferriss' blog, figured he knew what he was talking about, and eventually went to Barnes & Noble looking for his book. When I first got my mitts on a copy of *The 4-Hour Workweek*, I was so enthralled I spent a good half-hour reading through it before I even bothered heading up to the cash register. I found it *that* compelling.

And what I found compelling about *The 4-Hour Workweek* is its underlying philosophy, which is so subversive I can't believe Ferriss actually got the book published. The book is ostensibly about how to join the ranks of the "New Rich," a class of entrepreneurs who spend most of their time traveling the world, having fun and goofing off and *still* make more money than you, but here's the less PC summation of Ferriss' beliefs:

The only way to survive and make money is to rebel against the system, even if you end up screwing over your fellow man in the process.

Now, Ferriss doesn't advocate breaking the law or doing anything illegal. He's not stupid. But most of his advice is based around cutting corners and bending rules to your advantage and everyone else's disadvantage. For example, in the second chapter, Ferriss details how he won the Chinese Kickboxing National Championships in 1999 by exploiting two of the competition's rules:

1. Since the weigh-in was the day before the competition, Ferriss used the time between the weigh-in and the championship to hyper-hydrate his body above the max weight limit after hyper-dehydrating to meet it.

2. His principal tactic when fighting was to try to push his opponent off of the elevated platform, as any fighter who fell off three times in a round lost by default.

Nothing Tim did was against the rules, but no one with a

sense of fair play would dare argue that he was behaving in an ethical fashion. He didn't train harder, he didn't fight better, he didn't go beyond his sciolistic understanding of the sport he was competing in. He was the equivalent of those annoying brats who, when we were kids, would invade our personal space to annoy us. When we told them to stop touching us, they'd start waving their hands an inch in front of our heads and holler, *"I'm not touching you! I'm not touching you!"* And in Ferriss' case, "not touching" his opponents won him the gold:

> "The result? I won all my matches by technical knock-out (TKO) and went home national champion, something 99% of those with 5-10 years of experience had been unable to do."

He then goes on to brag about how his methods have become standard tactics for kickboxers competing in the CKNC. The lesson? Being aggressively passive-aggressive gets you what you want.

Virtually all of *The 4-Hour Workweek's* practical money-making advice follows this formula: read the fine print, identify the loopholes and jump through them on the road to riches and glory. The very first chapter of the "A is for Automation" section is devoted to the wonders of virtual assistants, outsourcing all your busywork to a drone in India so you can free up time for yourself on the cheap. Ferriss even relays the personal story of one New Rich sadsack who used his virtual assistant to settle a dispute with his wife:

> "I can't tell you what a thrill I got from sending that note. It's pretty hard to get much more passive-aggressive than bickering with your wife via an e-mail from a subcontinent halfway around the world."

What a pussy.

This ethos of subtly ripping people off continues right down to Ferriss' ideas of starting new businesses. For example, one of his suggestions is to create an info product (like an instructional DVD) by paraphrasing information from other, authoritative sources. If that isn't the definition of a con, the word has no meaning. But never fear, the rationalizations are here, as Tim explains why masquerading as an expert on a topic is no big deal:

> "First, 'expert' in the context of selling product means that you know more about the topic than the purchaser. No more. It is not necessary to be the best – just better than a small target number of your prospective customers...
>
> [...] "Second, expert status can be created in less than four weeks if you understand basic credibility

> indicators. It's important to learn how the PR pros phrase resume points and position their clients..."

Sorry all you folks who've spent years becoming experts on particular topics the old-fashioned way, any yahoo with an Internet connection and a copy of Microsoft Office can do what you've done in the span of a month. I can't help but think that most of the seduction community hucksters hocking overpriced, bogus PUA advice followed this method to the letter.

The really sad thing about *The 4-Hour Workweek* is not that it could get published by a major company, or praised by anyone of importance (like Jack Canfield of *Chicken Soup for the Soul*, a quote from whom is proudly featured on the inside of the book jacket), it's that *there's very little to disagree with in its philosophy of living*. Oh sure, there's plenty to nitpick with its practical advice. During the chapter about virtual assistants, I was rolling my eyes every other paragraph: outsourcing tasks to a half-literate foreigner on the other side of the world is a really stupid move if you care about getting things right. But no one who has descended into the rabbit hole of this part of the blogosphere can disagree with Ferriss' core beliefs.

Over a year and a half ago, I wrote this explaining why I christened this site *In Mala Fide*:

> "When the pseudonymous *Asia Times Online* columnist Spengler unmasked himself last April, he

stated his reason for choosing that nom de plume was as a joke: the name of the German scholar who wrote *The Decline of the West* appropriated for a column in an Asian newspaper. A bad joke, but it has a point. The name of this blog, *In Mala Fide*, can be thought of as a jab in that vein. The moral configuration of Western society, as chronicled on this blog and others, requires its best citizens to rebel, to go against the grain, to behave *in mala fide* in order to secure their own fortunes."

That's the central point of *The 4-Hour Workweek:* screw conventional wisdom and ethics to get rich. Leverage go-fuck-yourself Calvinist capitalism for your own benefit. Plagiarize other peoples' work and pass it off as your own. Outsource your work to India like a good little free marketeer. Then spend all your newfound free time on vacation instead of raising a family, creating a useful invention, or otherwise contributing to society in any way. Be a parasite, a tick burrowed in the hairy ass of Western civilization, getting fat from sucking blood and giving nothing but Lyme disease in return.

You can argue that Tim Ferriss is a degenerate whose advice would bring the country down if enough people followed it, and you'd be right. But at the same time, he's got the freedom to go tango dancing in Buenos Aires, scuba diving in Panama, or anything else he wants, whenever he wants. You, on the other hand, are working eighty-hour weeks doing a monkey's job, with a dictatorial boss pulling on your nuts and IT weirdos reading your emails, all for a comparative pittance. He broke the rules and he's happy and enjoying life, while you followed them and are a miserable sack of shit. Whose lifestyle sounds more appealing?

Examples of entrepreneurs going *in mala fide* to great success abound in our world. For example, take the infamous music video "Friday" that went viral two weeks ago. Everyone agrees that there's nothing redeeming about it.[5] The first time I watched it, I had to stop around the 1:30 mark, Rebecca Black's droning and the awful lyrics were so grating to my ears. Hell, the part at 2:06 with the strobe light notebook gave me meningitis seizure flashbacks. What sort of moron would give this nauseating wench a microphone, let alone an entire music video?

Turns out that "Friday" was produced by the record label *Ark Music Factory*, whose business model revolves around bilking the rich parents of snotty suburban brats out of their hard-earned cash. For a mere $2,000, Ark will write a song for your little pumpkin, film a music video starring her, and then Auto-Tune the shit out of her voice to mask her inability to carry a tune. It's the brainchild of entrepreneurs Patrice Wilson and Clarence Jay.

I simultaneously want to punch those guys and buy them beers. The punch is for inflicting talentless munchkins like CJ

Fam on the world, making my eardrums bleed with their bullfrog-like throat noises masquerading as genuine music. The beers are for discovering a way to make easy money off of wealthy idiots who spoil their lazy kids. I can't think of a demographic who so richly deserves to be dicked over in the most insulting way possible.

Or take this story about a American who fled to Canada to avoid having to pay off his onerous student loan debt:

> "Bottom line – there are many, many people who, like me, feel they have done the right thing all of their lives. We went to school, studied hard, started at the bottom and worked crap jobs for starvation wages. We did this all in exchange for the promise of a better life down the road. Those promises have turned out to be empty. We now have nothing to show for it but massive amounts of debt with little to no hope of ever repaying. We don't even have access to basic, affordable health care! Since they haven't held up their end of the bargain, I don't see why I can't opt out of holding up mine."[6]

"But but welching on your debts is immoral and unmanly!" Fuck you, wage-slave! Fuck you and your masters with a rusty pitchfork! The student loan scam is highway robbery,

and anyone who kicks those assholes in the nads is doing the right thing.

In a corrupt world divided between suckers and those who do the suckering, your only duty is to yourself and your kin. You can choose the sucker's path, the normal path, the path your parents and friends and co-workers took. Or you can break free, flip the bird to convention and do what *you* want, on your own terms and nobody else's. Freedom is within your grasp; you just have to reach out and take it.

In the meantime, if you want fuel for your dreams, *The 4-Hour Workweek* is a must buy.

March 28, 2011

Dead Meat

Whoever said the only things guaranteed in life are death *and* taxes never heard of the Koch brothers. Fortunately, the Grim Reaper is one specter even the ultra-rich can't buy off. Death is nature's own form of egalitarianism, because everybody dies. Oh sure, some will get it sooner than others, some later, but in the long run, everyone is dead meat. Maybe Charles'll be in his study alone, counting the billions he and David stole from the American taxpayers, when he'll feel a tightness in his chest, a twinge in his left shoulder. An hour later, he'll collapse on the floor, drooling and catatonic. His man-servants will call 911, try to get his heart beating again, try to get that dam of cholesterol in his artery to burst free, but it'll be too late. Time of death, 8:44 pm.

That's part of the perverse beauty of death. It's so much easier to destroy than to build. It takes nine months of incubation in a sack in a woman's abdomen to create a life, but you don't even need nine seconds to end it. Take a bullet in the brain or a knife to the throat. Trip, fall down the stairs, and break your neck. Have a cranial hemorrhage, your cerebrum drowning in your own blood. What was decades in the making, gone in an instant. Meat.

Of course, maybe you won't be so lucky. Maybe Death will have some fun with you by stretching your torment out for years and years. Maybe you'll get cancer and watch as your own cells turn on you and devour you alive. Maybe you'll die of Alzheimer's, forced to suffer your own brain turning into oatmeal, not even able to recognize your family, remember your name, or wipe your own ass. The journey may differ, but the destination is the same. Dead meat. No different than a slab of steak in the supermarket. Except that instead of being eaten, you'll be pumped full of chemicals, dressed in your Sunday best, and paraded about town in a wooden box while every sap you ever fucked over for a pittance bites their tongue and waxes poetic about what a great guy you were.

In a society full of pious liars, death is an opportunity to resuscitate the reputations of scumbags and sociopaths, no matter how much they stole or how many lives they ruined. It wasn't always like this. Back during the Middle Ages, death was a opportunity to laugh. The Black Death fueled the creation of the "Dance of Death" motif, from where we get much of our Grim Reaper iconography. The sole point of the Dance of Death was to remind everyone of its universality; no matter how rich, powerful or prestigious you were, Death came for you as readily as the starving serfs:

> "Sir Emperowre / lorde of al the grounde
> Soueren Prince / ande hyest of noblesse
> 3e most forsake / of golde 3owre appil rounde
> Sceptre and swerde / & al 3owre hie prouesse
> Be-hinde leue / 3owre tresowre & richesse
> And with other / to my daunce obeie
> A3ens my myght / is worth noon hardynesse
> Adames children / alle thei mosten deie."

That's pure motherfuckin' magic, right there: peasants taking solace in the fact that while they may be dying, so are the fat cat nobles. We'll see how high and mighty you think you are after your daughters start vomiting blood and growing pus-oozing tumors on their arms.

There's another beautiful thing about death: the way it reduces your life accomplishments down to nothing. So you did all the right things. You got married, you had four beautiful kids, you went to church and worked a steady job and waved a sign at all the Tea Party protests. You were a model citizen. But when you die, you'll end up in the exact same place as a layabout who spent his life banging skanks, popping Percocets, and sponging off his friends. All your triumphs, victories, and material possessions mean nothing because you're no longer around to enjoy them. The maggots don't discriminate; to them, you're all just dead meat.

  I'm coming up on the second anniversary of my grandfather's (my father's father) death. He didn't have a "good" death, a predictable death, the kind of death where everybody knows its coming and gets their licks in before the flatlining. He was driving with my uncle one day down the street from his house out in the boondocks when a driver on a side street ran a stop sign and T-boned their truck. My grandfather spun out of control and landed in a ditch, the impact severing several major arteries around his heart. He was dead before the medevac chopper touched down at the hospital.

  Seventy plus years of raising a family, serving in the Army, and generally being a pillar of the community in small-town America, ended because some asshole from the next county over had crappy peripheral vision. I'm not going to lie and say we were close or anything, because we weren't. I liked and respected him —he was a genuinely good man—but living hundreds of miles away tends to limit social interaction. The last time I'd seen him was the month before at a party thrown for my cousin, who had joined the Army National Guard and was being deployed to Iraq.

The wake was five days later. I took off from work early and made the two-hour drive from home to join the proceedings. Per usual, everyone in the funeral home was spinning the cliche about how my grandpa looked "peaceful" lying in his casket. To me, he didn't look peaceful, he just looked *dead*. He'd been dressed in his formal Army uniform, had had embalming fluids pumped into him that gave his skin an unhealthy, ghostly pallor, and had his arms folded around his chest in that stereotypical corpse pose. This wasn't a person anymore, it was a *thing*. An object, a piece of matter, same as a lamp or a chair or a table. A slab of dead meat.

Some people wonder why I'm hyperbolic, why I don't take my writing too seriously, why I'm a joker and a smartass. Why? Why not? What's the point of being so serious? Life is nothing but a sick joke played on us by God, a long march to the grave and oblivion. Decades of pushing a boulder up the hill, and for what? So your kids can give their inheritance away while you lie on your deathbed? So everything you accomplished can be undone by the goosestepping of time?

It's not worth it. I'll do what I can with the power I have, but I'm not going to suffer for any lost causes, and I'm not going to live in fear of the future. Racer X offers this inspiring message to bloggers who take themselves too seriously:

"Instead of the hopelessness of so many of today's

web sites, and their message of fear, I prefer the message from John Paul II: "Be not afraid." It is a message the Pope used to recite quite often, a message he himself learned while, as a young seminarian in occupied Poland, the Nazi soldiers searched his underground seminary. He hid in a closet and evaded capture. If captured, he probably would have been killed. After that terrifying experience the Pope learned first hand what true fear is, and it became a source of strength for him, renewed through Christ. Don't be afraid, because even in the worst of situations, God is still there.

"Now being hunted down by soldiers who want to kill you is a bit more of a serious situation and cause for concern than most of what our heroic warriors out there in the blog fantasy world are fighting against. That was real. That was true fear. Today's online warrior is often afraid of a female boss at work, among other things.

"Yes, the world is filled with pain, evil and injustice. It always has and it always will. Living in America or the West in general does not somehow magically exempt us from that. But there is hope too. Be not afraid."[7]

Man, those are words to live by.

So, by all means, fight for whatever you want. Try to change the world, or not. Live for any reason of your choosing. But remember that no matter who you are, what you do, what you accomplish and what you believe…

…in the end, all of us are dead meat.

April 8, 2011

The War on Mediocrity

One of the Big Problems of our epoch, according to smart people, is how nobody's reading books anymore. This is horrible, no good, and very bad for the future of Uh-Mare-Eca. Those durned kids spend all their time on Facebook and playing *World of WarCraft* instead of reading books, and as a result they're getting dumber and dumber with each passing year, so dumb their tongues hang out of their mouths and they can't tie their shoelaces or keep score for a bowling game by hand or recite the Gettysburg Address from memory. Y'know, because the best way to ensure someone understands a famous speech is to force them to memorize it and have them repeat it back to you.

Smart people who lament the end of fancy book-learnin' are retarded. Yes, it's true that people don't read books as much as they used to. But the average schmuck back then wasn't reading *War and Peace*, he was thumbing through the likes of *The Thin Man*, *The Long Goodbye*, *True Grit* or any number of mass market paperbacks aimed at the lowest common denominator. No preaching, no philosophizing, no complex themes or symbolism for tenured college professors to force their students to write fifteen-page papers about; just action, adventure, mystery and sex. Even the likes of Horatio Alger or Ayn Rand have had far more impact on American culture than F. Scott Fitzgerald, Robert Creeley or any of the other unreadable hacks that the lit-crit types gush over.

And yet we're supposed to pretend that Creeley's illiterate free verse poems on buying tampons for his girlfriend represent the height of American letters. That's why nobody reads anymore: the writers you idiots are pushing suck, suck, suck. Take this excursion to Parnassus by Sherman Alexie as an example of the sheer awfulness of modern literature:

On the Amtrak from Boston to New York City

"The white woman across the aisle from me says 'Look,
look at all the history, that house
on the hill there is over two hundred years old, '
as she points out the window past me

"into what she has been taught. I have learned
little more about American history during my few
days
back East than what I expected and far less
of what we should all know of the tribal stories

"whose architecture is 15,000 years older
than the corners of the house that sits
museumed on the hill. 'Walden Pond,'
the woman on the train asks, 'Did you see Walden
Pond?'"

Forget the whiny racial identity politics of the poem and simply concentrate on the structure. Doesn't this poem seem a bit off to you? There's just something wrong with it, but you can't tell exactly what? Here, let me help:

"The white woman across the aisle from me says
'Look, look at all the history, that house on the hill
there is over two hundred years old,' as she points
out the window past me into what she has been
taught. I have learned little more about American
history during my few days back East than what I
expected and far less of what we should all know of
the tribal stories whose architecture is 15,000 years

older than the corners of the house that sits museumed on the hill.

"'Walden Pond,' the woman on the train asks, 'Did you see Walden Pond?'"

That's right, take away the line breaks and this "poem" becomes a bunch of run-on sentences. Not only does it not rhyme, it doesn't even have any meter. The number of syllables in each line is completely random. This Alexie guy wrote a few paragraphs, hit the Enter key a few extra times, and tried to pass it off as legitimate verse. And the Beigeists in the publishing world lapped it up and begged for more.

Speaking of which, since this guy loves to sermonize about the evils of the white man and the suffering of "Native Americans," I'd love to know which Indian language the name "Sherman Alexie" comes from. I'm guessing it's from the Fullashit tribe, who live on the Ur-Anus Reservation in northern Idaho, but I'm no expert in Indian linguistics, so someone feel free to correct me in the comments.

But "On the Amtrak" is small-time hackery: there are far more sob-squirters, schlockmeisters and all-around frauds out there with completely undeserved fame and critical reputations. But thing is, I can't really blame them too much. It's a fact that you can't spell "stupid" without "U," and it's thanks to U that these fools are allowed to run around mass-murdering trees for their banal, bathetic books. Snake oil salesmen can't ply their trade without credulous dullards to give them their money and praise, and that's what U've been doing.

So, in an effort to help push back the tide of blandness and idiocy (and put my college degree to use), I've decided to start reviewing books more often. My first book is one of my all-time favorites: *The eXile: Sex, Drugs, and Libel in the New Russia*.

This is honestly one of the few books I've read that changed my life, and one of the few I make a point to re-read once a year. I'd wager that 100% of the people who poo-poo me for liking Ames and Taibbi haven't read it. My opinion may be skewed by the fact that I picked it up as a teenager, but even guys like Roosh who've had their own share of foreign adventures have been blown away by *the eXile*.

The book is divided into eight chapters, half by Ames, half by Taibbi. Fans of muckraking will appreciate Taibbi's contributions, which deal with the unbelievable amount of corruption and fraud in late 90's Russia. The mainstream narrative about Russia is that Boris Yeltsin was a great capitalist, pro-Western reformer unexpectedly decapitated by the 1998 economic collapse, and that Vladimir Putin is an evil fascist who hates freedom and probably eats cute puppy dogs. The reality is that Yeltsin was a venal bastard who aided and abetted the rape of his own country by capitalist oligarchs (both Western and Russian), and Putin is beloved by the Russian people because he had all the looters murdered, imprisoned or driven into exile (heh). The reason you don't know about this is because the entire Western press corps in Moscow, with the exception of *the eXile*, either turned a blind eye to the corruption or actively collaborated with the oligarchs. Hmmm, this all sounds kinda familiar... but nah, it can't happen here.

To this day, Mark Ames and Matt Taibbi are despised by the mainstream media because of the way they caught them with their pants down. To give just one example of how far ahead of the curve they were, *the eXile* was one of the only newspapers in the world that predicted the Russian financial meltdown of 1998. Particularly eye-opening is Taibbi's chapter on Michael Bass, an American crook who symbolized the worst of nineties expat excess. Bass was a convicted felon who came to Moscow to pimp Slavic nubiles for quick cash while simultaneously trying to present himself as a respectable public figure, writing a society column for a now-defunct expat rag, *The Moscow Tribune*. After *the eXile* ran a story on how he sold an aspiring Californian runway model into sex slavery to an Arab sheik, Bass gave Taibbi what may be the most passive-aggressive death threat of all time:

> "'I don't know... My roof wanted to kill you right away, but I really don't know what to do. I mean, what are my options? I can have you killed, or I can pay someone a couple of hundred bucks to have your legs broken, or I can just let it go. And I don't

like any of those options.'

"'Michael, I can't believe you're threatening me like this. What is this, the Solntsevo gang? You're talking about having me killed.'

"'I'm not threatening you,' he insisted.

"'You're sitting here, saying you don't know what you want to do, and talking about having me killed as one of your options! That's a threat from where I sit.'"

The tale has a happy ending, with Bass humiliated and exposed for all of Moscow's expats to jeer at.

All this isn't to argue that Ames and Taibbi are saints: Ames' half of the book will dispel that notion pretty quickly. Beginning with his contracting the worst case of scabies ever from a one-night stand in St. Petersburg, Mark Ames takes us from his early years living in a run-down California nursing home with his Czech girlfriend to his first months hustling in Moscow, and his eventually founding *the eXile* with a pair of proto-SWPL faggots from Seattle. The passage where he fantasizes about their violent deaths at the hands of Chechen gangsters may be some of the most disturbingly funny writing in the history of the English language.

But Ames doesn't hit his stride until the book's midway point, with the chapters "Our God is Speed" and "The White God Factor." "Our God is Speed" details his adventures with drugs and is full of sick, graphic detail (such as his junkie pal Kolya's "shooting bloodied water from his infected needle across [their friend's] floor"), but "The White God Factor," about his experiences with Russian women, is of particular interest to us manospherians. In between recounting his sexual encounters in Russia and Belarus, Ames tears feminism and American women to itty-bitty pieces:

> "Out in Russia, you gain a little perspective, which can be dangerous. Deep down, as it turns out, even the most emasculated, wire-rimmed glasses, cigar-smoking and martini-drinking American guy fantasizes about living in a world full of... well, I'll let you guess:
>
> "a) self reliant women who are also your friends
>
> "b) sluts
>
> "Okay, still stuck? I'll amend it. All men – that's right, all sane men – fantasize about a world populated with:

"a) self-reliant androgynous women who are also your friends

"b) young, beautiful sluts

"Envelope please... Whoah! This is a shocker, folks! Hold on to your seats! Turns out, when you scrape away the surface implants, every single sane man wants... drum roll, maestro... young, beautiful sluts!

"CUT TO: Young, beautiful sluts seated in third row, hands cupped over mouths in shocked surprise... They stand, crying-laughing, hugging each other, then slowly make their way towards the podium, kissed by vigorously applauding men on their way there..."

And of course, no book on late 90's Russia is complete without a mention of the Hungry Duck, a Moscow expat bar whose nightly bacchanalia made *120 Days of Sodom* look like a church social:

"...Ladies' Night is another word for rape camp. On Ladies' Night, only girls (generally ages 12 through 25) are allowed in, while all men are kept at bay from 7:00 P.M. to 9:00 P.M. The girls are offered free drinks, as much and as fast as they can down them. Not just offered free drinks, but pumped full of free drinks…Russians aren't known for their moderation when it comes to liquor; your average five-foot-one *dyev* could put any NFL lineman under the table. The point of Ladies' Night is to get the girls as drunk as possible in a two-hour period, then to open the floodgates to the guys and let the rape camp festivities begin. It was a brilliant idea to raise the volume of vomit and semen to levels yet unseen even in the Duck."

Ames then relays the story of the time he and Taibbi tended bar during Ladies' Night, where he "drunkenly slobbered into seven or eight different teenage mouths" and there was a "river of vomit coming out of the stalls" of the women's bathroom.

When I posted an excerpt of Ames' in which he bragged about threatening to murder one of his girlfriends if she didn't get an abortion (and convinced another to have her little bastard vacuumed out) a few months back, commenter PA referred to him as a "piece of shit" and claimed he "ruined" the girls. Ames is a piece of shit, to be sure, but Russian women are as equally vile, as he shatters the fantasies of white knights and mail order bride-site cruising beta schmucks with this passage:

> "...[Russian women] live it up to the max while they have the upper hand, when nature is good to them. They know that time is working against them. Youth is a dirty word here – most go straight to adulthood by the age of 14. I can count five women I've slept with who lost their virginity at age 11; they treat it as dry fact, like when their first teeth grew, and not as a psychology-loaded tragedy. A Russian woman is at the peak of her power from about age 13 to until 20. After that, beauty is subjected to the cruel forces of entropy, which renders them unrecognizable beasts – Division II noseguards – by the age of 30. That's why most have been married at least once by the time they hit 20 – in the provinces, the age is more like 17."

To hammer home the point, Ames quotes Edward Limonov (another great, underrated writer, and one of Ames' intellectual inspirations): "Russian women are usually, physically speaking, attractive, but morally – they are repulsive creatures, cripples."

One of the nice things about *the eXile* book is that it comes in a nice big 8 1/2 by 11 inch size, allowing the editors to toss unabridged reprints of *eXile* articles, cartoons, and covers in the margins. It adds value to an already action-packed title, but you definitely don't want to read this one in mixed company, unless you want to explain away a picture of a *dyevushka* with a champagne bottle jammed in her asshole or a prank cover with the headline "NIGGERS! Where Do They Come From... and Why Are They Here?"

When I first read this book a decade ago, it planted a germ in my mind, a desire to see the world beyond my country's shores. Mark Ames' Russia no longer exists, as shown by the collapse of *the eXile* itself three years ago. This is a good thing for both the Russians themselves and for proponents of nationalism across the globe. But the grip of go-fuck-yourself Calvinist conservatarianism and its hanger-on ideologies is still choking the life out of America and the West at large. Even with the Occupy protesters pushing back against the state religion, I doubt Americans can snap out of their stupor in time to halt the coming collapse. One decade later, I'm closer than ever to breaking out of the asylum.

Some will argue that Mark Ames and Matt Taibbi are bad men, and they'd have a point. But as is the case with so much of human history, it's not a case of good vs. bad, it's bad vs. worse. Ames and Taibbi are slime, but they're far more honest, truthful and talented than their detractors, the defenders of everything that's wrong with the world. People like them make the world a far more interesting place. If the choice is between them and you amoral, two-faced cocksuckers, I'll take them.

November 10, 2011

The Last Honest Fascist

Four years of college taught me that not only does the ivory tower have no idea what makes good literature, they couldn't care less; they'll erase truly talented writers from the history books if they wander off the plantation. Case in point: the 20th century's most reviled and imitated novelist, Louis-Ferdinand Céline. Ask an English professor about Céline and half of them will have no idea who you're talking about, and the other half will react like you just snapped off a Hitler salute. I still remember how my junior year Early American Lit professor reacted when I told her I was reading *Rigadoon:* "Wasn't Céline a Nazi?"

I may be *biased* on this front, but Céline is arguably the finest Western novelist of the past hundred years. With the publication of this, his debut novel, in 1931, Leon Trotsky wrote that Céline "had walked into the pantheon of great literature like a man walks into his living room." But with the rise of Nazi Germany, Céline made the fatal error of becoming a fascist, and like magic, he was suddenly a non-person in the world of books. Of course, he wasn't alone in joining the losing team: Ezra Pound gave anti-Semitic propaganda speeches on Italian radio and was arrested for treason when the war ended. But Pound is still taught in the universities while Céline is a leper.

    Don't give me the argument that it's because of Pound's influence on literature, because Céline was just as influential if not more. Numerous writers up to the present day have mimicked or outright ripped off the bad doctor, from the good (Bukowski, Miller, Burroughs, Houellebecq) to the awful (Kesey, Heller, Vonnegut). It's not hard to see why when you pick up *Journey to the End of the Night.* Like Mark Twain, the first great American novelist, Céline is less of a formal writer than a *storyteller:* he pulls you into his world as assuredly as your best friend bragging about the crazy adventures he had last night. His prose explodes with energy and life, never shying away from the dirty details, holding you captive in its grotesque grip. So the quality of Céline's writing has nothing to do with his being blacklisted from the curriculum.

    Nope, the reason why Pound is still loved and Céline is hated is because the latter was honest. Like all popular hacks, Pound was a better entrepreneur than a writer, a charmer who knew how to say all the right things at all the right times. Like the trendy lefties who lined up to root for the Republicans in the Spanish Civil War while they were disemboweling Catholic priests, Pound converted to fascism because he thought they were the winning side, then staged a public repentance to avoid having to face a firing squad. Céline, the poor sincere bastard, never surrendered to the jeering hordes. An open supporter of the Vichy regime and author of anti-Semitic pamphlets, Céline wore his convictions on his sleeve even when public opinion shifted against them. He went to the grave without apologizing for or recanting anything he'd ever written.

But more than that, Céline is *persona non grata* in the literary world because he alone confronted the nihilism and emptiness of the post-WWI West. Oh sure, Fitzgerald and Hemingway wrote about the aimlessness of the Lost Generation, but they were strictly amateur hour, bedtime stories for the kids. Céline was dead serious. His books were glorified accounts of his own life, with the boring bits taken out and new details added in. In *Journey to the End of the Night*, he grabs you by the back of the neck, shoves your face in it and doesn't let go.

Journey begins with Céline's protagonist, Ferdinand Bardamu, shooting the breeze with his buddy in 1910's Paris. Bardamu joins in a passing military parade to mock his patriotic countrymen and ends up being drafted into the war. Deserting the front lines, he flees into the jungles of French colonial Africa to escape punishment. Bardamu's bizarre odyssey takes him all the way to New York City, Detroit to work for Ford and fall in love with a prostitute, and finally back to France where he establishes a medical practice caring for poor Parisians who are always looking for ways to cheat him. Along the way, he is continuously dogged by Robinson, an off-and-on-again friend whose own escapades never end happily.

By Célinean standards, *Journey* is mild stuff, a gateway

drug for his later nihilism. As is the nature of geniuses, however, even his less-exemplary works are miles ahead of everyone else. The translation by Ralph Manheim does a fantastic job of preserving the unpretentiousness and humor of the original French, as shown by the excerpt where Bardamu runs into a communal toilet in New York:

> "Men among men, all free and easy, they laughed and joked and cheered one another on, it made me think of a football game. The first thing you did when you got there was take off your jacket, as if in preparation for strenuous exercise. This was a rite and shirtsleeves were the uniform.
>
> "In that state of undress, belching and worse, gesticulating like lunatics, they settled down in the fecal grotto. The new arrivals were assailed with a thousand revolting jokes while descending the stairs from the street, but they all seemed delighted.
>
> "The morose aloofness of the men on the street above was equaled only by the air of liberation and rejoicing that came over them at the prospect of emptying their bowels in tumultuous company.
>
> "The splotched and spotted doors to the cabins

hung loose, wrenched from their hinges. Some customers went from one cell to another for a little chat, those waiting for an empty seat smoked heavy cigars and slapped the backs of the obstinately toiling occupants, who sat there straining with their heads between their hands. Some groaned like wounded men or women in labor. The constipated were threatened with ingenious tortures."

Of course, a true artist like Ezra Pound would *never* have written about something as plebeian and low-class as the sight of Americans straining to shit in a public restroom. But that was the reality of post-WWI West: it was Shit World, everywhere, and Céline chronicled it like no writer before or after. In a way, I'm thankful that "respectable" people don't dare touch Céline; it makes it easier for me to separate the wheat from the chaff. It's the reverse of the Hunter Thompson Idiot Test; anyone who likes Céline is usually intelligent and worth paying attention to, even if I disagree with them.

One thing that annoys me about this edition of *Journey* is the glossary. Céline's writing was steeped in the vernacular of interwar France, and he frequently employed wordplay that doesn't accurately translate into English. For example, in an early part of the book where Bardamu is recovering in an army hospital, he shares a room with a Sergeant Branledore, whose name is derived from *branler*, the French verb "to masturbate." Instead of using footnotes, this edition forces you to flip to the back of the book whenever you come across an asterisked term. But this is a minor ding and won't stop you from enjoying yourself.

November 16, 2011

Sci-Fi for the Rest of Us

The sad thing about true geniuses in the literary/art world is that their genius usually isn't recognized until after they're dead or otherwise unable to turn a profit on it. Philip K. Dick is the poster boy for this sort of thing, as he labored most of his life in utter poverty and died in his early fifties just months before the first film adapted from his work, *Blade Runner*, was released to theaters. Now nearly three decades later, Hollywood is rushing to adapt every goddamn thing he ever wrote into a movie: *Total Recall, Minority Report, A Scanner Darkly, The Adjustment Bureau*, the list goes on. Not to mention all the other films that were inspired by Dick either directly or indirectly (*Vanilla Sky, The Matrix, Inception* etc.)

Most genre fiction is trash, and the nerd-dominated genres of science fiction and fantasy are the worst of all. The basis of all entertaining fiction is writing what you know and making sure what you know is interesting. The nerds who dominate sci-fi can't produce anything but garbage because they don't grasp this, substituting character development and plot for masturbatory exposition and futuristic gimmickry pulled out of their asses. There's no verisimilitude or ethos, which is why most nerd fiction rings hollow. For instance, I can't think of a single memorable novel or character by Asimov, Heinlein, or Herbert that stuck with me after I read the last page, and years afterwards, everything those tedious, overpraised failures wrote has slipped down the memory hole for good.

Dick sticks with me. Philip K. Dick stands alone among sci-fi writers as being worth reading, because he doesn't use sci-fi elements to prop up bad storytelling; he doesn't need to. His stories and characters stand on their own as being poignant and memorable. Dick's milieu was the rapidly-changing social landscape of mid-century California, caught between the free-love hippies on the coast and the hateful, miserable Calvinists in the suburbs, Nixon's "silent majority." His writing is rooted in this conflict, along with his understanding of the nature of reality and his drug use, with the science fiction element nothing but glorified drapery. Dick saw modern Calvinist conservatism in its larval stages–its fixation on "law and order," its willful ignorance, its hatred of beauty and glorification of ugliness–and feared it.

Flow My Tears, the Policeman Said is one of his finest works in this vein, and one of my favorite novels. The setting is pure Dick, a futuristic police state America that is slowly liberalizing. Think the Soviet Union under Gorbachev. Radical college students are condemned to live in poverty in collective camps. Blacks have been given a ridiculous amount of social status after a eugenics program designed to ethnically cleanse them was reversed; early on, while driving through Los Angeles, a hotel clerk muses about how he would get the death penalty if he ran a black person over:

> "'They're like the last flock of whooping cranes,' the clerk said, starting forward now that the old black had reached the far side. 'Protected by a thousand laws. You can't jeer at them; you can't get into a fistfight with one without risking a felony rap – ten years in prison. Yet we're making them die out – that's what Tidman wanted and I guess what the majority of Silencers wanted, but' – he gestured, for the first time taking a hand off the wheel – 'I miss the kids. I remember when I was ten and I had a black boy to play with...not far from here as a matter of fact. He's undoubtedly sterilized by now.'
>
> "'But then he's had one child,' Jason pointed out. 'His wife had to surrender their birth coupon when their first and only child came... but they've got that child. The law lets them have it. And there're a million statutes protecting their safety.'

THE TAO OF FERD

> "'Two adults, one child,' the clerk said. 'So the black population is halved every generation. Ingenious. You have to hand it to Tidman; he solved the race problem, all right.'"

Our hero is Jason Taverner, a popular TV talk show host who, after surviving a murder attempt by his mistress, wakes up in a run-down hotel to discover that all evidence of his existence has been wiped from the Earth. His IDs are gone, his friends don't recognize him, and his name is nowhere to be found in the government's databases. And in a world where you're asked "Papers, please," every other mile, being a nonperson is a one-way trip to the gulag.

On the run from the law, Taverner hooks up with Kathy, an ID forger and police informer with a batshit crazy streak. In the process, he catches the eye of LAPD chief Felix Buckman; thinking that Taverner is some kind of high-level government agent, Buckman has the police track him down. Taverner himself flees to Las Vegas to hide out with Ruth Rae, an Elizabeth Taylor-esque has-been actress with fifty ex-husbands. Cornered by the cops, Taverner is taken back to L.A. to be interrogated by Buckman and subsequently falls under the wing of his sister Alys, a slutty, drug using bisexual who has an incestuous relationship with her brother. Alys also happens to be the only person in the world who knows who Jason Taverner is.

THE TAO OF FERD

Flow My Tears is one hell of a riveting book, but there's one chapter that particularly resonated with me, the chapter that most clearly elucidates Dick's anti-Calvinist sentiments. Near the midway point of the novel, police are ransacking Ruth Rae's apartment building looking for Taverner when they come across a Mr. Mufi, a fat, pathetic slob with a predilection for pubescent boys. While preparing to cuff him, the corporal on duty discovers that Mufi's paramour is thirteen years old, and that as part of a campaign to take all victimless crimes off the books, the age of consent has been lowered to twelve. Frustrated that they can't legally charge him with anything, the police leave the cowardly bastard with this:

> "'I hope,' the corporal said, 'that someday you do commit a statute violation of some kind, and they haul you in, and I'm on duty the day it happens. So I can book you personally.' He hawked, then spat on Mr. Mufi. Spat into his hairy, empty face."

If that paragraph doesn't sum up mainstream Calvinist conservatism—unknowing, unthinking, with no higher principles than the desire to be the topper in the cell block of American society, getting off on raping the already weak and despised—I don't know what does. Dick even makes it clear who he's talking about when he describes the carpet in Mr. Mufi's living room as "depict[ing] in gold Richard M. Nixon's final ascent into heaven amid joyous singing above and wails of misery below."

If there's one criticism I'd level at *Flow My Tears*, the narrative sort-of disintegrates in the final third. The ultimate plot twist is relatively weak by Dickian standards, and the action doesn't really build to a climax, instead plodding along to its conclusion. The book also never explains the backstory of Felix and Alys' relationship; they have a son, Barney, who apparently grows up to be a normal man, not suffering the physical and mental retardation you'd expect the child of *siblings* to have. It's not important to the story, but I found it a bit odd. Still, I'd recommend *Flow My Tears* as a great introduction to the only good science fiction writer of the past century.

November 22, 2011

Roadmap to Freedom

It was a chilly January day when I logged in to my vanity Facebook account and found this waiting for me in my private messages:

> "Hey Ferd,
>
> "Long-time listener, first time caller. I've been a fan of *In Mala Fide* for a while now, but your post on Roosh Syndrome in particular nailed my life to a T.
>
> "I'm writing to ask you to have a look at my blog. Here's a summary from the intro page:

THE TAO OF FERD

"'This blog's mission will be to narrate and inspire my rise from what I am – a content and conventionally successful young guy, one year into his tenure at a prestigious, but soul-destroying desk job – into what I want to be: An Artist. A Man. A genuinely happy and fulfilled person, whose life is spent creating and experiencing the sublime.'

"I haven't written about politics yet, but I am a close follower of you, (obviously) Steve Sailer, Mencius, Roissy, Mangan, OneSTDV, Derbyshire, etc.

"I'd like to jump into the alt-right blogosphere in the near future, so I'm putting together a few sample posts and sending them around to gauge reactions.

"I would really appreciate if you would consider recommending a specific post to your readers. It's titled 'How radical politics can save your life' and I'd be happy to email you a draft if you can send me your address.

"Cheers,

"[CENSORED]

"(I also guest-posted as "Zdeno" at 2Blowhards a while ago)"

Another kid brownnosing me for a favor. It's one of the side effects of fame. Two plus years of venting my rage and frustration on this website and giving all my fellow bloggers virtual reach-arounds in the form of weekly linkage posts means I get a lot of up-and-comers asking me to promote their work. Every week, my inbox fills up with bloggers new and old asking me to plug one of their posts or take a look at their sites. It's like picking up women. When you're a nervous chump starting out, you have to approach the girls yourself; after you've gotten your share of notches and straightened your life out, they start coming to you. I'm practically the Andy Warhol of the manosphere, giving everyone who passes through my doors their fifteen minutes of fame.

This was the response I sent:

"Hey [CENSORED],

"Sorry for the delay, been busy. I did add your blog to my roll, though. My advice – forget about reactions and just publish the post. If I like it, I'll link to it. Blogging isn't about achieving perfection on the first draft – it's about working out your flaws through repetitious practice and feedback. Putting the post up publicly and allowing lots of people to read and comment on it will do you far more good than mailing it around privately.

"Ferdinand"

Shortly thereafter, Frost took *Freedom Twenty-Five* live, and the rest is history.

One year later, this Bardamu Superstar has accomplished everything that he set out to do. He's quit his job, he's moved to Thailand, and now he's written a book on how you too can liberate yourself from the sexless, carb-loaded capitalist rat race: *Freedom Twenty-Five: The 21st Century Man's Guide to Life*. And it's required reading for everyone in the manosphere.

Full disclaimer: I had a small role in proofreading the draft for *Freedom Twenty-Five*, enough so that Frost gave me a shout-out in his Acknowledgments. I must admit, it's a little weird seeing yourself credited in a printed book under a pseudonym, but there are stranger things in this world. But just because I helped edit the book doesn't mean I'm gonna go easy on it.

First off, if you're expecting *Freedom* to be a fully-detailed tome in the style of *The 4-Hour Workweek*, you're going to be disappointed. Frost's book could have easily have been titled *The Red Pill Reader*, because that's what it is: a brief introduction to paleo dieting, gold investing and other strange stops along the road less traveled. To compensate for *Freedom's* brevity (152 pages), Frost has both priced it cheaply ($15.99 for paperback, $9.99 for Kindle) and assembled an Online Companion to supplement the main text.

The book opens with a brief introduction in which Frost explains why he's just so damn qualified to tell you to change your entire life; he was an aimless wanderer like the rest of us:

> "Most importantly, I realized that I had almost completely lost the sense of purpose and drive that had once animated my life. Several half-finished novels lingered on my hard drive. A box of business cards and promo material from a failed entrepreneurial venture collected dust in my closet. Waking up in the morning and falling asleep at night became difficult. I caught myself making excuses to avoid life – friends, girls, new experiences and challenges – so I could sit at home and watch my limited hours in this world slip away."

While Frost and I come from different walks of life, his writing about the ennui and hopelessness he felt plugging away at *his* makework government job was eerily familiar. It's been nearly a year since I walked into that hideous neo-Soviet compound for another day of mindless drudgery, and knowing that I'm not alone, that there's another guy my age who was in the same situation, is a nice reassurance.

Freedom is organized into five chapters in the order of Maslow's Hierarchy of Needs: "Health," "Wealth," "Sex," "Wisdom," and "Purpose." The first three are self-explanatory, covering the ground of diet, exercise, game, and frugality. Frost backs up his assertions with citations from expert sources from Ramit Sethi to Roissy, as well as his own methods and experiences. For example, knowing full well that one of the rationales that fatties give for being fat is that healthy eating "takes too much time," Frost relates that going on the paleo diet means you'll be spending *less* time eating and cooking:

> "I eat 1–2 meals per day, and I'm almost never hungry. The conventional wisdom states that you should eat five meals a day, which is true if you're eating a typical American diet and need to constantly snack to maintain your blood sugar. On a high-fat Paleo diet, your body gets used to using dietary and stored fats as its primary energy source, meaning you can go long periods without feeling tired, 'hangry' (hungry + angry) or like your stomach is eating itself.
>
> "I now frequently go 18 hours without a meal, and

> by the 17th hour, I feel a vague sense of "Oh yeah, food would be nice right now, wouldn't it?" But I could just as easily work out, play a game of hockey, or take a nap."

As you can see, the tone of *Freedom Twenty-Five* is the same as the blog: like reading Tim Ferriss' excitable, caffeine-bombed younger brother. While I was reading, I could practically feel Frost standing behind me clapping me on the shoulder, trying to gauge how impressed I was with his genius. *"So Ferd, how'd you like it? Huh? HUH?"* Well okay, it's not that bad, but too often he veers into the happy-go-lucky condescension that defines modern self-improvement writing: *"I'm ripped like Arnold, I'm richer than Solomon, and I'm getting laid like a bathmat and SO CAN YOU!"* Maybe it's just because I'm a cynical burnout, but I find this attitude off-putting after a while.

Still, when you've got the factual goods to back up your boasting, style isn't such a huge deal. Chapter 4, on "Wisdom," deals with actually getting off your rear-end to make something of yourself. The section on "information diets" is nothing new if you've read *The 4-Hour Workweek*, but Frost injects some manospheric wisdom by bringing up the anti-male nature of mainstream media. I also chuckled at this swipe at political junkies:

> "Finally, if you follow the news, not out of some sort

of grade-11-civics-induced Calvinist guilt, but because you actually ENJOY it, because you feel that doing so makes you HAPPY...then you have no idea what true happiness is. Go get a girlfriend or ride a bike or something."

The final chapter, "Purpose," is a manifesto encouraging us Millennials to rebel against the various forces weighing us down, seeking to chain us to a mindless existence of office drudgery, fast food and the mediocrity of marriage:

"We are rebelling against a culture of laziness, mediocrity and spiritual poverty. We are rebelling against a world that encourages us to be passive, risk-averse and unremarkable.

"The most effective way to rebel against that is to become remarkable. Become excellent. Become the best possible version of yourself you can be, and then share your story with others who want to do the same. In a culture that has purged itself of confidence, let's create a counterculture organized along the exact opposite ideals: Pride. Courage. Self-respect. Strength."

A-fucking-men, brother.

To help you along, Frost includes a "Getting Started" section at the end of the first four chapters giving you simple, practical instructions for putting his advice into action. And of course, the book's Online Companion, hosted at Frost's blog, is stuffed with authoritative sources to ease your journey into the real.

My biggest criticism of *Freedom* is the Companion itself, or at least the way Frost handled it. The book is skimpy and short by design; rather than load it up with quotes and filler, he simply directs the reader to the *Freedom Twenty-Five* website if they have any burning questions that can't be answered in the space of 150 pages. While I think Frost's lean prose is a big plus for the book, and he's also promised to continuously update the Companion with new info, he doesn't go into as much detail as I would like in some sections, such as the investing portion of the "Wealth" chapter. Also a little annoying is the lack of endnotes in the book corresponding to sections in the Companion. I don't see how it would have hurt the book to tack on the Companion as an index instead of exiling it to an online ghetto.

Another wrong note with *Freedom* is the forward by Roosh. He's ordinarily a funny and frank writer, but this forward reads like a failed freshman writing workshop submission, going into very little detail about anything and doing nothing to enhance your experience of the book as a result. It's the literary equivalent of watching two men masturbating in a hot tub: gay, unnecessary and awkward. Because this is Frost's first book, I can grade him on a curve; not so with Roosh.

Still, the short length of *Freedom Twenty-Five* may end up being one of its greatest assets. I believe that too much information in these scenarios leads to paralysis; awash in pointless facts, you become unable to make a decision, too busy running the calculations in your head. Frost's approach is to arm you with some knowledge and the means to inform yourself further, giving you just enough to get started but not so much that you get lost in mental calculus.

More importantly, Frost's book is invaluable not just because of his practical advice but because of the attitude it presents. Notwithstanding his occasional forays into condescension, Frost reinforces an important idea that most self-improvement shysters don't: *self-improvement is a roadmap, not a guided tour.* There is no 100 percent foolproof method to becoming rich, getting a six-pack or having women line up to suck your dick. You need to seek out the facts yourself, test them, find out what works for you and what doesn't. Everyone is different enough that they'll need to chart their own paths to prosperity.

"Living well is the best revenge" is a tired cliche, but it's the truth. The manosphere takes heat from all corners: from feminists upset that the PC apple cart is being overturned to Christian "conservatives" eternally seeking out marks for their never-ending con game. The thin red thread connecting these disparate groups of haters is that they are all failures in their personal lives. Oh sure, some of them may be outwardly successful, healthy, wealthy or otherwise. But deep down inside, all of them feel inadequate, even if they won't admit it. Whether it's the barren-wombed lawyer termagent who labors eighty hours a week with nothing to look forward to but another drunken one-night stand, or the married eunuch putting himself into an early grave to provide for a wife who hates him and children who don't respect him, mediocrities can't stand excellence. Like crabs in a bucket, they'd rather drag down anyone who rises to the top instead of figuring out how to escape themselves.

What gives me satisfaction when these types hate on me and my comrades is not only knowing that I'm healthier, more financially secure and sexually satisfied then them, but knowing that I have one thing they don't and never will: *freedom*. While I'm still working on achieving my dreams, unlike the termagent or the eunuch, I don't have to wait until arthritis sets in to realize them. I'm not tied to my job, my house or my city. I don't get out of bed every morning dreading the day to come. I don't work a job I hate to pay off a stream of credit card debts. I don't put up with disrespectful women out of some misbegotten sense of loyalty to a society that abandoned me long ago. While I'd never say I'm happy (because "happiness" is a fleeting emotion, not a state of being), I can look at myself in the mirror and claim to be fulfilled, something none of my detractors can honestly say.

Are you fulfilled, or are you going to content yourself with mediocrity? Are you going to go through life on *your* terms or will you let the government, the church, the culture or the women dictate who you should be? If you were driven enough to find and read a blog like this or any other in the manosphere, you're already more intelligent, driven and capable than 99% of the human herd. The tools to build a better life for yourself are at your fingertips; you just need to get off your ass and learn to use them. *Freedom Twenty-Five* is an excellent place to start.

Just remember that defeatism is the province of impotent and old men. A weakling cries about what was and what could be; a man molds the future with his own hands. So long as you are driven, inquisitive and always moving forward, everything will be all right.

December 1, 2011

In Praise of Self-Loathing

Accusing someone of being a self-loathing [fill-in-the-blank] is one of the most popular insults on the Internet, almost up there with Godwin's Law in its predictability. The minute someone inveighs against a particular social class that we all know to be annoying and stupid, that someone is almost immediately called a self-loathing member of that class, projecting his self-loathing on his brethren. And in a world that worships at the altar of Self-Esteem, being "self-loathing" is a grievous sin, almost as bad as being a Nazi!

For example, a couple months back, I published a couple of articles by Chad Daring, "The No Fat Chicks Challenge" and "Why I Hate Fat People," in which he explained his disdain for the fatties of the world; he was a fatty himself and has spent the past few years working himself out of that hole. Both here and at his blog, Chad got slammed by fatty apologists with the "self-loathing" line, as exemplified by this comment:

> "There's an error in your blog post.
>
> "The title is currently – 'Why I Hate Fat People'
>
> "But the title should be – 'Why I Hate Myself'
>
> "The sooner you realize that you are projecting a personal element of self-loathing and fear out on to people of size or 'fat people' and, more importantly, WHY you are doing this, the closer you may become to achieving true inner peace.
>
> "The answer you are looking for (and the catalyst that is driving this post and this entire blog) might not be in the gym or the kitchen but in therapy session/s. Because right now the only battle you are fighting is one with yourself (despite what you

may believe)."

The same goes for anyone who opposes shameful and despicable behavior: they are immediately shamed with the "self-loathing" label. Whenever I point out that nerds are repulsive wastes of skin, some joker always claims I'm secretly a self-loathing nerd, the same moronic train of thought that also says that guys who bash fat chicks do so because they're stuck dating them. When a homo decides he *doesn't* want to be a hysterical, foaming-at-the-mouth maniac like 99% of homos, he's labeled a self-loathing gay man. When a black man aspires to be more than a uneducated ghetto gangbanger, he's derided as an "oreo," shorthand for "self-hating black person."

The "self-loathing" epithet says a hell of a lot more about the person hurling it then the one it's getting hurled at. For starters, note the contexts in which it's deployed. I've written countless articles denouncing, mocking and beating down feminists, yet no one's ever accused me of being a secret, self-loathing feminist. The use of the "self-loathing" epithet is revealing in that *it's a tacit acknowledgment that whatever's being discussed is inherently shameful and wrong,* but the person wielding it wants the accused to shut up about it, to ignore the fact that the emperor is naked.

But this doesn't approach the heart of the "self-loathing" insult; why's being self-loathing so bad anyway? I'd argue that if you're fat, socially retarded or otherwise a failure in life, *you damn well ought to be self-loathing.* If you feel guilty about your problems, that means you're cognizant of them and more likely to work to get rid of them. Having self-esteem when you've done nothing to earn it is a sign of delusion. Since when did being proud of being a loser become socially acceptable?

Since the rise of the Self-Esteem Cult, that's when. In our anti-hierarchical, egalitarian society, everyone is supposed to be equal, no better or worse than anyone else. By this logic, anyone who is rightfully ashamed of their lot in life and working to improve it is a blasphemer. *"It's not YOUR fault for being fat, it's society's fault for not accepting all 350 pounds of you! Stop blaming yourself for things you can't control!"* It's a strictly deterministic view of the world, in which people are trapped in their social roles and unable to climb their way out of them.

And it's a total lie, which is why the "self-loathing" line is deployed to shame people into giving up on themselves. When someone accuses you of being self-loathing, this is what they're really saying:

"You've recognized that you're deficient in some way (physically, mentally, morally) and are trying to improve yourself. I resent you for this, because your efforts make it more difficult for me to rationalize my complete failure to do the same, and it's far easier to blame everyone else for my problems instead of taking responsibility for them."

That's right: the people who hate on others for being

"self-loathing" are all losers right down the line. The weak always despise the strong and will try to tear them down, to drag them back into the mediocre masses. A fat person trying to lose weight, a nerd who puts down the video games and gets out of the house, a gay man who tries to integrate himself into heterosexual society; these people have more determination and willpower then all of their detractors combined. And their detractors know it, which is why they dedicate their lives to trying to destroy their superiors, so they can continue wallowing in their own misery and neuroses.

Going back to Chad Daring's posts, the reason he was so violently opposed by fat apologists was because he demolished their most precious, their prettiest lie: that they were completely powerless to get in shape. Let's look at another comment from one of them:

> "Wow... so many gene pools in dire need of filters.
>
> "You people should be ashamed, stop trolling internet forums, and seriously seek out the sunlight.
>
> "So much unnecessary hate. Whether you want to admit to it or not, you all are either related to or close to at least one person whom is overweight. Just imagine how that person would feel if they would come to learn your horrible views on fat

people?

"Fat or not, people are people and all deserve the same respect. I hope some of you end up in the fat pool one day, receive a dose of your own bitter medicine, and truly regret your way of thinking."

Just look at the language this heffalump used: "end up in the fat pool." The implication is that being fat is something that just happens to you, like tripping and falling down the stairs or catching a cold, and *not* the result of bad choices on your part. Chad and the countless men and women who hit the gym and cut down at dinnertime are living proof that *the easiest way to get over the pain of being fat is to STOP being fat.* The butterballs would rather blame the world for not accepting their sweaty, disgusting selves instead of taking the initiative to solve their problems.

I'm not some 15-year old Randroid idiot. I recognize that if you're a young, straight white man, there are incredible forces pushing against you, trying to make you fail. But these forces are not insurmountable. Sitting on your ass all day whining about how the 1%, the wimmenz, or the government are trying to keep you down is the mark of a loser, and won't get you anything more than a shoulder to cry on. If you want to solve your problems, you have to get up from the computer and work on them yourself; no one else gives a shit about you.

And if someone accuses you of being self-loathing, laugh at them; they're going nowhere in life, no matter how loudly they bray at you.

January 17, 2012

How to Stop Masturbating

Every man masturbates. Every day, multiple times a day, every other day; the frequency may vary, but every man is lubing up his salami for a spank session on a regular basis. Married, single, swinging, it doesn't matter how often he plows his tool into Vagina Fields, he's beating his meat. Everyone knows all this.

And you need to stop masturbating.

Well okay, you don't *need* to, just like you don't *need* to stop shoveling Big Macs down your throat. It's just that your quality of life will noticeably improve if you aren't slapping your cock around three times a day.

I'm not religious. I was raised as a Catholic, but I've gone to Mass exactly once in my adult life, and that was because it was part of a funeral. I'm not here to tell you that masturbation is bad because it makes Jesus cry, I'm here to tell you that it's bad because it has negative effects on your body and mind. Not jerking off confers all kinds of benefits:

1. You have more energy.

Your body is smarter than you think; it can tell the

difference between fool's gold and the real deal. While it's tempting to say that ejaculation is ejaculation, there's a world of sensory difference between jerking off in front of a computer and having sex with an actual woman. The former just gives you visual and auditory stimulation; with the live woman, you're not only seeing her naked body and hearing her moans of ecstasy, but inhaling her pheromones and feeling her physically. Medical science bears this out; unlike actual sex, beating off kills your testosterone levels, sapping your physical strength and turning you into a logy, limp lump. If you smack it with regularity, you aren't aware of this because your body has become accustomed to it, but if you abstain for a few days, you'll easily notice the difference. A 2003 study by the *Journal of Zhejiang University SCIENCE* showed that men who refrained from masturbating for at least seven days had a noticeable increase in their testosterone levels.[8]

For example, I've noticed that when I jerk off, I'm noticeably weaker afterward. When I first started experimenting with abstention, I went for about three weeks before giving in. The day after, I had to help load broken snowmobiles onto a trailer, and I could barely lift anything, I felt so tired and groggy. I never feel this way whenever I bang a girl; I'll get winded and sore maybe, but never lethargic. My BMI is on the healthy side; I exercise at home regularly and I watch what I eat, but I'm not particularly muscular. For me, not masturbating is like gaining ten pounds of muscle without having to spend a day in the gym. I can lift heavy objects more easily and exercise for longer periods of time when I'm not gratifying myself. In fact, I have so much energy when I don't fap that sometimes my leg will start jittering when I sit down, which usually only happens when I drink caffeine.

2. You have more focus.

Do you procrastinate like a stoned college student? Need to get an important project done? Keep your hands off your rod and watch your attention span rise on its own. When you avoid jacking off, your ability to concentrate and focus shoots through the roof, allowing you to do things like read books or fill out boring paperwork for longer durations. You also become more resistant to wasting time. For example, in the first weeks after I stopped pulling it, whenever I cleared out a block of time to do something mindless like play video games, I found myself quitting and restarting repeatedly due to a nagging voice in the back of my skull saying *"Don't you have something better to do? There's laundry to fold, taxes to finish, and all kinds of work to get done, and here you're playing some bullshit RPG you don't even really like."*

3. Women find you more attractive.

This is two-fold. The movie *There's Something About Mary* popularized the idea of popping off a load before you go on a date to take away your nervousness. The problem with this is that while playing with your little priest may make you less nervous, as noted above, it kills your energy and drive as well, making you more complacent and less assertive.[9] But this isn't the only thing about masturbation that turns girls off. Women can actually sniff out habitual weiner-whackers from the pheromones they give off, and they don't like them.[10] Not one bit. Rubbing one out before a date is basically castrating yourself. Abstention makes you sexier on both a conscious and unconscious level.

4. You find women more attractive.

It's well-known by this point how excessive porn usage deadens the pleasure men get from actual sex. Here's a good article about men who were able to cure erectile dysfunction and rediscover their desire for their wives/girlfriends by giving up porn.[11] I can confirm this in my own life; fapping to porn drains me of sexual desire in a way that sex doesn't. Whenever I get done turning my crank to whatever clip I've dredged up on *YouPorn*, the images that I once thought were sexy become boring, even disgusting; I want to take a piss, a shower and forget about it. In contrast, unloading an eight-roper on a girl's breasts doesn't make her any less attractive to me. If you're having trouble in the bedroom, ceasing your nightly smack sessions will halt and reverse the deadening effects of porn. The bad news is that you'll start fantasizing about fat chicks. The good news is that already hot girls will seem even hotter, and if you're not already in a relationship, you'll be way more motivated to meet girls period to sate your cock hunger.

5. You dream more vividly.

Not sure how this works, but when I'm not spilling my seed on pr0n, my dreams are more memorable and striking. I'm not big into dream interpretation, but I still enjoy this. And speaking of dreams...

6. You start having wet dreams again.

Ah, you remember those days? You were a horny 14-year old dreaming about slamming Nicole from biology class, motorboating her luscious double Ds, when you suddenly woke up in your bed in the middle of the night all alone. Dismayed, you got up to go to the bathroom when you noticed that your boxers were already damp. Chances are you can't remember the last time you had a nocturnal emission, because you started masturbating instead, relieving your testicles of the need to empty themselves. When you stop bopping your bishop, your chance of reliving this part of your wasted youth increases exponentially. (This may not be a selling point for some guys, but I'm apparently "immature," so it works for me.)

7. You'll save time.

If you spend a good deal of time watching porn, you inevitably end up wasting huge amounts of time finding the perfect clip to rub one out to. The sheer amounts of smut on the Internet these days paralyzes our brains, making us sift through hundreds of thousands of videos until we find the one that perfectly aligns with our desires at that moment. *"Let's see, do I jerk off to Gianna Michaels today? Or that Latina chick with the curly hair? Maybe a nice petite Asian..."* No more masturbating means no more porn.

The simple fact of the matter is that masturbation is the sexual equivalent of junk food. If you stuff your face with Starburst and Pepsi, you'll feel great for a little bit, until the sugar crash comes and you just want to curl up on your couch and take a nap. Similarly, if you squeeze off a shot to *Big Blonde Anal Sluts 6*, you'll enjoy the orgasm for a few minutes before you realize the life has been drained from your bones. Sanctified onanism is the seamy side of consumerism, a doctrine that encourages us to become addicted to short-term indulgences no matter the long-term costs.

But now that you know the pluses of masturbation abstention, how can you stop being a willy whacker?

Answer: *suck it up.*

I'm serious. While I have a number of tips that can make your journey easier, no amount of tricks can help you if you don't have the willpower to resist your base urges. There's no magical, instant solution to achieving anything worthwhile, just work, pain and sacrifice. Just like all diets require you ignore your grumbling stomach and not pig out like a slob every night, avoiding the abominable sin require you to have enough restraint to not rush off to the bathroom every time you get a stiffy. To put it another way, you're going to have to man up. Also, the younger you are, the harder it'll be to kick the masturbation habit, flush as you are with hormones and the energy to go all night. Nonetheless, here are some ways to help you wean yourself off of the teat.

1. Get rid of your moisturizing lotion.

The problem with giving advice like "get rid of everything you could potentially masturbate with" is that a man can grease his dick up with almost *anything* if he's desperate enough, regardless of how much pain it causes him afterward. Vaseline takes forever to clean up and smells bad; shampoo causes the skin on your cock to molt, like a bad sunburn; doing it raw, unless you're uncircumcised, works for all of two days in a row before the soreness mounts. The point is that a man's who sufficiently horny can get his rocks off with just about any household liquid substance imaginable.

However, there's one item that basically exists to make masturbation easier: moisturizing lotion. It's cheap, smells good, doesn't have any nasty aftereffects and dries up on its own, minimizing the amount of cleanup you have to do. It's the male equivalent of the Hitachi Magic Wand. Stop buying this shit; it serves no purpose other than helping you inflate *Spankwire's* hit counts. If you actually need this stuff for whatever reason, stop pussyfooting around and find an actual cure for your problem. If the backs of your hands crack and bleed in the winter, like mine used to, move into a building with radiator heat (which retains more moisture than convection heat) and/or wear gloves outside whenever the temperature is below 40 degrees (or 5 degrees Celsius for you non-Americans). If you've got severe eczema, go to the doctor.

2. Delete all your porn.

A no-brainer: find your secret code-locked smut folder or USB stick and wipe it clean. You don't have to delete *every* picture of a naked woman on your hard drive, but if it serves no artistic purpose aside from helping you catch a nut, it's gotta go. To determine whether it's artistic or not, ask yourself this: does it have a penis in it? If yes, it goes straight into the Recycle Bin.

3. Go to bed earlier.

Maybe it's just me, but I have a complex about manhandling my crotch-wrench during daylight hours. If you're the kind of person who has to wait until nightfall to pinch off a loaf, moving your bedtime earlier in the evening will help. You should be doing this anyway, because staying up late fucks with your body's natural rhythms once you get past a certain age. When I was a teenager, I pulled all-nighters doing classwork, partying or playing video games easily; now in my twenties, I feel awful if I don't drag my ass into bed by 2am at least.

If you have trouble sleeping, try using antihistamines like Benadryl, over-the-counter allergy pills that make you drowsy as a side effect. I pop two of those little pink pills a night and I'm out cold in twenty minutes. A $3-4 bottle from Walmart or any supermarket will last you more than half a year. Alternately, you can just drink more. Don't, I repeat, *do not* combine alcohol and antihistamines under *any* circumstances. Both substances slow your breathing and heart rate, and putting the two together can cause you to pass out and stop breathing altogether.

Some guys recommend using melatonin to cure sleep problems; I've personally become a big believer in the stuff myself. Melatonin is naturally secreted by the brain at night, a hormone that signals your body to gear down for bedtime. However, the presence of artificial lighting from computers, lamps and the like often fools your brain into thinking it's daytime, slowing melatonin production and causing you to stay up late. Taking supplements will force your body into sleep mode, helpful if you want to get your bed schedule under control. Melatonin can be bought over-the-counter in the U.S. at organic grocery stores like Whole Foods, as well as the organic sections of regular supermarkets like Price Chopper or Fred Meyer.

If you're on the computer a lot, try installing *F.lux*, a program that will automatically raise and lower your monitor's temperature to coincide with the sunrise and sunset, helping you gear your body into sleep mode.[12] It's available for Windows, Mac, Linux, iPhone and iPad.

4. Buy a standing desk.

This is also something else should be doing anyway, because sitting down is extraordinarily bad for you. How bad?

Sitting on your ass for long periods of time interferes with the blood circulation in your legs, slows your calorie burning to basically nothing (contributing to obesity), doubles your risk for cardiovascular disease, and causes a whole raft of other serious health problems. Another benefit of standing desks is that they take up less space than regular ones; if you live in a small apartment, like I do, you need every inch of space you can get.

For our purposes though, sitting down when using the computer makes it that much easier for you to wank it. Standing up decreases your comfort level and makes it easier for you to resist. At home, I use a Safco Stand-up 35"-49" Adjustable Height Computer Workstation, which retails for around $350-400 at office supply stores like Staples and Office Max. It's pricey, but the health and space benefits it provides are well worth it.

5. Get off your ass and work out.

It's damned difficult to slap your salami when you can't even muster the energy to get hard. Whenever you feel the need to blow your load, get up and exercise instead. Going to the gym every time you get horny isn't practical, so if you don't have one already, buy an exercise mat and do sit-ups and push-ups until the urges pass. If you live in a decent neighborhood and the weather is nice, going for a walk or jog around the block works too. Whatever you choose to do, you have to make sure that it burns off enough excess energy so that you don't have any left over for Mrs. Palmer and her five daughters.

6. Pee instead of masturbating.

This can work at any time of the day, but it's particularly useful when you wake up in the morning, confronted with a throbbing, wood-splitting boner. When I'm just coming out of sleep and my mind isn't at full working capacity, the temptation to rub one out right then and there is strong. Instead of abusing your king and crown, roll out of bed and relieve your bladder. After you've had a good pee, your erection should deflate on its own. Alternately, train your wife/girlfriend to give you early-morning blowjobs.

7. Block your computer from being able to access porn sites.

A friend of mine suggests installing *X3 Watch* on your computer to help deter you from fapping.[13] It's a program that reports any questionable sites you visit to an "accountability partner" of your choosing, like your mom. That's a bit extreme for my tastes, but it might work for you.

If you're using Windows and want to get more direct, you can outright ban porn sites from being accessed on your computer without installing any software. It's a simple procedure:

1. Navigate to the "hosts" file on your computer (C:\Windows\System32\Drivers\etc\hosts) and open it up with Notepad.

2. When you've opened up the file, you'll see a line reading

"127.0.0.1 localhost" (sans quotes). Add a line below it with the webpage you want to block (e.g. "127.0.0.1 www.youporn.com", again without quotes). Repeat this for all websites.

3. Save the file.
4. If you have any web browsers open, close and reopen them.

If you've done this properly, attempting to open the sites you blocked in your browser will get you nothing but an error message. *BAM!* No more faptime for you.

8. If you're worried about premature ejaculation, switch up positions during sex.

This is possibly the biggest problem with curbing your stack-whacking: you'll blow your wad much quicker when doing the dirty deed. A guide to Tantric sex is outside the subject matter of this book, so my quick recommendation is to change positions frequently to keep you from detonating right off the bat. You might be doing this already, but if you're not going to jack off, you'll need to take it to the next level. For example, I might start out in missionary, switch to cowgirl to recuperate, then go to doggystyle and back to missionary for the grand finale. If you're a student of "game," the art of seduction, think of switching positions as the sexual equivalent of a venue change; it makes it seem like you've been banging for longer then you actually have.

And of course, abstaining from spanking it will make your loads noticeably bigger when you finally do blow one out. There's nothing like unloading half a cup of cum on your girl's face to make you feel like a boss. One-man bukkake!

9. Don't get religious about it.

Have I stopped jerking off entirely since I began my crusade a year ago? Of course not. I still enjoy a nice fap session once every month or so. I'm human, I'm imperfect, I succumb to temptation like everyone else.

Once you've managed to get your urges under control, pinching one off every so often isn't a big deal. It's like dieting: once you've lost thirty pounds and can climb a staircase without passing out, it won't kill you to enjoy a double-fudge sundae on occasion. You won't be styling yourself a "recovering masturbator," unable to look at another photo of a naked woman lest you relapse and find yourself doing the 12-step program all over again. The point is to master your urges and not let them rule you. As the old cliché goes, everything in moderation.

Like everything else worth doing in life, combating your masturbation addiction will be hard, not just because you're giving up something that feels good, but conventional wisdom and society itself are working against you. Sloughing off short-term pleasure for long-term gain is never easy, but the benefits are more than worth the struggle. Best of luck to you in your journey.

THE TAO OF FERD

February 20, 2012, revised and expanded March 2012

The Case for Gassing New York

God, what an unreadable piece of shit.

I recall stumbling across a used copy of *City of Glass* when I was a kid and liking it for some inexplicable reason. I never bothered reading the two following installments in *The New York Trilogy*, so when I saw them all bundled together in a single Kindle volume, I jumped for joy. That was an Amazon gift card well-spent.

As soon as I laid eyes on Luc Sante's introduction, I knew I was in trouble:

> "Paul Auster has the key to the city. He has not, as far as I know, been presented with the literal object, traditionally an oversized five-pound gold-plated item, dispensed to visiting benefactors and favored natives on a dais in front of City Hall by a functionary in top hat and claw hammer coat, but I doubt he needs one of those. Auster's key is like the key to dreams or the key to the highway. It is an alchemical passe-partout that allows him to see through walls and around corners, that permits him entry to corridors and substrata and sealed houses nobody else notices, as well as to a field of

THE TAO OF FERD

variegated phenomena once considered discrete, but whose coherence Auster has established. This territory is a realm within New York City, a current that runs along its streets, within its office buildings and apartment houses and helter-skelter through its parks—a force field charged by synchronicity and overlap, perhaps invisible but inarguably there, although it was never identified as such before Auster planted his flag."

Recognize this? It's the overwrought diction of every "real" literary novel published in the past quarter-century. You've got the run-on sentences, the padding, and the highfalutin vocabulary. I mean, "passe-partout?" Do you even know what that means? I didn't, so I looked it up; it's French for "master key." Now that's how "real" writers write: using obscure terms to remind us all how smart they are and what dumbfucks we are in comparison. If a student handed this in to me for a grade, I'd strike out half of it with a red pen: *"Too much filler. Needless repetition. Drop the David Fuckster Wallace act and write like a normal human being."* And this is only the first paragraph!

Since this is a trilogy, I'll review each book on its own.

City of Glass

The lengthiest book in the series, it's also the only one worth reading. The plot concerns Daniel Quinn, a hermit mystery novel author who gets embroiled in an actual detective case after being mistaken for Paul Auster. Oh yes, Auster is a character in his own novel. I smell postmodern hijinks!

> "The following night, Quinn was caught off guard. He had thought the incident was over and was not expecting the stranger to call again. As it happened, he was sitting on the toilet, in the act of expelling a turd, when the telephone rang. It was somewhat later than the previous night, perhaps ten or twelve minutes before one. Quinn had just reached the chapter that tells of Marco Polo's journey from Peking to Amoy, and the book was open on his lap as he went about his business in the tiny bathroom. The ringing of the telephone came as a distinct irritation. To answer it promptly would mean getting up without wiping himself, and he was loath to walk across the apartment in that state. On the other hand, if he finished what he was doing at his normal speed, he would not make it to the phone in time. In spite of this, Quinn found himself reluctant to move. The telephone was not

his favorite object, and more than once he had considered getting rid of his. What he disliked most of all was its tyranny. Not only did it have the power to interrupt him against his will, but inevitably he would give in to its command. This time, he decided to resist. By the third ring, his bowels were empty. By the fourth ring, he had succeeded in wiping himself. By the fifth ring, he had pulled up his pants, left the bathroom, and was walking calmly across the apartment. He answered the phone on the sixth ring, but there was no one at the other end. The caller had hung up."

You can pretty much guess how the rest of the book reads from this one paragraph: lots of exposition, adjective abuse, and page-long paragraphs. Still, unlike the following two books, *City of Glass* is interesting because it at least tries to conform to the structure of a narrative, with a discernible plot, dialogue and a character arc, detailing Quinn involving himself in the case to the point where he descends into gibbering insanity. At the very least, I was motivated to keep reading. You can spout all kinds of babble about how *City of Glass* is about breaking down the boundaries between truth and fiction and questioning the relationship between author and reader, but none of it matters. If you want a good, vaguely Coen-esque mystery story, *City of*

Glass is a decent read.

Ghosts

I was plodding my way through this godawful novella (the shortest installment of the trilogy) trying not to fall asleep, when I came across this paragraph:

> "One night, therefore, Blue finally turns to his copy of Walden. The time has come, he says to himself, and if he doesn't make an effort now, he knows that he never will. But the book is not a simple business. As Blue begins to read, he feels as though he is entering an alien world. Trudging through swamps and brambles, hoisting himself up gloomy screes and treacherous cliffs, he feels like a prisoner on a forced march, and his only thought is to escape. He is bored by Thoreau's words and finds it difficult to concentrate. Whole chapters go by, and when he comes to the end of them he realizes that he has not retained a thing. Why would anyone want to go off and live alone in the woods? What's all this about planting beans and not drinking coffee or eating meat? Why all these interminable descriptions of birds? Blue thought that he was going to get a story, or at least something

like a story, but this is no more than blather, an endless harangue about nothing at all."

There's nothing like a book that insults you for even bothering to read it. I almost think Auster threw this in to make fun of the lit-crit hacks who gush over him: *"Ha ha, you idiots are actually READING this? I farted this crap out between watching reruns of Happy Days!"* As for me, I just jabbed my Kindle's next page button until I was at the end.

The plot of *Ghosts* is nearly identical to *City of Glass:* a private detective is assigned to tail some guy and eventually spirals into madness in the process. The main difference is that with *Ghosts*, Auster decided to dispense with such irrelevant distractions as "action" and "dialogue," instead burying us in a nonstop monologue of the protagonist's thoughts, which naturally wander all over the place and have nothing to do with the story. Even better, all of the characters are named after colors (e.g. Blue, Black, White, Gold), which combined with Auster's squid-ink prose means you'll need a flow chart to keep track of everything. That individual paragraph might not seem so bad, but imagine reading a hundred straight pages of this drivel.

The few short segments of *Ghosts* that *aren't* Blue's inane exposition are like oases in a desert, but even then Auster can't resist the urge to fuck things up. Take this segment where Blue is confronted by his fiance (just about the only character who isn't given a color for a name, but incessantly referred to as "the future

Mrs. Blue"), who has understandably gotten sick of his undercover games and found another man:

"You! she says to him. You!"

No quotation marks. Who do you think you are, Cormac McCarthy? And of course, that's the only dialogue in that section; "the ex-future Mrs. Blue's" physical assault on Blue is written in *more fucking exposition!* Skip this.

The Locked Room

I made it all of two chapters into this before giving up. *The Locked Room* is written in the exact same dialogue-free expository style as *Ghosts*, and I was so burnt out from trying to make it through *that* one that I couldn't take it anymore. The plot is at least different; it concerns an unnamed narrator's search for his childhood friend Fanshawe.

> "Fanshawe had never had any regular work, she said, nothing that could be called a real job. Money didn't mean much to him, and he tried to think about it as little as possible. In the years before he met Sophie, he had done all kinds of things–the stint in the merchant marine, working in a warehouse, tutoring, ghost writing, waiting on tables, painting apartments, hauling furniture for a

moving company—but each job was temporary, and once he had earned enough to keep himself going for a few months, he would quit. When he and Sophie began living together, Fanshawe did not work at all. She had a job teaching music in a private school, and her salary could support them both. They had to be careful, of course, but there was always food on the table, and neither of them had any complaints."

Perhaps I'm just being unfair. Perhaps *The Locked Room* is actually a really good read and I was just so put off by *Ghosts* that all of Paul Auster's writing is forever ruined for me. But I seriously fucking doubt it.

The New York Trilogy is a encapsulation of everything I hate about modern literature. It's turgid, condescending, obtuse, and pointless. But the sad thing is that Luc Sante got it right in his intro: Paul Auster is the poet laureate of New York City, though not for the reasons he thinks. *The New York Trilogy* is the perfect book for the New York of Rudy Giuliani and Michael Bloomberg, a stultifying police state run by over-educated SWPLs who think *All Things Considered* is really deep and get the vapors whenever anyone says anything vaguely controversial. It's perfect for the New York of the hipsters, pencil-necked dweebs from Seattle or Milwaukee thinking they're going to be the next Thurston Moore or Lydia Lunch while they snack on artisan bread courtesy of their trust funds. It's perfect for a New York defanged, declawed and stripped of everything that made it interesting and unique, made safe for underemployed Midwestern brats and bored Australian tourists. The New York everyone romanticizes–the New York of danger, intrigue and passion–is dead and buried.

And this neutered New York has produced a literati that spends all day sniffing its own farts. Jonathan Safran Foer, Colson Whitehead, Nicole Krauss, Gary Shteyngart, Jhumpa Lahiri, David Foster Wallace (actually wait, he's dead; I've never derived so much joy from a suicide in my life), and all the rest: worthless hacks devoid of curiosity, humanity or talent. There's more merit in a single Roosh Tweet than in the entire American literary establishment.

Sorry, but I went through four years of this horror, and I've got the diploma to prove it. I'd rather gargle battery acid than write another ten page paper analyzing Melville's "Bartleby the Scrivener," and I'd never read any of this garbage in my free time. I would love nothing more than to see the mainstream publishing world collapse, along with the toxic, insular culture that gave birth to it. This is why I'm such a huge booster of self-made writers like Roosh, Frost and English Teacher X: for all their flaws, they understand what makes good writing, and they don't water down their books to make some soccer mom–fearing suit happy. I refuse to support a world where pretentious puff words and navel-gazing are considered the stuff of great literature.

As for *The New York Trilogy?* The only reason I can see to buy this flaming turd is if you're an adjunct English professor looking for new ways to torture your students. Alternately, give it to them as an example of how *not* to write. If there was a version of *City of Glass* available on its own on Kindle, I'd recommend you buy that instead.

And here's the final joke. When I sat down to write this review, I was suddenly struck with a thought: *"Is Paul Auster related to Lawr–. No, he can't be. That would just be too convenient."* Ten seconds of research and my suspicions were confirmed:

> **"Paul is the older cousin of conservative columnist Lawrence Auster."**[14]

It pains me to say this, but Paul should have taken some writing tips from his little cousin. Larry Auster is a senile old dork, but he can at least write. He's not *great*, but he can make his points clearly and concisely, without feverishly masturbating all over the page.

February 29, 2012

Advice for Young Men

"Sir, could I see your ID please?" the cashier blurted out.

THE TAO OF FERD

As a former retail wage slave, I know better than to read anything into this. Officially, I was required to card everyone who bought alcohol, no matter how old or young they looked. Most registers require the cashier to punch in a date of birth whenever an alcoholic item is scanned. In reality, most cashiers don't bother carding people unless their supervisors are watching, because they don't get paid enough to care. Still, I played along.

"Geez, how old do you think I am?" I chuckled, pulling my drivers' license out of my wallet.

"Just making sure," he wheezed, keying my DOB into the computer. "$24.58."

I swiped my ATM card as he bagged my stuff. "Thanks for shopping at Hannaford," he droned, handing me my receipt.

"Yeah, thanks. Take it easy." I grabbed my groceries and left.

Young men are at the absolute bottom of the American/Western totem pole. You have no money and no life experience. Society, the media and the government tries to neuter you at every opportunity. If you have a scintilla of independent thought, they diagnose you with some phony disorder like "ADD" and pump you full of Ritalin to shut you up. If you get picked on and defend yourself, you get punished by being labeled a "problem child" and sent to juvie hall. If you're white, you have the additional cross of "white guilt" to bear, made to constantly genuflect for the "crimes" of your ancestors.

You're forced to sell yourself into debt slavery so you can get a job that pays more than minimum wage, if you're lucky: if you don't have the right connections, you're back to waiting tables and living with mom and dad.

Girls get every leg up in life. The education system from pre-K to graduate school is designed to cater to them. When they fuck up, they always get a shoulder to cry on; when you fuck up, you get laughed at. When you behave the way society tells you to, the obedient little worker drone, the girls your age reward you by calling you "creepy" and running off to get fucked by jerks in their late twenties. The government, the church, and the corporate machine view you as pack mules, good only for making them richer.

And despite punishing you in every way conceivable for being a man, they still have the audacity to slap you around with the "man up" line. After repeatedly cracking you in the shins with a shovel, they tell you to get up and run a marathon, calling you a "kidult" or a "manboy" when you don't jump up on command. That's your lot in life as a young man; a cubicle slave for your boss, a bottomless purse for your girlfriend/wife, a mindless pew-warmer for your pastor, an expendable sack of meat for the government. All of the obligations of manhood, none of the perks or respect.

You *should* be pissed off. Hell, I've made a decent life for myself and I'm still pissed off. You've been shit on from the

THE TAO OF FERD

moment you were pulled into this world; you damn well ought to be enraged. Anyone who thinks anger is a sign of weakness can go fuck themselves to death. But just because you're going through the trials of Job doesn't mean you can't triumph.

I'm old enough to have carved out a comfortable life, but young enough to remember the torturous journey getting there. Advice from men older than 35 is questionable to flat-out worthless, both because they're too removed from the experience of being a young man and because they had it way easier than you do. Here's some advice from a guy who's been there, done that and has the mental scars to prove it.

1. Cultivate a lifestyle.

You won't be the same man in ten years that you are today, but the foundations for the man you will be are being laid right now, if not by you, then by the people around you. If you want to change yourself, you need to retake control of your life today and start shaping it in the way you want. If you want to lose weight or get ripped, start going to the gym. If you want to be in a rock band, buy a used Stratocaster and amp and start taking lessons from the music store. If you want to visit a foreign country, save up your wages and learn the language with a *Pimsleur* audio course. If you want to get laid more, grab a copy of *Day Bang* and start working on your elderly opener. Life doesn't "get" better; you have to *make* it better.

The big advantage to being invisible is that there's no one

to catalogue your fuck-ups, and trust me, you *will* fuck up. The younger you start shaping yourself, the better shape you'll be in down the line, as you'll have acquired a bounty of information and skills that will serve you until the day you die. Don't even tell me that you don't have enough time for any of this, because *all* human beings only get 24 hours to a day. If you've got time to fart around on the Internet or play *Call of Duty*, you've got enough time to do something constructive and useful.

If you want some motivation, check out Littlepdog (beware, as his blog has some images of nude women), a Aussie manosphere blogger who's only 17, yet he's already building his own online business and planning to travel the world slaying beautiful women, among other things. He's got his life together in a way I didn't when I was his age. If a kid who's not even out of high school can pull all this off, the rest of you have absolutely no fucking excuses.

2. Start reading.

There are two ways to learn about the world: experience it yourself or read about someone else's experiences. Since you're not going to come close to experiencing everything the universe has to offer in an 75+ year lifespan, you need to pick up a book, or two, or three. Not just nonfiction, but fiction, quality fiction, not trashy genre crap or ivory tower masturbation. Reading good books keeps your mind sharp and expands your horizons. I highly recommend picking up a Kindle so you can save money (and space) or books.

3. Tune out the mainstream media.

If you're wasting more than an hour a week on mass media, you're murdering your brain cells. They call it television "programming" for a reason. Ditch your cable and Xbox Live subscriptions and spend that time playing the guitar or reading instead. If you feel you need to pay attention to sports or reality TV in order to not come off as a social retard, you're hanging out with the wrong kinds of people.

4. Associate with winners.

Success and failure are contagious. If you hang out with people who are healthy, wealthy and sexually satiated, you'll be motivated to improve yourself so you can join their ranks. Conversely, if you hang out with fatties and nerds, their loserness will rub off on you and make you more miserable. If someone is subtracting from your life instead of adding to it, cut them off. Be loyal to your friends and help them out in their times of need, but don't repeatedly bail out someone who can't get their act together. Find a mentor, someone you look up to and admire, learn their secrets and use them for yourself.

5. View girls as a side course, not the main dish.

Telling young guys surging with hormones to not worry about getting laid or some variant thereof is a fruitless enterprise. Only a gelding or a clueless Christian traditionalist would neglect this vital part of a man's life. Whatever you want from women (one-night stands, a long-term relationship, or a threesome), you should go out and make it happen. But the focus of your life should never be getting girls, but being the best man you can be. The more energy and time you put into building a cool lifestyle, the less you'll ultimately have to expend on women, as they'll be natively attracted to who you are.

6. Go to bed earlier.

Yeah, you might be able to spend all night doing keg stands and making out with sluts right now, but this habit will fuck you hard if you don't snap out of it by the time you're 25. Try to get to bed by 1am on weekdays; you'll have more energy and feel better then when you stay up all night.

7. Beware of entangling alliances.

Before you get involved with any political, ideological or religious causes, read the fine print first. It's nice to work for a cause you believe in, whether it's the Ron Paul Revolution or ensuring that the beauty of the white Aryan woman doesn't perish from the Earth, but all groups have their own agendas, parts of which may not align with yours. The only person who will ever look out for your interests 100% of the time is you. If you want to go join a party or church, make sure you're doing it for the right reasons.

8. Be prepared to bleed.

It's easy to get swept up in the boundless optimism of the Tim Ferriss crowd. While Ferriss and the lifestyle design gurus have useful ideas to impart, the road to paradise is long, winding and painful. You'll be working shit jobs for low pay, you'll be striking out with the ladies and/or getting into relationships with crazy bitches, you'll be suffering in countless ways. Pick yourself up, grit your teeth and keep on trucking. In order to accomplish anything worthwhile, you need to bleed. But if you put in the work, you'll get the results.

9. Always have a Plan B.

The world is unpredictable and your plans can (and will) go up in smoke. Always have a stack of Fuck You Money stuffed under the mattress and a booty call you can dial up for a deep dicking. The more options you have, the better you'll be able to weather the crises that life will throw at you.

10. Finally, always look after yourself first.

I've said this already, but it bears repeating: *the only person who will ever look out for your interests 100% of the time is you.* No one—not your wife, your priest, your friends, your children, your parents, your boss—will be able to understand your needs like you do. If you lean on anyone else to solve your problems, you will get burned every time. Ultimately, you should always put yourself before anyone else. This doesn't mean be a narcissistic amoral asshole (necessarily), it means you should be cognizant of your goals and wants and not rely on anyone else to fulfill them for you.

One of the most rewarding things about running *In Mala Fide* is knowing that I've changed lives for the better. Every so often, I get a heartfelt letter from a young man telling me how I've directly helped him when it comes to women or other issues. The manosphere is plugged into the needs and desires of young guys today in a way that no other entity—not the church, not the media, not anything—is. If I've encouraged even one guy to put down the Jergens, start lifting and transform himself, I consider *In Mala Fide* a success.

There's a whole world out there full of morons and mediocrities. You guys are smart, motivated and savvy. Go out there and get yours.

April 17, 2012

IV

HUMOR AND SATIRE

One Splotch of Yellow

Yesterday afternoon was my office's Christmas party, held at a nondescript chain restaurant in the suburbs. You wish you were me. Anyway, after four chicken wings, three mozzarella sticks, and a pint-and-a-half of Yuengling had worked their way through my system, I burst into the bathroom for the mother of all excretions. I squeezed my way into the sole stall and prepared to assume my place on the porcelain throne when I saw urine stains on the seat. Dozens of them. Distraught, I was forced to go to the gas station across the street in order to relieve myself.

There is a loathsome plague that has spread across the continent. Everywhere I go, from Schenectady to Syracuse, Newark to New Hampshire, Montreal to Manhattan, lazy men are pissing all over public toilet seats, making them unsuitable for shitting. As recently as five years ago, you could enter most public restrooms and plant yourself on the nearest bowl confident that the seat at least *looked* clean enough to eat off of. Now, such an action is akin to jogging into a minefield, a minefield of dried urine stains.

Why have the men of this great land become so careless as to spray the contents of their bladder over perfectly good porcelain seats? Has the women's eternal whine of "don't leave the seat up" become so ingrained that the guys refuse to put the seat up when they *need* to, in a *men's only* bathroom? If so, our civilization truly is lost to us! Get thee to a foreign country, preferably one where the menfolk know to lift up the seat when they only need to go number one!

If you are a man reading this and you ever need to whip it out and let it fly, put the fucking seat up before you commence the golden showers. Be considerate. And if you find out if any guy, even your friend, has been drizzling urine all over a toilet seat, tell him off for being an lazy dickhead. If every man who splashed his piss on a restroom seat was publicly embarrassed for it, the epidemic would end overnight, and those of us with sensitive stomachs could relieve our pain without fear of sitting in a stranger's liquid waste product. Isn't that a world you'd want to live in? Isn't that a world you'd want your *children* to live in?

The ball's in your court, my comrades. The choice is yours.

December 24, 2009

Everything I Know About Life, I Learned from PSAs

In Syracuse, there's a brand new radio station calling itself CNY Talk Radio and billing itself as "the new alternative for talk." The station takes that "alternative" part very seriously. For instance, instead of having a website like every other ordinary business in the year 2009, CNY Talk Radio has a Twitter page! Not only that, instead of having boring commercials, the station airs cool, informative PSAs! While on my Christmas vacation, I got to listen to a lot of radio while I was driving about, and I want to share with you the unique wisdom that can only be gained from listening to PSAs that radio stations air when they can't get paid advertisers. Sit back and prepare to have your brains blown out of your skulls.

If you want to encourage kids to read, tell them that you can make new friends from opening a book. Yes, you can apparently talk to and establish relationship with fictional characters as expressed through ink printed on the remains of dead trees. And they'll buy this, because as you all know, kids are too fucking stupid to know when they're being condescended to.

You should be worried about your child being diagnosed with autism, because one out of every 150 children has it. That's right: two-thirds of one percent of all kids are on the spectrum. Fear!

White children are born racists. Your little boy or girl may seem tolerant and loving, but behind that naive smile is the heart of a stone-cold bigot. Don't believe me? Take your daughter to work and watch as she points out that your co-workers have differently colored skin and funny accents, traits that the residents of your white flight suburban neighborhood don't have. On the other hand, you can use this opportunity to educate her about the limitless joys of diversity.

Inner-city high school dropout black youths are huge fans of news/talk radio. Why else would all those PSAs that encourage kids to stay in school, delivered in ebonics and played with cool hip-hop music, be played during the Laura Ingraham show?

Don't go drunk driving this month, because you're all but guaranteed to get busted. After all, cops are cracking down coast to coast this month. They were also cracking down last month, and the month before that, and the month before that too. Apparently, there has never ever been a month in recorded history when the cops *weren't* "cracking down."

Speaking of which, buzzed driving is drunk driving. It doesn't matter if you only had a couple of drinks and are within the legal blood alcohol limit, *BUZZED DRIVING IS DRUNK DRIVING, MOTHERFUCKER.*

See, what did I tell you! Public service announcements tell the unvarnished truth about the world, more so then your pathetic little blogs. Sadly, Santa Claus brought me a replacement CD player for my car, so I won't be able to experience these paid-for nuggets of honesty again for a long, long time. *sniff*

HUMOR AND SATIRE

December 30, 2009

Saving the White Race with Sexual Degeneracy

A thought occurred to me the other day. Lots of folks among the right make lots of noise about how low white fertility will spell the doom of the West. According to the doom-sayers, the higher birthrates of the filthy darkies, brownies and slanty-eyed devils from the East will inevitably make white people into minorities in their own lands, unless Joe and Jane Paleface start cranking out crotch-droppings ASAP. To this end, much agonizing is done in the right-o-sphere on the ways white fertility can be raised. I'm highly skeptical of these claims, considering they're all based on linear demographic projections that assume social conditions will remain frozen in amber (which they never do), but I'll play along and assume current trends are cause for concern.

I've stated in the past that it's far easier to destroy then to create. In light of this truth, why bother trying to raise white birthrates? You rightists should be focusing your efforts on lowering non-white birthrates. And I'm not talking about forced sterilization or anything reprehensible like that, but identifying the conditions that have led to whites forsaking family for shallow pleasures and replicating them in third-world countries and communities. In other words, you fight them by forcing them to swallow the poison pill of sexual liberation that has so devastated your own cultures.

Let's review. The current dystopia of the West is the result of the Four Sirens of the Sexual Apocalypse:

1. "Effective and widely available contraceptives (the Pill, condom, and the *de facto* contraceptive abortion).

2. "Easy peasy no-fault divorce.

3. "Women's economic independence (hurtling towards women's economic advantage if the college enrollment ratio is any indication).

4. "Rigged feminist-inspired laws that have caused a disincentivizing of marriage for men and an incentivizing of divorce for women."[1]

Societies which lack any or all of the four horsemen have higher birthrates and more quickly growing populations then those that suffer from them all. Therefore, our objective is to bring the Sirens to the third world. But how? I've got a fully fleshed-out plan the government can carry out.

We begin by mass airdropping "sexual humanitarian aid" packages into third world countries. Porn mags, hand lotion, and condoms for the guys, vibrators and the Pill for the girls. When Achmed from Fallujah gets a look at this month's Playboy

Centerfold, he'll be too busy cranking his little Muhammad to spare a drop of love juice for his hairy, burqa-clad wife. And if Maria from Santo Domingo doesn't have to worry about getting pregnant, she'll be free to spend her *quinceanera* getting her Virgin Mary desecrated by all the hot boys in the barrio. It'll be like a sweatier, sexier, more sallow-faced Berlin Airlift.

But merely mass exporting our tools of decadence won't be enough. Give a man a back issue of *Hustler* and he'll jerk off for a day; give him an Internet connection and he'll jerk off for a lifetime. Therefore, we should start constructing the physical and social infrastructure required to turn the teeming melanin-infused hordes of the world into the weak, hedonistic pieces of shit that we white people are. If we're going to have a Berlin Airlift to give temporary relief, we need a Marshall Plan to affect long-range change in the third world.

We start by getting the sanction of governments the world over to implement our plan. How? Simple: we require, as a condition for continuing to receive foreign aid, governments of developing countries to liberalize all laws pertaining to sex and marriage. Won't legalize abortion and no-fault divorce? Ban porn sites from being viewed on the interwebs? No more evil colonial oppressor aid money for you! Given that the IMF has been able to force debtor countries like Argentina and Bolivia to upend their economies with neoliberal policies in exchange for financial assistance, getting the same governments to loosen up their marriage and divorce laws should be easy.

Next, we invest in constructing electrical grids and high-speed internet access in third-world countries, all the better to download *Bangbros* clips from *The Pirate Bay*. The erection and maintenance of these grids and networks can't be entrusted to the kleptocrats in charge, so we fly in German and Japanese engineers to do all the legwork. We then subsidize the sale of laptops, smartphones, and broadband internet plans to the masses. We fund all of this ourselves, allowing us to not only sell our enemies the jizz-smeared rope with which they will hang themselves, but look like selfless saints in the process.

Finally, we offer up aid grants to encourage third-world women to pursue higher education, preferably in feminist institutions. When they graduate, we fund useless makework jobs to employ them and give them wealth and status they haven't earned. With their hypergamous instincts eliminating ninety percent of their male peers as potential mates, a whole new generation of girls will head straight to the alpha cock carousel. To facilitate this, we give a massive grant to Planned Parenthood so they can construct free abortion clinics on every block from La Paz to Islamabad. Decline of civilization, here we come! (These proposals can also be implemented on a smaller scale in third-world immigrant communities in the West.)

Some of you will balk at my ideas. *"Why the fuck should my money be pissed away on condoms and internet porn for third-worlders?"*, you might ask. Think of it this way: *if you live in the West, your money is already being pissed away on third-*

worlders. Afghan war anyone? Operation Iraqi Freedom? Every other military operation the U.S. has fought in the past sixty-plus years? That's trillions of dollars gone with nothing to show for it. And even if you don't live in the U.S. (and even if you do), your government throws millions of dollars yearly at corrupt turd-world governments that only ends up lining the pockets of the people in charge. My proposals will replace those failed operations and will not only be cheaper, *they will actually work.*

My plan is genius, which is why it will never be implemented. Neither side of the political spectrum will find it palatable. Liberals will reject my proposals because they will destroy the "vibrant" cultures of the turd world with Western imperialism. Conservatives will reject my proposals because they're anachronistically moralizing, dysfunctional prudes who oppose abortion and contraception and think anything outside of missionary sex through a garbage bag is immoral and degenerate. Hence the white race will be outbred into extinction because of the stubbornness and ignorance of the people who claim to want to save it.

June 15, 2010

She's Pure, He's a Loser: The Sexual Double Standard

From the book She's Pure, He's a Loser by Ferdinand Bardamu. Reprinted by arrangement with Lambskin Press, a member of the Odysseus Books Group. Copyright © 2011.

HUMOR AND SATIRE

If you have a penis, chances are someone has called you a loser at least once in your life. There's just no getting around it.

I remember the first time I heard the word "loser": I was in my fifth-grade science class. A certain little boy (terror) named Tashawn had been making my life miserable all year in a way that only mean little boys can. He had turned all my friends against me, spread rumors and the like. He walked up to me at my desk and said, "You called me a loser." I had absolutely no idea what the word meant. I just sat there, silently. He repeated himself: "You called me a loser, but you're the loser." I don't remember how long after that I found out exactly what "loser" meant, but I knew it had to be terrible and I knew I didn't want to be it.

Naturally, I'd be called a loser many times over later in life: not unlike most guys. I was called a loser when my penis grew faster than others'. I was called a loser when I had a girlfriend (even though we were having sex). I was called a loser when I didn't have a girlfriend and banged a random girl at a party. I was called a loser when I had the nerve to *not* want to talk about sex. I was called a loser when I wore a Speedo on a weekend trip with high school friends. It seems the word loser can be applied to any activity besides white knighting, putting women on pedestals, or bending over and greasing up lest any sudden movements be deemed weird.

Despite the ubiquity of "loser," where you won't hear it is in relation to women. Women can't be losers. Sure, someone will occasionally call a girl "a prude," but women simply aren't judged like men are when it comes to sexuality. (And if they are, they're judged in a positive way!) Women who don't have any sexual partners are maidens, Madonnas, chaste, and virtuous. Never losers. In fact, when I just did a Google search for "female losers," the first result I got was a page asking why so many women stay with losers! I know, should have seen that coming. The point is, there isn't even a word–let alone a concept–to signify a female who's a loser.

But it makes sense when you think about what the purpose of the word "loser" is: controlling men through shame and humiliation. Men's volition is always the one that is being vied over for control: whether it's false rape accusations, no-fault divorce, or domestic violence hysteria, it's our choices that are the battleground, not women's.

And if you don't think it's about control, consider this little bit of weirdness. The most recent incarnation of the sexual double standard being played out in a seriously creepy way is through hypergamy. This lizard hindbrain event basically has all women lusting after and having sex with only 20 percent of men. If a beta guy can get a girlfriend or wife, it's only after her prime years have passed and she's sat on a big bucket of dongs. Where is hypergamy for women, you may ask? Oh, it's there, but it's about controlling men too! Men are shamed for wanting a woman who is "out of their league," but women are encouraged to never settle and to keep holding out for men who have more options then they do! Women are given a pass for behavior that is discouraged in men. Unbelievable, really.

Outside of the masculist implications of the sexual double standard, the loser/pure conundrum has always been my favorite because it just makes no sense logically. Why is a man less of a person, or (my favorite) "creepy," because he has not had sex? (Heterosexual sex, that is; somehow gay sex isn't "real.") Does a vagina have some bizarre normal-making power that I'm unaware of? Every minute my cherry remained unpopped, did I lose a bit of my moral compass? *"Sorry to mug you, Grandma, but I didn't have sex at all this week!"*

And let's face it: the loser stigma isn't just dangerous to our "reputations" or to some strange-ass notion of normalcy. How many times have false rape accusations been accepted because a man was deemed a loser? How many times are men called losers while their partners beat them? How often are men's relationship histories used against them in workplace harassment cases? The sexual double standard is a lot more dangerous than we'd like to think.

So... What to Do?

First and foremost, stop calling other men losers! It doesn't behoove us to bash each other, guys. And speak out when you hear women do the same. I'll never forget in college overhearing a conversation that my girlfriend's roommates were having. They both had been asked out by the same guy over the course of the

HUMOR AND SATIRE

day: they called him a loser and made a joke about his right hand being "callused." I asked them why he was the bad person in this scenario: after all, they had spoken to him, too. They couldn't provide an answer, but that didn't stop them from continuing to laugh. I always regretted not saying anything more. Outside of calling ourselves and others out on perpetuating the double standard, it's a hard battle. But I think if we recognize the hypocrisy of the loser/pure nonsense when we see it—whether it's an anti-male law or a movie that makes men who don't have sex look like deviants—we're on the right road.

July 5, 2010

The Right to Get Laid

One of my readers asked me to comment on this story about the British government paying for a drooling retard to lose his virginity to a Dutch hooker:

> "A 'man of 21 with learning disabilities has been granted taxpayers' money to fly to Amsterdam and have sex with a prostitute.
>
> "His social worker says sex is a 'human right' for the unnamed individual – described as a frustrated virgin.
>
> "His trip to a brothel in the Dutch capital's red light

district next month is being funded through a £520 million scheme introduced by the last government to empower those with disabilities.

"They are given a personal budget and can choose what services this is spent on.

"The man's social worker, who spoke on the condition of anonymity, said his client was an 'angry, frustrated and anxious young man' who had a need for sex."[2]

What do I think? I think this is monumental. Declaring sex to be a human right is simply following the socialist program to its absurd, logical conclusion. If we have the right to eat, have a decent standard of living and a roof under our head, why can't we have the right to get laid? Oh wait, the feminists will have a collective embolism: *"YOU DON'T HAVE A RIGHT TO MY BODY I CAN HAVE SEX WITH WHOEVER I WANT YOU MISOGYNIST WOMAN-HATING DOUCHEHAT!!!!"*

My solution to this problem, that won't involve violating the sovereignty that women have over their vaginas, is twofold:

1. Legalize prostitution, Nevada-style, across the country. Treat brothels like other legal red-light businesses like

adult video stores and strip clubs.

2. Establish a program giving out vouchers to undersexed dudes, redeemable at the whorehouse of their choice. Call it Poonicaid.

Why not? Under my plan, the only women who'll be required to sex undesirable dudes are the ones who get paid to do it anyway. And they and their pimps will get monetarily compensated for doing so. Everybody wins. If you're a conservative, libertarian, or feminist who's upset at the prospect of having to pay losers to get some action, think of it as insurance against the next spree shooter, bread and circuses for the unloved masses. It's certainly a more sensible way for the government to spend money then half of the crap they do these days.

Not to mention that we could establish an outreach division for divorced men. The news article mentions a guy whose wife ran out on him who also got "serviced" under this program:

> "Another man who has a brain injury has even had sex work built into his council care package.
>
> "This is designed to teach him to become sexually 'self-reliant' after his wife left him and took all their money."

Want to help husbands whose bitchy wives have cleaned

them out in divorce court and taken their kids away? An appointment with Sexy Sally at the Beaver Ranch will do more for them than all the happy pills and counseling in the world.

Of course, Poonicaid is just a stopgap measure. The sickness that has destroyed relations between men and women—feminism and by extension liberalism—needs to be addressed. But until then, give me your tired, your poor, your unfuckable masses yearning to come free, the wretched refuse of your teeming shore, send these, the woman-less, tempest-tost to me: I lift my lamp beside the golden vaj!

August 18, 2010

Fuck or Be Fucked

At the *Pro-Male/Anti-Feminist Technology* blog, David Collard writes:

> "Just an addendum, why do men refer to women 'fucking [someone]?' Women don't fuck – they are fucked. Passive. Masculine men should resist this kind of expression.
>
> "Men fuck women. Women don't fuck. They are fucked."[3]

Good question. The reason is because men have been pussified by feminism. The egalitarian nasties have so thoroughly indoctrinated us into their sexless, fun-free horror chamber that they've gelded the very language we use. And by controlling how we speak, they have poisoned our minds into denying the fundamental truths in front of our eyes.

I say no more. David is right: women by nature cannot fuck. It's a matter of anatomy. You stick the plug in the outlet, not the outlet in the plug. The nail goes into the wall; you don't pound the wall into the tip of the nail. So it is with the act of conjugal pleasantness. Women can't fuck because they are the holes and men are the objects to be inserted. Men are the fuckers and women are the fuckees.

Some joker is inevitably going to bring up cowgirl position. Well dummy, even if I were to rip the electrical outlet out of my living room wall and insert it around my plug, that doesn't change the fact that the plug is still the object going in and the outlet is still the object being filled. It is the possessor of the penetrating object who is the active player in these situations. I win.

So men, work to excise this linguistic inaccuracy from your language pronto. You fuck her, she doesn't fuck you. I'm way ahead of you all, because I've done this for years. If you go back through the hundreds of posts I've written over the past twelve months, you'll notice that I almost never refer to a woman as "fucking" someone. She "gets fucked," but she never "fucks." With small steps, we can reclaim our culture and our manhood from the femisandrists and improve our day-to-day lives. *Forward!*

August 19, 2010

What is Up with White Boys?

Greetings, Ladies and Germs, it is I, the one and only Onyx, here to provide you with a TRULY different perspective on the issues you know and love. And as a Black Man living in 2010 America, I have to ask a question: what is WRONG with you white boys? For example, me and Ferdi were hanging at a Starbucks a few months back when I asked him this:

O: Say Ferdi, mind telling me why you white boys are so obsessed with the Sexuality of Black Men?

F: Um, I don't care about how much sex Black Guys are having or who they're doing it with. Nobody does but you. The only reason we talk about it is because you keep bringing it up.

O: Nuh-uh Ferdi, you ain't gettin' off that easy! It's a historical FACT that during the Jim Crow era, jealous white boys would hang Black Men from trees and mutilate their genitals because they thought they were trying to get with white girls. Have you ever seen Rosewood? That film, based on real events, is an excellent example of what I'm talking about.

So, you were saying?

F: Uh dude, Rosewood happened in 1923. No one's

hanged a Black Man from a tree or mutilated his genitals for decades. I, and no white person I know has ever lynched any Black Men for anything.

O: You've lynched Black Men?! DIE YOU SKINHEAD CRACKA!!!!

And then I threw my boiling hot cup of coffee in Ferdi's face.

That's another thing too: why are you white boys so whiny? You've had everything handed to you on a silver platter and you keep blubbering like a bunch of losers. Like what happened with Ferdi. After I threw the coffee in his face, he fell out of his chair screaming and yelling, "HELP!" "AMBULANCE!" like a crybaby bitch. A grownassed man yelling to go to the hospital for second-degree burns: beyond pathetic.

So I leaned over and told Ferdi that it was HIS fault his face was burned all the way to the dermis, and that if he didn't want to look like one of the mutants from *Total Recall*, he'd have to stop whining and DO SOMETHING ABOUT IT. He responded by grabbing me by the collar and screaming, "You threw hot coffee in my FACE, YOU FUCKING IDIOT!!!" It was clear to me that Ferdi just wanted to moan and complain, so I shrugged him off and left.

SMH...

But back to the Sexuality of Black Men, and why you white boys are so threatened by it.

It is an established fact that Women of all races and nationalities find Black Men to be the most attractive. Women love men who are Cool, and Cool is a uniquely Black concept. On average, Black Men are Cooler than nerdy STEM white boys and even nerdier STEM Asian boys. The proof? Barack Obama. If he wasn't in a committed marriage with a Beautiful Black Woman, Girls from around the world would gladly worship his Ebony Rod. And if you doubt me, who do you think could get more girls: Denzel Washington or Steve McQueen? Will Smith or Cary Grant? Samuel L. Jackson or Clark Gable? Hmmm?

Some sexually frustrated white boys have tried to claim that Asian girls, particularly Koreans, don't like Black Men. I have personally proven this wrong. Years ago, before I met Muscovado, the love of my life, a Korean Gal loved me long time. She set up a blind date with me that took place at her house. I came over at three in the morning on a Sunday and we made Love in her bedroom with the shades drawn and lights off. Then She told me to leave before the sun came up, which I did. It was clear to me that she preferred the Ebony Spear to the Ivory Thimble, but didn't want to hurt the feelings of you white boys.

What I want to know is why you white boys get so bent out of shape by the fact that we Brothas can pick up pretty Women of all races. We live in a Free Sexual Marketplace now, where you need Game to get some action. You want to get laid today? Stop whining, Man Up or Shut Up. We Black Men are doing great in this new world, and if you white boys don't like it, get therapy.

I challenge anyone to prove me wrong on anything I've said in this post, with exact quotes, citations and statistics. I'll wait. ;)

Now adjourn your pasty, pussy-less, crybaby asses...

The Onyx

September 27, 2010

National Fuck a Ginger Day

Hi, my name is Ferdinand, and I used to be a gingerphobe.

For a long time I thought I'd always been afraid of redheads. That it was perfectly normal, nay, *natural* to heap derision and abuse on those pale-faced, flame-groined hellspawn. But a bit of soul-searching has revealed to me when the hate began.

It was that day in third grade when John Gavone, the 300-pound mulatto kid who'd been held back a couple of grades, had stolen all my crayons. I was pissed off and needed to reassert my place in the savage school hierarchy. Then I saw *him*. One of my classmates. I forgot his name, but I'll never forget his face:

freckled, cherubic, with a lustrous mane of rust-colored hair. I knew I had to act.

I wasted no time, running up to him and slamming his innocent, dimpled mug into his locker door. He screamed and struggled in vain against my grip, and with each yell of pain I pounded his face harder and harder.

Ferdinand Bardamu (bashing kid's head between words): That's... what... you... get... for... being... a... curly-haired... ginger... freak!

Ginger Kid: But Ferd, *you* have curly hair!

F (shoving kid's face against the locker): *Did I say you could speak, loser?!*

I then let him go, satisfied with proving my superiority over a weaker, slower member of the herd. He ran off sobbing, blood from his nose leaving a trail behind him. I had won.

Despite being taken to the principal's office for a stern talking-to, the foundations were laid for a lifetime of tormenting gingers. With my droogs at my side, I roamed the halls and grounds of Dachau Elementary making the lives of gingers young and old a living hell. We gave the boys wedgies, swirlies, and weekly beatings; we taunted the girls by calling them ugly, fat, and a multitude of other insults that made them cry. We cut them in the lunch line, we ganged up on them in dodgeball, we yelled nasty words at them as they walked home from school to be suckled in the nurturing arms of their mammies. With my blonde hair and blue eyes, I was like a kid version of Rutger Hauer kicking the shit out of Harrison Fords everywhere. And I loved it.

And while my blonde hair may have since faded into a robust brown, and my pale blue eyes perpetually hidden behind a pair of polarized sunglasses to keep the fuzz from discovering my smack addiction, I carried my fear and hatred of gingers right into adulthood. Until one day.

I was coming home from college one year and seeing my family for the first time in months when I noticed my kid sister, Cécile, had an unusual tint to her hair. Unlike Claire, who had a curly blonde mop like I had had, Cécile had straight brown hair and some freckles. I used to tease her by saying she was adopted because of her hair, which wasn't like either of our parents (my dad had jet-black hair, and my mom was a blonde-turned-brunette like me). But Cecile's hair looked almost… *red*.

Ferdinand: Um, sis, what's up with your hair?

Cécile: What do you mean?

F: It's kinda… red.

C: Ferd, it's been like this for a while. If you'd stopped doing drugs for once in your life, you'd have noticed before.

I then realized what I was seeing wasn't a opioid-fueled hallucination. My little sis was a ginger.

It was then I learned the truth about redheads. Gingers

aren't ungodly devil children to be punished every day in preparation for their eternal burning in hellfire, nor are they mistakes of evolution to be weeded out of the gene pool through mockery and derision. They are human beings like you and me, and are no less deserving of respect. Gingers have contributed greatly to American history and culture. From Carrot Top to Kari Byron, your world today would not be the same were it not for gingers.

And yet, as my life as a young bigot shows, gingers are the one group that is still acceptable to discriminate against today. Gingers are routinely harassed, abused, and denied employment and educational opportunities because of the color of their hair. And unlike other minority groups, gingers have no one to speak in their defense. Blacks have the NAACP, Jews have the ADL, Mexicans have La Raza. Even the filthy dirty cheating Gypsies have their own advocacy groups. Who do the gingers have? Who will be the Morris Dees of fair-skinned fire-crotches everywhere?

I will. No, no need to thank me, for I have decided that it is my calling in life to speak out for this underprivileged, long-suffering group. And I will start by taking back a celebration of ginger oppression that occurs every year. I, Ferdinand Bardamu, hereby decree that November 20th is no longer "National Kick a Ginger Day": it is National Fuck a Ginger Day!

That's right. For one day out of the year, my blonde, brunette, and raven-haired brothers and sisters, you get to appreciate the contributions gingers have made to society by seducing one and fucking his or her brains out. Why not? Ginger girls are beautiful and have a reputation for being passionate lovers. And ginger guys are great in the sack due to pent-up aggression from being picked on their whole lives. The rarity of redheads in the wild (only one percent of humans have red hair) is proof positive that they don't get much action, so let's give 'em a leg (and something else) up!

So tell your friends and spread the word: November 20th is National Fuck a Ginger Day! And if your friend doesn't like gingers, be sure to educate the bigotry out of him. With your help, we can end the scourge of gingerphobia and secure equal rights for *all* Americans.

November 10, 2010

ENDNOTES

I: Sexuality

1. Ross, Chuck. "From the Mouths of Babes." *Gucci Little Piggy*. WordPress.com, 30 Jan. 2009. Web. 20 Jan. 2014.

2. Fedders, Rob. "When Shit Gets Sold as Soap..." *NO MA'AM*. Blogger, 27 Sept. 2010. Web. 20 Jan. 2014.

3. Heartiste. "Sexual Dystopia: A Glimpse at the Future." *Chateau Heartiste*. WordPress.com, 01 June 2009. Web. 20 Jan. 2014.

4. The Futurist. "The Misandry Bubble." *The Futurist*. The Futurist, 01 Jan. 2010. Web. 20 Jan. 2014.

5. Derbyshire, John. "It's a Woman's World." *John Derbyshire*. John Derbyshire, 28 Aug. 2001. Web. 20 Jan. 2014.

6. "Erection Killerz: Hipster Chicks Once Again Politicize Sex and Think it Makes Them Edgy." *The Exiled*. The Exiled, 07 Oct. 2009. Web. 20 Jan. 2014.

7. V, Roosh. "Idiot Model Gets Taught an Important Lesson." *Roosh V*. Roosh V, 28 Oct. 2009. Web. 20 Jan. 2014.

8. Mercer, Ilana. "Update II: Conservative Chicks." *Barely a Blog*. Ilana Mercer, 16 Nov. 2009. Web. 20 Jan. 2014.

9. Mercer, Ilana. "Updated: 'Sluts Galore: Scenes from 2006.'" *Barely a Blog*. Ilana Mercer, 21 Dec. 2006. Web. 20 Jan. 2014.

10. Mercer, Ilana. "Sluts Galore: Scenes from 2006." *Ilana Mercer*. Ilana Mercer, 22 Dec. 2006. Web. 20 Jan. 2014.

11. McDonell-Parry, Amelia. "Would You Go to Europe to Find the One?" *The Frisky*. SpinMedia, 13 Jan. 2010. Web. 20 Jan. 2014.

12. Heartiste. "Black Men, White Women." *Chateau Heartiste*. WordPress.com, 23 Jan. 2009. Web. 20 Jan. 2014.

13. Heartiste. "What Foreign Men Think of American Women." *Chateau Heartiste*. WordPress.com, 15 July 2009. Web. 20 Jan. 2014.

14. Longman, Phillip. "The Return of Patriarchy." *New America Foundation*. New America Foundation, 01 Mar. 2006. Web. 20 Jan. 2014.

15. "Jersey's Bachelor Tax." *The New York Times*. Arthur Sulzberger, Jr., 13 Feb. 1898. Web. 20 Jan. 2014.

16. "December 20, 1820 in History." *BrainyHistory*. BrainyHistory, n.d. Web. 20 Jan. 2014.

ENDNOTES

17. Raustiala, Kal. "Copyrighting Porn: A Guest Post." *Freakonomics*. Freakonomics, 05 May 2010. Web. 20 Jan. 2014.

18. "FSC All-Star Anti-Piracy PSA." *YouTube*. YouTube, 20 Apr. 2010. Web. 20 Jan. 2014.

19. *The Intactivism Pages*. The Intactivism Pages, n.d. Web. 20 Jan. 2014.

20. Young, Hugh. "The Rape of the Cock." *The Intactivism Pages*. The Intactivism Pages, 1998. Web. 20 Jan. 2014.

21. "Female Genital Mutilation." *World Health Organization*. World Health Organization, Feb. 2013. Web. 20 Jan. 2014.

22. Kay, Athol. "A Little More on Alpha and Beta Male Traits." *Married Man Sex Life*. Athol Kay, 20 Jan. 2010. Web. 20 Jan. 2014.

23. Stark. "Sending Studs to the Glue Factory." *Woeful Beauty*. WordPress.com, 09 Feb. 2010. Web. 20 Jan. 2014.

24. Walsh, Susan. "It's About Time: The New Reverse Double Standard." *Hooking Up Smart*. Susan Walsh, 28 Apr. 2010. Web. 20 Jan. 2014.

25. Heartiste. "Common Shit Tests." *Chateau Heartiste*. WordPress.com, 17 Dec. 2008. Web. 20 Jan. 2014.

26. "Berlusconi: I'm Too Old to Have All the Sex I'm Accused Of." *The Toronto Star.* John D. Cruickshank, 16 Mar. 2011. Web. 20 Jan. 2014.

27. Schopenbecq. "The Myth of Sex Trafficking." *The Anti-Feminist.* Schopenbecq, 28 May 2010. Web. 20 Jan. 2014.

28. Ross, Chuck. "Traffick911's Lies." *Gucci Little Piggy.* WordPress.com, 19 Jan. 2011. Web. 20 Jan. 2014.

29. "Another Day in the Life of an Unethical Prosecutor: Jenifer Yois Hernandez-Vega." *Crime & Federalism.* Crime & Federalism, 24 Apr. 2010. Web. 20 Jan. 2014.

30. Solomon, Dan. "Porn Star Rescues Man from Jail Sentence in Puerto Rico." *Asylum.com.* Asylum.com, 28 Apr. 2010. Web. 20 Jan. 2014.

31. "Legal Age of Consent by State." *Age of Consent by State.* Age of Consent by State, n.d. Web. 20 Jan. 2014.

32. "Canada's Age of Consent Raised by 2 Years." *CBC News.* CBC/Radio-Canada, 01 May 2008. Web. 20 Jan. 2014.

33. "The Campaign to Raise the Legal Age of Consent, 1885-1914." *Women and Social Movements in the United States, 1600-2000.* Thomas Dublin & Kathryn Kish Sklar, n.d. Web. 20 Jan. 2014.

34. Schatz, Joe. "Teen Pregnancy: Why the U.S. Lags Behind

Europe." *Examiner.com*. Philip Anschutz, 15 July 2008. Web. 20 Jan. 2014.

35. Garner, Richard. "The Big Question: Why Are Teenage Pregnancy Rates So High, and What Can Be Done About It?" *The Independent*. Independent Digital News and Media, 17 Feb. 2009. Web. 20 Jan. 2014.

36. Agnostic. "Corrupted by the Youth." *Dusk in Autumn*. Blogger, 26 Apr. 2008. Web. 20 Jan. 2014.

37. Dalrock. "Next Phase of the Hypergamous Arms Race: Revenge of the Nerds?" *Dalrock*. WordPress.com, 23 July 2010. Web. 20 Jan. 2014.

38. Dalrock. "Is Marcos Evil for Conning Women Looking to Trade Sex for Financial Security?" *Dalrock*. WordPress.com, 12 Oct. 2010. Web. 20 Jan. 2014.

39. Goldman, David P. "Spengler's Universal Law of Gender Parity." *Asia Times Online*. Sondhi Limthongkul, 24 Feb. 2004. Web. 20 Jan. 2014.

40. Wood, Laura. "Does Society Need Men's Rights?" *The Thinking Housewife*. Laura Wood, 11 Dec. 2010. Web. 20 Jan. 2014.

41. Diaboli, Advocatus. "Why Care About _____?" *Playing the Devil's Advocate*. WordPress.com, 14 Oct. 2010. Web. 20 Jan. 2014.

42. Mangan, Dennis. "Anti-Male Shaming Tactics?"

ENDNOTES

Mangan's. Blogger, 29 Sept. 2010. Web. 20 Jan. 2014.

43. Robins, Laura G. "Respect Men!" *Unmasking Feminism*. WordPress.com, 12 Jan. 2011. Web. 20 Jan. 2014.

44. Eve's Daughter. "A Man is a Rape-Supporter If..." *Eve Bit First*. WordPress.com, 18 May 2011. Web. 20 Jan. 2014.

45. *Fuck Yeah Self Shooters*. Tumblr, n.d. Web. 20 Jan. 2014.

46. "The Big GPS Location Thread: Pics with EXIF Info (Date, Camera Type, Coordinates)." *Dumpster Sluts*. Dumpster Sluts, n.d. Web. 20 Jan. 2014.

47. Diaboli, Advocatus. "Self Shots, GPS Enabled Smartphones and Data Mining." *Playing the Devil's Advocate*. WordPress.com, 13 Jan. 2010. Web. 20 Jan. 2014.

48. DeVoy, J. "Open Letter to Mr. Bardamu: Why Won't You Pay for Porn?" *The Legal Satyricon*. WordPress.com, 20 July 2011. Web. 20 Jan. 2014.

49. Heartiste. "Long-Term Cohabitation Is Just as Good as Marriage." *Chateau Heartiste*. WordPress.com, 23 Jan. 2012. Web. 20 Jan. 2014.

50. Rosen, Siobhan. "Dinner, Movie, and a Dirty Sanchez." *GQ*. Condé Nast, Feb. 2012. Web. 20 Jan. 2014.

51. Trunk, Penelope. "The Psychology of Quitting." *Penelope Trunk*. Penelope Trunk, 28 Dec. 2011. Web. 20 Jan. 2014.

52. Trunk, Penelope. "Zero Tolerance for Domestic Violence is Wrong." *Penelope Trunk*. Penelope Trunk, 01 Jan. 2012. Web. 20 Jan. 2014.

II: What's Wrong with the World

1. Heartiste. "International Truth Day." *Chateau Heartiste*. WordPress.com, 07 May 2007. Web. 20 Jan. 2014.

2. Lindsay, Robert. "'John Mearsheimer and the Future of Israeli Apartheid,' by Kevin MacDonald." *Beyond Highbrow: Robert Lindsay*. WordPress.com, 23 May 2010. Web. 20 Jan. 2014.

3. Margolis, Eric. "Right to Be Angry." *LewRockwell.com*. Lew Rockwell, 13 Feb. 2006. Web. 20 Jan. 2014.

4. Glass, Charles. "Is the French Burqa Ban Against Muslims, Patriarchy, or Liberty?" *Taki's Magazine*. Taki Theodoracopulos, 26 May 2010. Web. 20 Jan. 2014.

5. Udolpho. "Why You Should Never Listen to Geeks, and in Fact Should Despise Them." *Udolpho.com*. Udolpho, 08 Mar. 2005. Web. 20 Jan. 2014.

6. Udolpho. "Why Do Geeks Have Such Bad Taste?" *Udolpho.com*. Udolpho, 19 Oct. 2004. Web. 20 Jan.

2014.

7. Savage, Matt. "When a Girl Says She Likes Nerdy Nice Guys..." *The Modern Savage*. Matt Savage, 27 May 2010. Web. 20 Jan. 2014.

8. Agnostic. "When Did Video Games Become So Boring? Around 1998." *Dusk in Autumn*. Blogger, 12 June 2009. Web. 20 Jan. 2014.

9. Lowe, Al. "Magna Cum Laude." *Al Lowe's Humor Site*. Al Lowe, n.d. Web. 20 Jan. 2014.

10. Zirin, Dave. "The Nation: Why the Far Right Hates Soccer." *NPR*. NPR, 14 June 2010. Web. 20 Jan. 2014.

11. Kaczynski, Ted. "The Unabomber Manifesto." *American Nihilist Underground Society*. American Nihilist Underground Society, n.d. Web. 20 Jan. 2014.

12. Khan, Razib. "Justify Judeo-Christianity!" *Gene Expression*. Discover, 13 Jan. 2009. Web. 20 Jan. 2014.

13. Prozak, Vijay. "Why I Am Not a White Nationalist or Neo-Nazi." *American Nihilist Underground Society*. American Nihilist Underground Society, 16 Nov. 2004. Web. 20 Jan. 2014.

14. Evola, Julius. "American 'Civilisation.'" *Julius Evola: Traditionalist Visionary*. Julius Evola: Traditionalist Visionary, n.d. Web. 20 Jan. 2014.

15. Moldbug, Mencius. "A Gentle Introduction to Unqualified Reservations (Part 1)." *Unqualified Reservations*. Blogger, 08 Jan. 2009. Web. 20 Jan. 2014.

16. Benoist, Alain de. "Monotheism vs. Polytheism." *Alternative Right*. Richard Spencer, 22 June 2010. Web. 20 Jan. 2014.

17. Noah, Timothy. "Mister Landslide's Neighborhood." *Slate*. Graham Holdings Company, 07 Apr. 2004. Web. 20 Jan. 2014.

18. Moldbug, Mencius. "Why I Am Not a White Nationalist." *Unqualified Reservations*. Blogger, 22 Nov. 2007. Web. 20 Jan. 2014.

19. Brecher, Gary. "Homage to Haiti: A War Nerd Classic." *The Exiled*. The Exiled, 13 Jan. 2010. Web. 20 Jan. 2014.

20. "Nihilism." *American Nihilist Underground Society*. American Nihilist Underground Society, n.d. Web. 20 Jan. 2014.

21. "Paladino: I Don't Want Children 'Brainwashed Into Thinking That Homosexuality Is an Equally Valid or Successful Option.'" *All Over Albany*. All Over Albany, 11 Oct. 2010. Web. 20 Jan. 2014.

22. Boyajian, Michael. "The Mask Removed." *Room Eight*. Alley Media Ventures, 11 Oct. 2010. Web. 20 Jan. 2014.

23. "Deviant." *Dictionary.com*. Dictionary.com, n.d. Web.

20 Jan. 2014.

24. Taibbi, Matt. "The Truth About the Tea Party." *Rolling Stone*. Jann Wenner, 28 Sept. 2010. Web. 20 Jan. 2014.

25. Zernike, Kate, and Megan Thee-Brenan. "Poll Finds Tea Party Backers Wealthier and More Educated." *The New York Times*. Arthur Sulzberger, Jr., 14 Apr. 2010. Web. 21 Jan. 2014.

26. Alexander, Sam. "The Pay Ethic." *Xamuel.com*. Sam Alexander, 22 Nov. 2010. Web. 21 Jan. 2014.

27. Diaboli, Advocatus. "The Real Significance of Wikileaks." *Playing the Devil's Advocate*. WordPress.com, 30 Nov. 2010. Web. 21 Jan. 2014.

28. Bady, Aaron. "Julian Assange and the Computer Conspiracy: 'To Destroy This Invisible Government.'" *ZunguZungu*. WordPress.com, 29 Nov. 2010. Web. 21 Jan. 2014.

29. Gibson, Dan. "The Crazed Internet Rantings of Jared Loughner." *Tucson Weekly*. Thomas P. Lee, 08 Jan. 2011. Web. 21 Jan. 2014.

30. An Unmarried Man. "Jared Loughner and His Legacy of Despair." *Social Extinction*. An Unmarried Man, 10 Jan. 2011. Web. 21 Jan. 2014.

31. Wonka, Willy. "Ranting and Raving." *Willy Wonka's Adventures*. WordPress.com, 18 Jan. 2011. Web. 21 Jan.

ENDNOTES

2014.

32. Freddie. "The Blindspot (Updated)." *L'Hôte*. Blogger, 15 Jan. 2011. Web. 21 Jan. 2014.

33. Sigma, Half. "Murder Rates by State." *Half Sigma*. Half Sigma, 30 Mar. 2011. Web. 21 Jan. 2014.

34. Colletti, Jaclyn, and Joel Weber. "The 100 Best (and Worst) Places to Raise a Family." *Men's Health*. Rodale Press, n.d. Web. 21 Jan. 2014.

35. *American Juggalo*. Sean Dunne, n.d. Web. 21 Jan. 2014.

36. Mangan, Dennis. "Juggalos." *Mangan's*. Blogger, 28 Sept. 2011. Web. 21 Jan. 2014.

37. Cook, William. "Self-Esteem and African Americans." *Suite101*. Suite101, 22 Jan. 2010. Web. 21 Jan. 2014.

38. Fry, Richard, D'Vera Cohen, Gretchen Livingston, and Paul Taylor. "The Rising Age Gap in Economic Well-Being." *Pew Research Center*. Pew Research Center, 07 Nov. 2011. Web. 21 Jan. 2014.

39. Cheese, John. "5 Ways We Ruined the Occupy Wall Street Generation." *Cracked.com*. Demand Media, 10 Nov. 2011. Web. 21 Jan. 2014.

40. Hill, Catey. "Things Baby Boomers Won't Say." *Yahoo! Finance*. Yahoo!, 10 Nov. 2011. Web. 21 Jan. 2014.

41. Proph. "We Have to Vote, Don't We?" *The*

Orthosphere. WordPress.com, 20 Feb. 2012. Web. 21 Jan. 2014.

42. Moldbug, Mencius. "A Gentle Introduction to Unqualified Reservations (Part 1)." *Unqualified Reservations*. Blogger, 08 Jan. 2009. Web. 21 Jan. 2014.

43. Waldman, Steven, and John Green. "It Wasn't Just (or Even Mostly) the 'Religious Right.'" *Beliefnet*. BN Media, Nov. 2004. Web. 21 Jan. 2014.

44. Edsall, Thomas B. "The Future of the Obama Coalition." *The New York Times*. Arthur Sulzberger, Jr., 27 Nov. 2011. Web. 21 Jan. 2014.

III: The Tao of Ferd

1. S., Kamal. "Blast from the Past ('You Can't Survive Without Being a Rebel...')." *Initium, or How I Learned to Love the Kali-Yuga*. Kamal S., 25 July 2009. Web. 21 Jan. 2014.

2. Kachka, Boris. "What Is Jhumpa Lahiri's Hook?" *New York*. New York Media, 27 Mar. 2008. Web. 21 Jan. 2014.

3. McCain, Robert S. "In Search of Right-Wing Gonzo." *Taki's Magazine*. Taki Theodoracopulos, 26 Mar. 2009. Web. 21 Jan. 2014.

4. Spike. "Why Blog?" *The Festival of Patience*.

ENDNOTES

WordPress.com, 08 Nov. 2010. Web. 21 Jan. 2014.

5. Black, Rebecca. "Friday: Rebecca Black – Official Music Video." *YouTube.* YouTube, 16 Sept. 2011. Web. 21 Jan. 2014.

6. "Fleeing the Country: From the Horse's Mouth." *But I Did Everything Right!* Blogger, 23 Mar. 2011. Web. 21 Jan. 2014.

7. Racer X. "Travis Would Be Blogging Today." *The Chase.* WordPress.com, 06 Apr. 2011. Web. 21 Jan. 2014.

8. Jiang, M., J. Xin, Q. Zou, and JW Shen. "A Research on the Relationship Between Ejaculation and Serum Testosterone Level in Men." *National Center for Biotechnology Information.* U.S. National Library of Medicine, Mar.–Apr. 2003. Web. 21 Jan. 2014.

9. V, Roosh. "Jerk Off Management 101." *Roosh V.* Roosh V, 08 Oct. 2008. Web. 21 Jan. 2014.

10. Tomassi, Rollo. "The Pheromonal Beta." *The Rational Male.* WordPress.com, 17 Nov. 2011. Web. 21 Jan. 2014.

11. Robinson, Marnia, and Gary Wilson. "Guys Who Gave Up Porn: On Sex and Romance." *Psychology Today.* Psychology Today, 01 Feb. 2012. Web. 21 Jan. 2014.

12. *F.lux.* N.p., n.d. Web. 21 Jan. 2014.

13. *X3 Watch*. N.p., n.d. Web. 21 Jan. 2014.

14. "Paul Auster." *Wikipedia*. Wikimedia Foundation, 21 Jan. 2014. Web. 21 Jan. 2014.

IV: Humor and Satire

1. Heartiste. "Sexual Dystopia: A Glimpse at the Future." *Chateau Heartiste*. WordPress.com, 01 June 2009. Web. 21 Jan. 2014.

2. Sims, Paul. "Councils Pay for Disabled to Visit Prostitutes and Lap-Dancing Clubs from £520m Taxpayer Fund." *The Daily Mail*. Associated Newspapers, 16 Aug. 2010. Web. 21 Jan. 2014.

3. Pro-Male/Anti-Feminist Tech. "The Experiment: Church." *Pro-Male/Anti-Feminist Technology*. Pro-Male/Anti-Feminist Technology, 14 Aug. 2010. Web. 21 Jan. 2014.

Made in the USA
Charleston, SC
10 August 2016